I0128211

Will Reason

University and Social Settlements

Will Reason

University and Social Settlements

ISBN/EAN: 9783742810731

Manufactured in Europe, USA, Canada, Australia, Japa

Cover: Foto ©Thomas Meinert / pixelio.de

Manufactured and distributed by brebook publishing software
(www.brebook.com)

Will Reason

University and Social Settlements

UNIVERSITY AND SOCIAL SETTLEMENTS

EDITED BY

W. REASON, M.A.

METHUEN & CO.

36 ESSEX STREET, W.C.

LONDON

1898

PREFACE

WHATEVER may be said as to the non-originality of the idea to which all University and Social Settlements owe their origin, the form in which that idea is embodied is essentially modern. It has been determined by those social forces of the Industrial Revolution which have made the several grades of rich and poor to live in separate quarters of our large towns. The Settlement is, therefore, a new feature of our civilisation, and deserves a close and careful study, not only as a result in itself, but as an experiment which contains the possibilities of other far-reaching results in their turn. In one sense it is more than an experiment; it is an accomplished fact. No doubt it will continue to develop, and it would be rash to predict that this development will be bounded by the lines which have already been laid down. But that the Settlements will go on increasing, both in numbers and in strength, we are assured by the experience of the thirteen years and more which have elapsed since the foundation of Toynbee Hall.

The present volume is a contribution to the study of this movement. Settlement literature in this country is not large, and will easily bear additions. Besides the annual output of reports, etc., there is only, so far as I

know, Mr Knapp's "Universities and the Social Problem."
Even in the few years that have elapsed since the publication of that book there have been large developments; and,
apart from this, the method of treatment left ample room
for another work on the subject.

There are still many people who ask with a puzzled air,
What is a Settlement? To such it is not easy to give a
brief answer that satisfies all the requirements of a logical
definition, for Settlements are living things, and differ in
proportion as they are alive. For this reason, no attempt
has been made to bring the different papers "into line"
in any way, save only in the distribution of subject-matter,
that the book might be as complete as possible within the
allotted limits. For the different Settlements have been
founded by bodies of people of widely differing kinds,
whose aims, as consciously set forth, seem at first to be also
far apart. The only candid method was, therefore, to let
each paper speak for itself. It will be seen that almost
all the writers have not only been engaged in Settlement
work, but have had the chief direction and the shaping of
the policy of the institutions which they represent. It
might well have been expected, under these conditions,
that the views expressed would have shown considerable
divergence, and they are, in fact, by no means uniform.
At the same time, there is easily discernible a strong
underlying unanimity of purpose, and a remarkable agree-
ment on fundamental points.

Hearty thanks are due to all who have contributed to

this book, for it has been with them all "a labour of love."
It was a disappointment to me that the late head of
Oxford House, now the Bishop of Stepney, could not
himself write the article on "Settlements and Recreations,"
for none could speak with such authority as he; but
pressure of other business forbade this. He very kindly,
however, allowed me to use whatever he had written on
the subject, and it will be seen that I have made free use
of this permission. The sections borrowed from his writings
are clearly distinguished in the text of the article, and it
must be distinctly understood that here, as in all other
places, each writer is responsible only for his own
words. I am also very greatly indebted to my colleague,
Mr Alden, at whose instigation I undertook this book,
for much help and many valuable suggestions.

One very important point remains to be noticed. There
is no article dealing with the religious aspect of Settlements.
This is not at all because there is no religion in Settlements,
or that none of them do religious work. On the contrary,
a glance at the Settlement Directory will show that a very
large proportion set out with this as their central aim. It
is rather because, as a second glance over the same section
will show, it would have been impossible to do justice
to the subject. For these Settlements have been founded
not only by Anglicans, Roman Catholics, Wesleyans,
Congregationalists, Friends, and other religious bodies,
but also by those who object to the association of any
form of distinctively religious work with Settlement activity.

It is obvious that there are very few indeed who could handle the subject with authority and ability, and at the same time fairly represent all the differing elements. At any rate, no one was available.

Still, in an account of what Settlements actually are, it ought, merely as a matter of fact, to be clearly stated that in a good number of them, and these by no means the least influential, the religious aim is the central one, round which the others find their places; or perhaps I should better express the minds of those concerned if I said that it was that which inspires all the rest. As to the particular form which this religious activity takes in each Settlement, and the nature and quality of the results, no one may judge the other, "To his own Master he standeth or falleth." Nor is it possible to judge from the outside, by religious statistics or inspectional visits, as to the "spirituality" of Settlement work. One thing is happily certain; within the Settlements and between the Settlements there is no religious strife. If any such unhappily arise, it will come from the outside, from those who are more ready at criticism and judgment than at lending a hand. The aim of the Settlement itself is not strife, but helpfulness.

In compiling the "Directory of Settlements," I have been much assisted by the "Bibliography of Settlements" compiled for the American College Settlements Association by John P. Gavitt of Chicago Commons. This is a most useful little work to all who are interested in the study of this movement, though, naturally enough, it has required considerable revision and correction as regards British Settlements. Any one who has tried to do the same kind of work will know how difficult it is to get the necessary information in the first place, and then to interpret it always correctly. In the case of the present "Directory," the aim has been rather to note the special characteristics of the different institutions than to give a description such as would be necessary if dealing with that particular instance alone. I have also confined myself to British Settlements, for convenience sake, but reference to Mr Gavitt's little book will show that the Settlement is now fully established in the four quarters of the world. In Far Japan there are two extremely interesting Settlements—one in Kyoto, called "Airinsha," or the "House of Neighbourly Love," and the other in Tokyo, known as "Kingsley House," after our own Charles Kingsley.

WILL REASON.

CONTENTS

xi

ON UNIVERSITY SETTLEMENTS

By Sir Walter Besant

[Inaugural Address at the opening of Mansfield House
New Residence, 5th December 1897]

THE new teaching concerning the relations of the cultured to the uncultured classes, which has taken
shape and expression in the University Settlements, is very
peculiarly the creation and the growth of our own time,
or, as those who have reached this year of the reign may
say, the creation and growth of the later Victorian age.
This movement will in the future, I am convinced, be
noted as the most remarkable outcome and result of all
the teaching and writing of this age. Also, there can
be little doubt that, since every human institution must
continually develop and increase, or as continually de-
crease and decay, since there is death in standing still,
the movement represented by these settlements, born but
yesterday though already so full of vigorous life, is destined
to grow and to spread, and to play a far greater part in
the elevation of our race than at present appears probable
to the casual observer. I do not say the elevation of
the masses, for a special reason—namely, that this work
means the elevation of those who are engaged in it, and
with them their own class, as well as the elevation of
those for whom they work. I look for the continual

A

appearance of unexpected developments, unhoped-for openings of new work, because such developments are the one sure and certain sign of vitality and reality. Therefore, we must not be surprised to find here and there, as the work of these settlements goes on, the appearance of lines of work apparently quite outside those originally contemplated by the founders. That such a settlement as this should have its own lodging-house; that it should provide legal advice for the working men and women; that it should give a deputy-Mayor to the borough : these are among the unexpected new lines of work which prove vitality and vigour. The settlement has come upon us unostentatiously; the Press at first spoke little about it, the new thing was not understood by journalists. It was wisely done. Had it come with trumpets and grand inaugurations and professions of work, it would have called upon its head that instinctive hostility of criticism which always awaits one who professes and promises great things. Safety lies always in the quiet seclusion of unpretending work ; and although we do, from time to time, find public mention of what is done by this or that settlement, yet its work continues, and will always continue, to be carried on quietly among the people for whom it is intended, by men, or by men and women, who seek not the ordinary rewards of name and fame and money, and are contented with the satisfaction that follows after effort that is not in vain, and with a life that in the end will prove not to have been wasted.

I am constantly reminded, not only by the University Settlement, but by much of the other work which is now going on in London, of the early days of the Franciscans. What St Francis commanded his followers was, that they should be obedient; that they should remain in poverty; and that they should be celibate. They were to be obedient because work of all kinds among men must be organised; very well, that law is in full force in the University Settlement. They were to remain in poverty— that law is also in force wherever work is done without reward or money. They were to be celibate—a custom, if not a law, which also prevails in the modern settlement. Thus equipped, with these three rules to guide him, the Franciscan friar went to live in the poorest and most miserable parts of the towns, and worked among the poorest and most miserable of the people. When, for instance, he came to London, he asked for a piece of ground in the shambles, where the cattle and the sheep were daily slaughtered; he put up his first buildings, where is now Christ's Hospital, beside the streams of blood that daily flowed along the kennel, and amidst the stench of offal and of skins. No record exists in detail of the success of their early work, but for two hundred years, and until the spirit of the order wholly died out, they were deeply loved and profoundly venerated by the people of London. That was 600 years ago. Between that time and the present generation, though there have been many men and women devoted to humanitarian work of different kinds—sporadic cases, such as those of Raikes, of Buxton, of Howard, of Elizabeth Fry — there has been no large organisation, such as that of the Franciscans, in the direction of personal devotion. We have attempted other forms of philanthropic endeavour; we have created schools and opened churches; we have founded alms-houses; we have written very fine essays on philanthropy; enormous sums—millions upon millions — have been given in charity. In spite of all,

there has been but little improvement; the slums seem
to grow only worse instead of better, until—when? where?
how?—we know not; but, suddenly as it seemed, unexpected as we thought, there ran through the minds of
men and women the same words, the same formula, at
the same time—"Not money, but yourselves." These
words rang out in trumpet tones in the minds of those
who heard—"Not money, but yourselves."

This is not a rhetorical *façon de parler*. It is literally
true. The note of the new philanthropy is personal
service; not money; not a cheque; not a subscription
written; not speeches on a platform; not tracts; not
articles in Quarterly Reviews; none of the old methods:
but personal service—"Not money, but yourselves." Now,
if we ask how this conviction—that personal service is
the one thing needful—arose, I think we need not go
farther back than to Carlyle. If you look into his "Past
and Present," into his "Chartism," you will find the germ
of the doctrine of personal service there. You will also
find it in Kingsley's "Alton Locke," but that author
could not wholly grasp the doctrine. You will find a
certain broad humanitarian view, which seems to include
this teaching, scattered up and down the pages of Robert
Browning; or you will find it plainly taught by Ruskin.
If, however, Carlyle preached this doctrine, it may be
asked why it was not carried into practice for fifty years
after he taught it. The reason is that Carlyle was that
much, at least, before his time. A prophet before his
time speaks to the winds. Carlyle's teaching has not
been entirely understood; some of it is only now appeal-
ing to a generation which has advanced so far as to
understand it. In the old days—I speak of my own

personal experience as a young man when first I read
Carlyle—his readers were lifted by certain of his chapters
or pages into regions of thought which were to them
purely imaginary—the lovely creation of a mere dreamer;
they wandered in those regions with the help and guidance of their prophet, but they never conceived the
possibility of the dream becoming realised. Kingsley
himself was in some respects before his age; but yet, as
I have said above of his "Alton Locke," his grasp of
what would now be the strong central thought was
hesitating. Carlyle, you see, was in advance even of
Kingsley.

It may be contended that literature does not inspire the
world so much as it formulates their thought and guides
them, by giving expression to the vague and floating
ideas of the time; or that upon these ideas the teacher
builds up a teaching or a philosophy which would be
impossible but for them. Carlyle, for instance, preaches
a humanity far in advance of his own time: the world
does not understand; a few here and there, and only a
few, understand; they understand in part; then they
preach and teach what they understand. Literature in
such a case has not directly inspired the multitude, but
only the few. These few were men like Maurice, Kingsley,
Frederick Robertson; they, in turn, preached what had
gone home to their own souls: and so the new doctrine
of the responsibility of man for his brother, and the duty
of personal service, spread and deepened, wave after wave,
over the whole nation, until it reached every one who
could be fired with noble impulses, who could be driven
forth to practical work based on these impulses. So that
now there is nothing strange, nothing new, nothing dreamy,

in the doctrine that the highest form of humanitarian work, the truest charity, one even thinks the only real charity, is the personal service for which this settlement exists. Let me only mention the names of those pioneers of personal service—John Richard Green, Edward Denison, and Arnold Toynbee: all, alas! dead, though all of them might well be living now. Consider only how great a flame they kindled in the hearts of the young and generous. They worked separately, because it was not possible for them to find fellow-workers; they worked in silence. Not till after their death did the world understand the nature and importance of their work; not till they had taken their hands from the plough did the world understand how straight and clean and deep was their furrow. They have found successors, no longer working singly, but in an organised company; and they have raised the level of humanity by the practical example of a teaching which the Protestant Church has always recognised and never understood. "Not money," was the voice in the air; "not money, but yourselves."

Literature, then, can only inspire minds already ripe for inspiration. Then, and then only, can the writer or the preacher speak with the certainty of success. For the word spoken at the moment when the mind is ready is like the light applied to the train of powder. Such a word spoken at such a moment is of rare occurrence, but it is not unknown. He who speaks it must himself be saturated with the ideas of the day. He then puts into shape, in the form of a sermon, or of an essay, or of a poem, or of a play, or of fiction, into words, into characters, into scenes, these ideals and these aspirations. Probably it is often done unconsciously. The writer knows his own ideals; he has worked them out for himself; he does not realise that they may also belong to the whole of the class which can think; he puts forth his work, and, lo! in a moment the blaze of light in response, for he has involuntarily given notice to, clothed with words, the thoughts of his own generation. Such an illustration is found in Mrs Humphrey Ward's "Robert Elsmere." The success of that book, quite apart from its very great literary merits, was undoubtedly due to the fact that it appealed in its aspirations and its ideals to the thoughts of thousands who were ready for broader views of humanity and religion, for proclaiming things which they themselves felt but wanted the power to clothe with words. And the book succeeded the more readily because its views were presented in the form of fiction. The national mind at this time is accustomed to that form of expression. It is more easily moved by fiction than by poetry, by teaching, or by the sermon. It succeeded practically, and with a success far beyond the mere delight of the moment, as is proved by the establishment of the University Hall and the Passmore Edwards Settlement. But above all, and to repeat, the success of "Robert Elsmere" was in great measure due to the fact that the book and the moment were ready for each other.

Let us turn from the influence of literature to this Settlement itself. When one considers what is being done in this place—the group of societies scattered about this centre; the 3000 members of these societies; the eminently practical work that is going on; the public spirit of its leaders; the lectures, classes, concerts; the clubs; the lodging-house; the benefit societies; the music; the brotherhood society—one is tempted to compare the privileges and advantages enjoyed at the present day by the working-classes of this great city with the utter neglect under which they laboured a hundred years ago.

I have recently had occasion to investigate the condition of the riverside population of the last century. I venture to afflict your ears with a very brief description of that part of London. You will believe me when I assure you that I am not able—simply not able—to set forth the whole truth, or anything like the whole truth. The population of London between the Tower and Shadwell, where houses then ceased, was wholly engaged upon work connected with the Port of London and its shipping. That is to say, they were boatbuilders, mast and rope makers, block makers, sail makers, and so forth. This part of London also provided all the men engaged in loading and unloading the ships which at that time took in and unloaded cargo in the middle of the river. The people, taken as a whole, were the most abandoned and dissolute ever known. Every man of the stevedores, of the barge and lightermen, of the boatmen, was a robber and a thief: all together daily plundered the cargoes of the ships. They robbed the cargoes of big things; they stole little things; every day they went ashore with the goods they stole; every other house was a receiving-house and a tavern. The men spent their unholy gains in drink. Their children grew up without the least tincture of education, in an atmosphere of crime and drunkenness; while of virtue, modesty, honesty, there was not a trace. Nobody was any the better for the money gained by robbery, but only so much the worse. Their personal habits were to the last degree disgusting. The women wore a gown of some thick stuff which they never

changed; they wore no hat or bonnet, but in cold
weather a kerchief over the head and tied under the
chin; they never combed their hair, which fell in rats'
tails on their shoulders; they fought with fists, like the
men, in a ring; they drank like the men; they cursed
and swore like the men; and like the men they all died
young by the diseases belonging to their way of life. It
will be asked if there were no churches. There were
several churches : that of St Katherine's by the Tower;
of St John's, Wapping; of St Paul's, Shadwell; of Limehouse; churches in the very midst of this delightful
society; churches with the machinery complete of clergy,
services, and schools. Why, then, was there nothing done
to check this state of things? One has no wish to attack
one's own grandfathers, but we must remember the theory
of the church of the last century. The doors were open
on Sundays, and sometimes on week-days, for *those who
chose to come.* The clergy were always ready to attend
the sick and the dying *when they were invited.* But they
waited, you see, to be invited; they waited for the people
to come to church. That they should themselves go
among the people and teach and testify and administer
and show by example was not yet part of their daily
work, or part of the work of the church.

Now all is changed. It is a missionary church: the
clergy go everywhere; they visit; they reprove; they relieve
want—they do, in a word, all that a clergy can be expected
to do, as much in every parish as any one man or any
two men can do. When all is done that they can do,
there remains so much. In this work the clergy of all
the churches should be united, for there is room for all.
Especially is there room for the efforts of young men, who

bring the light and beauty of ordered recreation into the
elevation of the people. Sometimes, I am told, these new
missionaries of a Christianity which makes the higher life
a part of their religion, feel discouraged among a mass
which seems to refuse their leavening. At such times let
them take heart by thinking what these people were like
before any personal efforts at all were made among them;
let them remember the changed conditions under which
the children are now brought up; let them remember the
thousands of good men and true who are now in their
societies, and so take heart. And as for myself and the
men like me, who feel in the presence of their great and
noble work that we are but drones outside the hive of
workers, we can but say, while we look round at the present
and look back at the past, that we thank God for the new
spirit that is abroad among us—the spirit which sends our
young men and maidens to carry light and healing and
a nobler life and higher thoughts among those who have
to dwell in the darker places of our great cities.

UNIVERSITY SETTLEMENTS *

FOURTEEN years ago a paper published in this Review suggested "University settlements in our great towns." There are now Toynbee Hall, Oxford House, Mansfield House, the Bermondsey Settlement, Cambridge House, Caius House, Chalfont House, Newman House, Browning Hall, the Passmore Edwards Settlement, the Southwark Ladies' Settlement, the Women's Settlement in Canning Town, and Mayfield House in London. There are settlements in Glasgow, Bristol, Manchester, and Edinburgh. There are Hull House in Chicago, Andover House in Boston, besides perhaps twenty others in different cities of America.

The paper was an expression of what was in many minds and of what others' work had prepared. The movement which followed its publication was an indication of a strong stream of thought already running.

After fourteen years, therefore, the question to be asked by those who would estimate the value of settlements is not, "What did the paper say?" but, "What did it mean, and how far have existing settlements carried out the meaning?"

Fourteen years ago there was a stirring in the waters of benevolence which are for the healing of the weak. Men and women felt a new impulse towards doing good,

* Reprinted, by kind permission, from the *Nineteenth Century*, with a few alterations to date.

11

and that impulse took shape in the creation of these Halls and Houses. What was the impulse? Why has "the plan of settlement" extended?

Three causes may be suggested.

I. Distrust of Machinery.—Many people become distrustful of the machinery for doing good. Men at the Universities, especially those who directly or indirectly felt the influence of T. H. Green, were asking for some other way than that of institutions by which to reach their neighbours. They heard the "bitter cry" of the poor; they were conscious of something wrong underneath modern progress; they realised that free trade, reform bills, philanthropic activity, and missions had made neither health nor wealth. They were drawn to do something for the poor. Charity organisation societies had taught them not to give doles; they had turned from preachers who said, "Give up your business and live as monks"; they were not contented with reformers who came saying, "Change the laws, and all will be well," nor philanthropists who said, "Support our charity to meet the need," nor with religious teachers who said, "Subscribe to our church or mission."

They felt that they were bound to be themselves true to the call which had summoned them to the business and enjoyment of life, and they distrusted machinery. The poor law, the chief machine, seemed to have developed pauperism, fostering the spirit which "bullies or cringes." Societies had become empty shells, occupied only by officials, who had found pleasant quarters in the forms created by the life gift of the founders. Missions in making proselytes seemed sometimes to corrupt men.

Philanthropy, indeed, appeared to many to be a sort

of mechanical figure beautifully framed by men to do their duty to their brother men—made with long arms, so as to reach all needs, and with iron frame, so as to be never tired. It saved its inventors all further care beyond that of supplying it with money. Drop in a coin, and the duty to a neighbour was done. But duty so done, proved often more harmful than helpful. A society acting by rules sometimes patched "hearts which were breaking with handfuls of coals and rice." The best-devised mechanism can have neither eyes nor feeling. It must act blindly, and cannot evoke gratitude.

Thus it came about that a group of men and women at the Universities distrusted machinery for doing good. They were between two duties. On the one side they were bound to be true to themselves and do their own work. On the other side they were bound by other means than by votes and subscriptions to meet the needs of the poor. They welcomed, therefore, the proposal for a settlement where they might live their own lives and also make friends among the poor.

II. Demand for more Information.—Alongside of this distrust of machinery was a demand for more accurate information as to the condition of the people, as to their thoughts and their hopes. The sensational descriptions of the ill-housed, the ill-paid, and the ignorant had roughly awakened easy-going citizens, but those descriptions did not give assurance that they represented facts or their meaning. A generation which had breathed something of the modern scientific spirit was not content with hearsay knowledge and with sentimental references; it required facts and figures—critical investigation into the causes of poverty and personal knowledge of the poor. Thus it was that many men and women received with favour a proposal that they themselves should go and live in a neighbourhood where they would come into contact with the industrial classes, see with their own eyes their houses and surroundings, and hear from their own lips how they lived.

III. Growth of the Human Spirit.—The human spirit is always growing in strength. It bursts traditions as the life in a tree bursts the bark which protected its tender age. It strains to reach beyond class distinctions, old habits, party lines, and anything which hinders man from helping man. Nowhere is the growth of this human spirit more evident than at the Universities.

Fourteen years ago there was a clear recognition that old forms of benevolence were often patronising in character, that charities and missions often assumed a superiority in their supporters, and that sectarian philanthropy often developed party bitterness. Many men and women, therefore, anxious to assert their fellowship with the poor, resented the ways which in the name of love made their brothers humble themselves to take gifts. They did not want to appear as "benefactors" or as "missionaries." They had no belief in their nostrum as a Morrison's pill for the cure of all evils. Their desire was, as human beings, to help human beings, and their human feeling protested against forms of help which put the interest of a class or of a party before that of individuals, reaching out handfuls of gifts across impassable gulfs and making party shibboleths the condition of association.

Working people, on the other side, under the influence of the same human spirit, had come more and more to resent exclusion from the good things enjoyed by other classes. They wanted to know more of what their richer neighbours did, and, at any rate, before heaving a brick at an aristocrat, they desired to find out something about him.

Thus it was that a way was prepared for a suggestion that members of the University might live as neighbours of the poor, and, without affecting the superiority of an ascetic life, or claiming to have come as teachers, or having any sectarian object, might form the friendships which are channels of all true service.

The establishment of settlements is the work of those who believe that the gifts to modern times are good; that culture is gain, not loss; that cleanliness is better than dirt, beauty better than ugliness, knowledge better than ignorance—Isaacs not to be sacrificed. Settlements stand as an acknowledgment of the claims of all the citizens to a share in these good things, and as a protest against meeting those claims by the substitution of philanthropic machinery for human hands and personal knowledge. They express the desire on the part of those "who have" to see, to know, and to serve those "who have not."

How far have Settlements succeeded ? — Settlements are not to be judged out of the mouths of their critics or supporters. Both try them by measures used for weighing and testing things seen and felt. They fasten, therefore, on what is done for education, for relief, or for entertainment, and they give praise or blame. They compare the lists of classes, the results of examinations; they count up the number relieved or converted; they get out accounts of entertainments, and say, "How small," or "How great." It may be, it probably is, the case that much of the strength of settlements has gone to such objects, and that some of the Houses and Halls have become identified with special methods and special objects. But my claim is that settle: ments are not fairly judged by such standards.

A Settlement as it seems.—Toynbee Hall, for example, is not what it seems. The visitor who, Baedeker in hand, is shown over the lecture-room, the library, and the class rooms, and hears that there are 1000 or 1500 students, imagines that the sitting-rooms and bedrooms are occupied by men who give up their time to teaching and lecturing. "All the residents are, I suppose, professors," is a frequent American comment. Such visitors are apt to go away regarding the place as a centre of education.

If, however, the visitor happens to be told that most of the residents concern themselves with other objects, he makes up his mind that this object must be "temperance" or "conversion." He asks, "What is the effect of the work on the criminal population?" "Are the lowest people attracted?" "What is the spiritual outcome of the movement?" He gets, perhaps, as an answer, "that spiritual results are not visible," "that the residents have friends and acquaintances of all sorts," "that there is no common action which could be called the work of the place." He feels that his questions may have been impertinent, and he goes away somewhat confused, but on the whole assured that the place is a sort of a mission.

If a visitor with more time or perseverance arrives in the evening, he finds, perhaps, the lecture-room filled by Dr Gardiner's history students or Mr Rudler's geology students, the class-rooms occupied by small groups studying English or foreign literature, the principles of science or economics, the laboratory in the hands of a few practical workers, the library in the use of its quiet readers, the club-room noisy with the hum of talk about excursions, entertainments, and parties to be undertaken by the Students' Union. He is told that the distinction of all the educational work is that it is for the encouragement of knowledge which is not saleable, that lectures and classes aim at adding joy to life rather than of pence to wages, that their object is the better use of leisure time rather than of work time. He then determines that the place is a sort of polytechnic, with "university" classes in place of "technical" classes; he wonders so much is done without endowment; he criticises or admires. But when, the next moment, he goes into the drawing-room to find a party of Whitechapel neighbours or of East London teachers in the hands of a host with whom they are making merry, and passes by the tennis-court, which is occupied by an ambulance corps, into the dining-room, to find a conference of trade unionists, co-operators, or friendly society members discussing with leading thinkers and politicians some matter of policy or economy, he is again confused, but still fits in what he sees to his conception of the place as a charitable institution.

Or, once more, if a visitor comes to stay for a few days, and gets into conversation with the residents, he will probably be surprised at the new knowledge he almost unconsciously acquires. He will, as he listens to some casual talk, shape for himself a new idea of what is done by guardians or vestrymen; he will discover the part which local government plays in life, and learn how trades unions, co-operative societies, and friendly societies are worked; he will get new light on clubs, and be set thinking about measures of reform and development. Further and more private talk with individuals will put him in possession of

B

strange facts and figures, clothed in humanity by reason of the narrator's intimacy with the lives of his neighbours. He will feel the importance of such knowledge to all who speak, write, vote, or legislate. He will no longer wonder at mistakes in philanthropy or legislation while such ignorance exists as to the hopes and needs of the poor. He will go away thinking that Toynbee Hall is a sort of bureau of social information.

A Settlement as it Is.—Toynbee Hall seems to its visitors to be a centre of education, a mission, a centre of social effort. It may be so; but the visitors miss the truth that the place is a club house in Whitechapel occupied by men who do citizens' duty in the neighbourhood. The residents are not as a body concerned for education, teetotalism, poor relief, or any special or sectarian object. Each one leads his own life, earns his own living, and does his duty in his own way. Catholic, Churchman, Jew, Dissenter, and Agnostic, they live together and strengthen one another by what each contributes to the common opinion. There is no such thing as a "Toynbee Hall policy," and it is never true to say that "Toynbee Hall" favoured one candidate in an election, or that it stands for any special form of religion. A few men with their own bread to earn, with their own lives to enjoy, with their own sense of social debt, come to live together. No one surrenders what he has found to be good for his own growth; each man pursues his own vocation and keeps the environment of a cultured life. There is no affectation of equality with neighbours by the adoption of mean or dirty habits. There is no appearance of sacrifice. The men live their own lives in Whitechapel instead of in West London, and do—what is required of every citizen—

citizens' duties in their own neighbourhood. If those duties seem to a man to include the preaching of his own faith, he delivers his own soul and tells his gospel when he visits in a club or teaches in a class. There is no limit put on any form of earnestness so long as it is the man, and not the place, who is committed.

The same impulse which has created settlements has led many men to take lodgings and, alone or with one or two friends, live in East London. They have thus found duties to their hands and made links with their neighbours; but, notwithstanding striking examples of success, my present judgment favours the plan of a community. In a settlement no resident loses his individuality, but the criticism of his peers keeps up his standard of order and cleanliness, while it checks the development of fads and of sloth. A place like Toynbee Hall may offer what seems to be more comfort than is possible in East End lodgings, but it requires what is often a greater sacrifice— the surrender of self-will and of will-worship. Moreover, although no man loses his individuality in a settlement, each is stronger as a member of a body in touch with many interests than as a lonely lodger; he gets strength by what his mates are, and he gives strength by what he is. In fact, true individuality survives, I think, better in a settlement than in lodgings, where eccentricities are often cherished, and where useful conventions succumb to the influences of East London.

Toynbee Hall is not what it seems. Imitators who begin by building lecture-rooms and by starting schemes for education and relief, make the same mistake as those who followed our Lord because He made the sick man take up his bed, and not because He forgave sins. True

imitation is when half-a-dozen men or women set on
social service go and live among the poor. They may
take a house or occupy a block in an artisans' dwelling, and they may begin without a subscription list or
an advertisement. Out of their common life various
activities will develop, and the needs they discover they
will meet.

Toynbee Hall seems to be a centre of education, a
mission, a polytechnic, another example of philanthropic
machinery; it is really a club, and the various activities
have their root and their life in the individuality of its
members.

Test of Settlement's Success.—It is as an effort of the
human spirit to do human work that a settlement must
be judged. Its classes, its social schemes, are not so
true a test of its success as its effect in establishing friendship between man and man.

If from this point of view I were asked what Toynbee
Hall has done, I should answer : (1) It has tended to
mitigate class suspicion; (2) it has helped to inspire local
government with a higher spirit.

1. It has tended to mitigate class suspicion. East
London and West London suspect each other. The
poor, when they hear of a rich man's philanthropy, say,
"Does he serve God for nought?" They reckon up
the activities of the clergy with the reflection that they
work to make converts or for promotion, and they imagine
that public men seek their votes in order to get place
for themselves. The rich on their side suspect the poor :
they are half afraid they may rebel; they think an act
of politeness is a sort of begging; they see vindictive
designs in their policy, and imagine that because they

have no stake in the nation, they have no common interests with themselves.

Toynbee Hall has puzzled its neighbours, who had such opinions. For a long time all sorts of motives were put to its credit. "Wait a bit," it was said, "and the people who go there will be called to a prayer meeting"; or, "you will see it is a dodge of Tories—of Liberals—of Socialists to get votes." It was five or six years after its opening that a speaker at a meeting of a friendly society confessed that up to that time his society had held aloof, suspecting some design to steal from people their independence. Up to the present time many neighbours remain unconvinced, and any appearance of special sympathy at times of crisis would be sufficient to get the place classed as Tory or Radical, Church or Chapel.

But on the whole the policy of the last thirteen years has shaken old prejudices. When in the same house is found both a Moderate and a Progressive member of the London School Board, when one resident is known as a Tory and another as a Radical, when at the dock strike service was rendered and no credit taken, when at times of distress the place has not been used as a centre of relief, and when it is realised that the residents give their time from a sense of duty, the belief is encouraged that it is not to advance any party interest that the place is established. When, further, it is realised that earnest believers in different creeds work together in friendship—remain true to themselves and yet push towards the same ends—another idea of the meaning of religion is developed.

A shake has thus been given to the habit of suspicion;

but, more than this, individual friendships have been formed, along which currents of good feeling run from class to class. At first men have met their neighbours as members of a committee; they have, perhaps, taken part in the administration of relief, or joined in a game at a club, or spoken in a debate. They have made acquaintance naturally on an equal footing, and in some cases acquaintance has ripened into friendship. Two men born in different circumstances, educated by different means, occupied in different work, have in such meeting felt . themselves akin. They have become friends and sharers in each other's strength. And because they are friends their eyes have been opened to see the good in their friend's friends. Poor men have seen that the rich are not what they are pictured by orators, and the rich have found that the poor have virtues not always expressed by their language.

There are few parties which have left happier memories than those at which some resident has received together friends made in the West and in the East. All the guests have felt at their ease. They have come with different pasts and different hopes, but the common intimacy with their host provokes such trust that they enjoy their differences. Many are the testimonies received as to the pleasure experienced in forming acquaintances in a new class.

It would obviously be absurd to expect that twenty men living in Whitechapel should make any evident mark on the public opinion of half-a-million of people, but for my part I am convinced that, as a result of their settlement, there is an increase of good-will.

2. In the second place, I think Toynbee Hall has

helped to inspire local government with a higher spirit. It is a true instinct which makes people distrust machinery, but it is obvious that if humanity is to operate effectively in raising society it must be by means of organisations and officials. Local government is in East London the most effective of such organisations, and is gradually absorbing many of the functions of the Church and of charity. It more and more has under its care the schools of the children and the classes of the adults; it provides for health and recreation, for the relief of the weak and the training of the strong. School managers are making the Board Schools delightful by the new interests they introduce. District Councils secure health by means of clean streets and sound houses; they open spaces, build libraries, and put public halls within easy reach of their constituents. Guardians are making their infirmaries model hospitals, their workhouses training homes, and their methods of relief a stimulus to exertion. People who are weary with the competition of charities, with the constant appeals and advertisements, turn with relief to the municipal system. They are pained by the quarrels of Church and Dissent, by the exaggeration and depreciation of efforts, and they more and more depend on Boards and Councils. Local Government is, indeed, the hope of East London, but the hope grows faint under pressure of the thought that East Londoners are too busy or too crushed to serve on boards and councils.

No one lives in East London of his own will. Its inhabitants are either striving to move out of it or unable to do so. The wonder, indeed, is that local government is as good as it is. But it is not good, and in some ᵕcases it is bad. It is often wanting in knowledge, and is therefore unconscious of abuses which would not be endured in West London; it rarely understands economy —the economy of wise expenditure or of business control —and it is wanting in the public spirit which breaks from old traditions. The faults are accidental, not inherent. If the abuses of smells, smoke, dirt, and noise are pointed out, they are recognised; if the needs of the people are put alongside of the old customs of the Board, they are often allowed; if someone appears who has knowledge of accounts, and shows faith in his policy, his lead is accepted.

Local government in East London needs the presence of a few people who will formulate its mission. To some degree this has been done by the residents of Toynbee Hall. / Some of them as members of boards, all of them as neighbours, have shown something of what is not done and of what might be done. Whitechapel has been moved to get a library; political parties have been induced to adopt a social programme; the police have been encouraged to enforce order in back streets. /

A new spirit is moving over local government. It is obviously impossible to put its presence to the credit of Toynbee Hall; but it is fair to say that its residents have contributed by the share they have actively taken as members of various boards, as well as by the influence they have exerted. What is still wanting to the efficiency of the boards is the business power which understands economy. Grants in aid of rates have developed a policy which doles always develop. Local legislators become more concerned in getting money to spend than in economical management. If business men, with the capacity which has created great private establishments, would come as residents, they might make local government strong enough to prevent some threatened evils.

A settlement, by bringing into a neighbourhood people whose training makes them sensible to abuses, and whose humanity makes them conscious of other needs, does what machinery as machinery cannot do. It fits supply and demand; it adapts itself to changing circumstances; it yields and goes forward; it follows or guides, according to the moment's need; it turns an organisation which might be a mere machine into a living human force. Above all, it brings men into touch with men, and, by making them fuller characters, enriches their work.

Thus up to a degree, taking Toynbee Hall as an example, settlements have put something human alongside the necessary machinery. But the end is far off; settlements are too few, and they have too often yielded to the temptation to rival other organisations with a show of their works.

It is a surprise to some of us that settlements are so few, and the question is sometimes asked, whether it is because the life is so interesting that it appeals to no sense of sacrifice, or whether it is because the sacrifice of leaving "a West End society" is too great.

I have written this paper believing in neither of these reasons, but believing rather that men do not understand the meaning of a settlement.

There is as much good-will to day as there was fourteen years ago; there is more knowledge. Men and women, conscious of other needs, are more conscious that machinery fails. They are anxious to avert the ills which threaten society, and are ready themselves to do their part. It is because settlements seem to be "a fad"—an experiment of "cranks"—or another mechanical invention, that they keep aloof.

I have, therefore, written this paper to show that a settlement is simply a means by which men or women may share themselves with their neighbours ; a club-house in an industrial district, where the condition of membership is the performance of a citizen's duty; a house among the poor, where the residents may make friends with the poor.

SAMUEL A. BARNETT.

SETTLEMENTS IN RELATION TO LOCAL ADMINISTRATION

OF late years a great change has come over the settlements, both in England and America. The primary idea of the settlement has always been, of course, to afford a centre from which the neighbourhood spirit and the spirit of brotherhood shall emanate; but a considerable amount of doubt has been expressed as to the part the settlement should play in the public life of the district. It is no longer under dispute that the residents of any settlement are justified in occupying positions on public bodies, although, even within my own recollection, criticisms have been made of the efforts of various settlements to influence through public work the life of the people in any locality. Such criticisms, however, may be for the most part neglected: they are extraneous, and seldom come from men who are actually engaged in social work either in East or South London, or in the poorer districts of any of our great cities. The critic usually contends that it is impossible to dissociate the work of social reform on a public body from ordinary party politics. His advice is to avoid even the appearance of evil — evil in this case being partisanship. The only answer to this is, that if party politics be so definitely associated with the work of local administration and municipal life, then the sooner we begin to discriminate and dissociate the two the better it will be for our great

27

cities. It behoves the settlements to prove that the con-
tention of Professor Bryce, who urged them to enter the
sphere of "pure politics," is sound and reasonable, and
all experience has emphasised the truth of his words. So
far back as the opening of Toynbee Hall the settlement
has been called upon to fill the gap which the absence
of men of leisure and education has left in our poor
districts. On that occasion Mr Lyttleton Gell pointed
out that underlying all our municipal life was the idea
of such a leisured educated class. We do not pay men
to take office and serve the people : the supposition is
that there are men only too glad to do it—willing, that
is, to devote a considerable amount of time to the
administration of public affairs. In East and South
London, if anywhere, there is need for such men, and
here comes in the value of the settlement, which can,
if it will, assist in educating the civic conscience in forming and crystallising public opinion, in supplying men
to initiate and carry out various social reforms. London
is too large ; the geographical distance which separates
the rich from the poor is almost commensurate with the
width of the gulf which yawns between the two classes so far
as sympathies and interests are concerned. Can there be
a more painful symptom of the disease which afflicts the
body politic than the army of unemployed to be found
on either side of London? The idlers of the East who
cannot find work contrasted with the idlers of the West
who have no need or desire to work. If the thousands
of men in West London who have little or nothing to do
except "moon" up and down Piccadilly and Regent
Street could only be persuaded that there is useful and
honourable work to be done in the great industrial centres

upon local bodies, it might possibly be *their* salvation, even if it did not contribute to the solution of any vexed social problem. But, as a matter of fact, these men of wealth and leisure could do very much if only they were very willing. It would be a good thing if the West and East could be brought together, and if the suburban North could be made to see the true inwardness, the utter sordidness of existence in Walworth, Southwark, or Bermondsey. The rich and well-to-do *ought* to feel their responsibility for the condition of the poor; *ought* to do something more than to give money in doles of charity; ought, in fact, to give *themselves*. I have often said that if one wealthy man with knowledge and sympathy consented to live in East or South London until the prejudice against him had been overcome, he might, both in his own individual capacity and as a member of some public body, do an enormous amount to change the environment and life of the district. It is quite true that he would find some difficulty at first in convincing the working-man that he had no ulterior motive, that he had no desire beyond that of serving and helping his adopted city and neighbourhood. But when he had once succeeded, when he had once convinced them that he was not seeking his own interest and emolument, he would have endless opportunities of useful service, and be enabled to shape and mould the character of the institutions which govern the lives of men. There is a great need for working-class representation on our public bodies. The working-man makes many mistakes, and often displays little judgment in his endeavours to attain the object that he has at heart. Nevertheless, he does represent the feeling of his fellows; and the settlement would do well to support all honest and intelligent labour candidates. When all is said and done, however, there is still room for the settlement resident who, by disinterested hard work and honesty of purpose, will sooner or later prove that any suspicion and distrust that may have been entertained was altogether unjustified. After all, the graduate from Oxford or Cambridge who goes to East London and settles there is less likely to be actuated by impure motives than many who offer themselves for election. Other things being equal, a man of education, provided that he be possessed of a fair amount of practicality and common-sense, ought to be extremely useful on any public body. His range of ideas gives him truer perspective, his horizon is more extended: it is quite possible that he is not an extreme supporter of the labour movement, but, just for that reason, if he be fairly advanced, he can give most valuable and unexpected help. To begin with, he is probably an educationalist, and is willing to spend money on our schools. He believes in free libraries, technical instruction, proper sanitation, well-built houses, recreation grounds, public baths, pure water, well-paved streets: in all these things he is at one with the labour member, and is in all probability more effective in the efforts that he makes. The late Professor Thomas Hill Green of Oxford illustrates my meaning in the best possible way. Although he was one of the profoundest philosophers Oxford has produced, he was also, at the same time, a practical and progressive reformer in the Council of that city. My knowledge of the municipal history of Oxford leads me to share the opinion of many of his colleagues on that Council, that Green was a real force and strength in all municipal undertakings. In those days University representatives were less common than they are now, especially in the city of Oxford; but as a pioneer in municipal reform his name ought not to be forgotten. The action of Green in Oxford might well be imitated in other cities and in the poor districts of London. Something has already been done at Toynbee Hall, Oxford House, Mansfield House, Browning Hall, and the Bermondsey Settlement: but the possibilities of such work are almost unlimited, and at present the settlements are only on the very threshold.

Municipal Work.—If municipal work is to be done at all successfully, it is a *sine qua non* that the resident should be fairly permanent—that is, he must be willing to stay at least three years. Even this does not give him time to win his way into the confidence of the people, and little and no good work can be done until he has that confidence. A successful administrator must always have a thorough knowledge of the social conditions under which the people of his district live. He must be cognisant with the trades, occupations, and industries which surround him.

To legislate for a country you must be in touch with the people, and know their requirements and desires. To administer the law for a municipality it is necessary that one should know what goes to make the life of a citizen in that town. He cannot properly administer the law unless he has something more than a nodding acquaintance with it; neither can he get it changed for the better without making a study of other and more advantageous townships, both in England and on the Continent. The nation has conferred upon the municipality certain powers for regulating the life, health, and well-being of the people, and the laws which make all improvement possible have to be mastered.

Toynbee Hall has rendered valuable service to the work of local government through Mr Henry Ward, member of the L.C.C. for Hoxton, who has for some years been working on that body as one who is specially interested in all matters connected with the housing of the working-classes and sanitary reform. He has three times been elected chairman of the Works Committee, and in that capacity has given his assistance to all judicious advances in the direction of municipalisation. Another resident is serving on the Mile End Vestry, and a third on the Local Administrative Board of Whitechapel.

Oxford House has no representative at present on any public body, but members of that settlement have given assistance to the Bethnal Green branch of the Mansion House Council on the Dwellings of the Poor, interesting themselves in many cases of overcrowding and insanitation which are to be found in their district.

Mansfield House has from the very first made an endeavour to influence the public life of West Ham, in the southern portion of which it is situated. For nearly six years the Warden has been working upon the Town Council in such ways as seem most likely to better the conditions and the life of the working-classes. West Ham is a borough with a population of over 270,000, and the southern portion would have rather the larger half. As it is a County Borough with large and extensive powers, it is obvious that the work is more complex and wide-reaching than that of a London Vestry. The influence of the settlement is most clearly seen in the work initiated by the Warden himself. Thus the Free Picture Exhibitions, which are being held this time for the fourth year, were adopted at his suggestion, and have been entirely organised by him. The exhibitions are open each Easter for a month, the time being divided between the two largest halls in the borough, the Town Hall, Stratford, and the Public Hall, Canning Town. Some of the finest pictures in England have been exhibited, and the average attendance of 130,000 seems to show that this piece of municipal enterprise is greatly appreciated by the working-classes. Toynbee Hall has a similar exhibition, but the whole expense is met by voluntary subscriptions, and the Vestry is in no way responsible. Canon Barnett, the pioneer of this movement, has for many years past organised these exhibitions, and he now has the great satisfaction of knowing that a permanent picture gallery, built by Mr Passmore Edwards, and maintained out of the rates, will be a fitting crown to the unselfish efforts of himself and his wife. Mansfield House has, also, through the efforts of the Warden, assisted by other members of the Town Council, succeeded in obtaining for the people the public baths, which have been for so long a crying need in the district. Baths are to be erected both in the north and the south of the borough, at a cost of about £18,000 each. The out-lying districts will in all probability receive assistance later on. This is paralleled by the action of Hull House Settlement in Chicago, which brought such pressure to bear on the City Council that an appropriation of 12,000 dollars was made for what was, I believe, the first free public bath in America. In the same way with the free library movement. Just as Mansfield House assisted in the canvass which obtained free libraries for West Ham; just as Toynbee Hall has, in a truly missionary spirit, assisted that and other efforts: so Hull House became, as it were, a branch of the Chicago Free Libraries, which

C

branch was maintained by the Board with two salaried librarians, and supplied with English and foreign papers, as well as books.

Another direction in which the residents of the settlement can devote considerable time and energy with much profit is in the work of sanitation. All except the largest towns of England have no option but to administer the Public Health Acts of 1875 and the Housing of the Working-Classes Act of 1890. The Public Health Acts especially are by no means perfect, and many Corporations have introduced improvements into their own private bills. The L.C.C. in 1891 obtained the Public Health Amendment Act (London). The first thing for the resident to do who serves on a Public Health Committee or a public body which has control of sanitation, is to see that the existing law, however imperfect, is properly administered. This is impossible without a sufficient staff, and, accordingly, Mansfield House pressed for an addition to the number of sanitary inspectors. I fear that it is absolutely inevitable that unsanitary conditions will prevail in all poor and working-class districts, unless the most drastic measures are taken to keep the landlord up to the mark. Such landlords are often of the worst type. One often finds street after street farmed out to an agent, who, however anxious he may be to keep the property in repair, has little or no power of spending money. A very flagrant instance of this was the case of a landlord who absolutely refused to allow his rent collector to do any repairs at all, preferring to employ another agent, who undertook to keep the houses in repair for a nominal figure, intending to do little or nothing himself. In new districts, the speculating jerry-builder has it very much his own way, for, however strict may be the bye-laws of a Council or Vestry, and however vigilant the building inspectors, it is next door to impossible to prevent a man who is determined to build a bad house from doing so. Sometimes houses become insanitary because they have not been built in a fit place. A considerable portion of the Isle of Dogs and of Canning Town is below the Trinity high-water mark, and in such cases it ought to be possible to prevent houses from being built until the marsh land has been raised above the river level by good brick rubbish or ballast. The London County Council obtained such powers. West Ham inserted a similar clause in their own Corporation Bill, and had it thrown out by a Committee of the House of Commons, with the result that men are at perfect liberty to build on wet marsh land that is sometimes as much as twelve feet below high-water mark. It may be said that the average resident of a settlement knows nothing about such matters ; if this be the case, the sooner he learns the better. But, as a matter of fact, we have illustrations which seem to prove the contrary. I have already quoted Mr Ward of Toynbee Hall as Chairman of the Works Committee of the L.C.C., and one who keeps a watchful eye on the Works Department of the Council. Two other residents also serve on the Local Sanitary Aid Committee—a body that endeavours to supplement in helpful ways the work of the local authorities.

Browning Hall, which has hardly been in existence three years, has taken an active part, through its members, in all civic effort. The sub-warden, Mr Bryan, is a member of the Vestry—one of six upon that body who are, more or less, in connection with the settlement. Mr Bryan has since his return rendered very marked service in the matter of sanitation. In particular, he brought to light the shocking state of affairs which prevailed in one district, which was proved by its death-rate to be the plague spot of the parish. The alarming prevalence of diphtheria led Mr Bryan, in the face of much discouragement, to press for investigation. And the result disclosed the remarkable, but not uncommon, fact that the sewers had been badly constructed with a reverse fall ; that they were broken and choked, and the whole ground was soaked with sewage. The sewers were, of course, relaid, and Mr Bryan was thanked by the Vestry for having called its attention to this serious scandal.

The settlements in America have not been behindhand in such work, and Hull House again affords a similar illustration. Situated as it is in the nineteenth ward, one of the poorest wards in the whole city, it was discovered that the garbage was rarely properly and systematically collected from the alleys and side streets. This work is always given out by contract, and Miss Jane Addams, the head of Hull House, on one occasion sent in a tender with other contractors. She did not succeed in obtaining the contract, and the obvious reason was that while they intended to "scamp" she meant to do the work. Thereupon she succeeded in obtaining the appointment of "garbage inspector," her business in that capacity being to see that the contractor did his duty. The result is that the nineteenth ward is one of the cleanest wards in the city. Another resident has taken the place of Miss Jane Addams, and other settlements are following in the footsteps of Hull House. My experience of settlements in America would enable me if necessary to give many other illustrations.

Another most important piece of work for the Settlement, a sphere in which the resident should find himself quite at home, is to be found in the provision of recreation grounds and parks for the people. Mansfield House, through its representative, has strongly supported the acquisition of these parks. Two of them have been purchased outright by the Town Council, and the third has been obtained by voluntary subscriptions. It seems to me that nothing could be more important than to give the Londoner a chance of breathing fresh air. The Metropolitan Public Gardens Association has done a noble work in providing open spaces for the people, and Settlements have often assisted them in their endeavours. But the work needs to be indefinitely extended and developed. It should be noted that Browning Hall made an attempt to obtain such opportunities for the people of Walworth, and failing that, they have, by the help of voluntary subscriptions, turned a little graveyard at the back of the hall into a public garden and recreation ground. Oxford House has treated in a similar way St Matthew's Churchyard, which is to be laid out by the M.P.G. Association. Philadelphia Settlement induced the Council of that city to improve very greatly, and enlarge, their garden; while Hull House has provided a fine playground for the children. As an extension of such work I should suggest that more attempts be made by the Settlement worker to beautify the district in which the House is situated. The warden of Mansfield House, as secretary of the Borough Relief Fund, and by the kindness and assistance of the Town Council, was enabled to employ a large number of men in laying out cricket pitches on Wanstead Flats and planting trees in some of the principal

streets in the town. There is no reason in the world why
the streets of East and South London should not be, at
least partially, redeemed from their utter sordidness by
the planting of plane and lime trees, which seem to flourish
even in the London smoke.

I have left to the last what I consider to be one
of the most important pieces of work that a Settlement resident could engage in—I mean the work of
technical instruction. On all sides we hear the cry for
more efficient education. Partly by design, and partly by
accident, funds are forthcoming, at any rate to some extent,
for the building of technical institutes or the conduct of
classes in manual training. But everywhere it is a case
of blind leaders of the blind. There is an utter lack of
knowledge as to the best method of procedure. The
Polytechnics have made many mistakes, chiefly owing to
the fact that they have looked only on the commercial
side. Here is the opportunity of a man with a University
education, who can, if he choose, become an expert in
this subject. His life at the Settlement makes it possible
for him to assist where assistance is most needed. In this
connection it might be mentioned that the warden of
Mansfield House, who is this year Deputy Mayor of the
Borough, is ex-chairman of the Technical Education Committee. It is not denied that this work requires men who
can give a fair amount of time to it, and who are in addition
thoroughly trained ; but while we are waiting for such men
the Settlement can do good work in strengthening the
committees that have control of technical instruction funds ;
and if they are wise they will discourage the attempts that
are being made, in forgetfulness of the ideal of education, to
make our technical schools mere grant-earning institutions.

Little or nothing need be said as to the School Board and Board of Guardians, as the ground has been traversed quite thoroughly in two other articles contained in this book, but it should just be pointed out that a great deal more work is being done than the outsider imagines. The warden of the Bermondsey Settlement has quite recently been elected to a seat on the London School Board. Toynbee Hall had for some years two representatives on the same body, and but for a mistake in nomination would still be represented there by Mr Bruce. Mansfield House had in the same way two of its members on the West Ham School Board ; though Messrs Newland and Reason have both left the district, the Settlement has this year succeeded in placing the sub-warden Mr D. S. Crichton in the same position. Oxford House, though unrepresented at present, has also taken a prominent part in the education of children on the London School Board, and other Settlements are moving rapidly in the same direction. It is needless for me to expatiate upon what is *par excellence* the sphere of the University man, and I content myself with adding that nearly all the Settlements have shown their interest in the education of the children by allowing their residents to act as School Board Managers : work, the importance of which cannot well be over-estimated.

To many Settlements the work of the Poor Law arises naturally out of the attempt that is sure to be made, almost at the inception of the Settlement, to relieve the distress of those who live in the immediate neighbourhood. It is perhaps a mistake, but it is a very natural one for the poor to make, to suppose that people who come to settle amongst them have come in the first place to relieve their poverty; and, as a matter of fact, some of the Settlements, and notably the Women's University Settlement in South-wark, have devoted an enormous amount of time to work of the Charity Organisation Society, believing that if help must be given it should only be after every possible pre-caution has been taken. It is not long, therefore, before the Settlement finds itself face to face with the question of how best to utilise the existing Poor Law, and it has been found of the utmost value to have representatives sitting on the Board of Guardians. Canon Barnett has represented Toynbee Hall upon the Whitechapel Board of Guardians, while another resident of the same Settlement has served on the Mile End Board. Mansfield House is represented by two of its members: Miss Cheetham, who is at the head of the Women's Settlement, and Miss Kerrison of the Co-operative Home. Bermondsey has a Guardian on the St Olave's Union in the person of the warden, who strongly believes that there is great need of improvement in our dealing with children under the Poor Law.

The Settlement, as it seems to me, has a unique oppor-tunity. It comes into a district that is chaotic and dis-organised, and proceeds to weld into one harmonious whole the broken, and often antagonistic, fragments of local life. It gives the people of the district an ideal to work for, and calls forth the reserve force which is always to be found even in the most apathetic and poverty-stricken locality. In this article I am concerned for the most part with the question of actual local administration, but I am very unwilling to admit that only representatives on public bodies are of much value. I can conceive of a Settlement greatly influencing the work of local administration without possessing a single representative. Reference has already been made to the work of School Board Managers, and, incidentally, to the help given to local authorities by voluntary Sanitary Aid Committees. I am of opinion that every Settlement should have in con-nection with it a committee of working men with a resident to act as secretary, who should devote themselves to assisting the medical officer and the sanitary inspectors of the locality. The Mansfield House Brotherhood has in this way caused hundreds of cases of insanitation to be examined into which otherwise might have altogether escaped observation. One practical example may well be given in illustration. A member of this society reported that at a certain house the tenants had been without water since they entered, a period of six weeks, although they had paid their rent regularly, and the agent did nothing in response to their appeals. Mr Reason, the president, at once investigated, and found a condition of things that can be better imagined than described. The stench was fearful, and several of the children were ill and feverish. Urgent representations were made to the Sanitary Inspector, who took up the case with prompt energy. Not only that house, but one or two neighbour-ing ones were inspected, with the result that the land-lord made a, to him, disastrous appearance before the magistrate, and the evils were remedied. Without such co-operation, it is impossible for the few inspectors to maintain control over several square miles of houses, which, experience shows, must all be considered as unsanitary until proved to be otherwise. The residents at a Settlement should endeavour to make themselves acquainted, not only with the laws that govern administration, and not merely with the transactions of the various public bodies, but also with the local officials, who are much encouraged and strengthened in their action if they feel behind them a strong consensus of public opinion. My own view is that nearly all the most important reforms of the next ten years will come by way of the Town Council, the Vestry, the School Board, and the Board of Guardians. Lord Rosebery seems, also, to think that this is the age of the Council and Local Administration as opposed to the House of Commons and Imperial legislation; but, even if it were not so, and your House of Commons were on the *qui vive* for every new and promising measure of legislation, what would it all amount to apart from capacity to administer the law when made? If the Settlements can supply the right men—men of tact and character with broad and generous views—there is the possibility of great advance, even in East and South London. We need men who would settle down and work for years at the problem of casual labour or the unemployed. We need men who would take pains to investigate the conditions of the poor, and, above all, men who are willing to apply the knowledge which has been thus obtained. It is not sufficient to collect facts, figures, and statistics, and then to use them as a sort of fetish to scare off the would-be social reformer. The man who is afraid to make a mistake rarely does much that is worth remembering. Why should not the "citizen student," as a resident at the Settlement has been called, devote himself to helping forward the solution of some part of this great poverty problem? On this point I feel inclined neither to add to nor detract from the opinion of two years ago, as stated in "The Universities and the Social

Problem." The poverty which results from casual labour and the lack of employment has become a national disease. From one point of view it is a national crime, and, as such, must be atoned for by long years of ceaseless effort to effect the necessary reforms in our existing social system. And if we are told that local and imperial legislation for these objects is paternal government, and ought not to be resorted to in the nineteenth century, let us answer, in the words of Sir Arthur Helps, "Never is paternal government so needful as when civilisation is most advanced." Here we are crowded together in a place that is "treeless, colourless, bathless, mudful, smoke-stained, its amusements coarse, the dress of its inhabitants hideous, its food adulterated, its drink pernicious," and, we may add, its houses insanitary. Poverty, as Stopford Brooke says, is not merely lack of food or clothes, but "that condition of things in which, for lack of means, no true development of the natural powers of any man or woman can be reached." Using the word in this very true sense, there are hundreds of thousands of men and women in England who, just because they are ignorant and apathetic about these necessaries of a higher life, must be raised to see their importance and assisted in the obtaining of them. Their environment tends to corrupt and demoralise, making the work of succeeding generations far more difficult. At present we are expecting an evil tree to produce good fruit, untilled and untended land to produce a rich harvest. If this is the soil in which the future generation has to grow and develop, will it develop or degenerate? This is the question we have to answer, and, having answered it in the only way possible, let the resident at the University Settlement continue to take an interest even in the petty details of local administration, or the unattractive person of the casual labourer, for, as Wordsworth says:

> " He who feels contempt
> For any living thing, hath faculties
> Which he has never used: that thought with him
> Is in its infancy."

PERCY ALDEN.

SETTLEMENTS AND EDUCATION

" A LL Settlements, both in England and America, seem
to be begun upon one uniform principle. The
first object, to which every other is subsidiary, is to make
friends with the neighbourhood—to become part of its
common life; to associate with the people on equal terms,
without either patronage on the one side or subserviency
on the other; to share in the joys and sorrows, the
occupations and amusements of the people; to bring
them to regard the members of the Settlements as their
friends."

These words of Sir John Gorst admirably sum up the
spirit in which a true settler approaches the problem he
has determined to grapple with; it may be called a spirit
of undifferentiated helpfulness.   But, as soon as he has
taken up his quarters, and become a veritable neighbour
to the living men, women, and children, that helpfulness
must necessarily take on some concrete shape.   The needs
that cry aloud on every hand must be met by something
more effective than mere sympathetic feeling; this must
be translated into action—the expenditure of positive effort
upon actual conditions, with the purpose of achieving a
definite result.

There are always two points to be settled: not only
" What needs to be done ? " but also, " What can I do ? "
For the power of universal helpfulness belongs to none
of us; we have to confine ourselves to those matters that

45

by reason of our differing abilities, opportunities, previous training, and many other considerations, we can do best, leaving the rest to comrades who are strong where we are weak.

Since the first impulse to settlement life came from the Universities, and these still supply most of the men, it is only natural that this question should have been answered in large measure by different forms of educational activity, for this is, as the writer already quoted puts it, the line of least resistance. The field is obviously immense, practically unlimited, and is just the one in which the man fresh from his own studies feels he can do the best work. It is true that actual experience often modifies this confidence in important respects. The scholar is not necessarily a teacher; a man may be able to absorb information as a sponge soaks up water, and yet lack the power of imparting it to others. He must have not only knowledge, but the ability to present it in a manner intelligible to the particular persons he has undertaken to instruct. This means he must speak their language, for which something more than a common mother-tongue is required. The best form of words, from an abstract point of view, will often fail to penetrate minds unaccustomed to that phraseology. I remember hearing a lecturer to an East End audience, who continually corrected ordinary phrases by a more classical diction: "If a glass of beer is allowed to stand for a time, it becomes thick, that is, it *attains a mucous viscosity*." The teacher must also have a tactful sympathy which enables him to discern just where difficulties are felt—difficulties that would never have been felt or suspected by himself. This is what I mean by "speaking their language."

It is pretty certain, also, that a little experience will considerably modify the teacher's estimate of his own educational superiority, without assuming at all that he was conceited about it to start with. He will find that even a University curriculum, with all its apparatus of tutors, lectures, classes, and libraries, leaves large provinces of knowledge untouched, and is in many ways not so successful in training the powers of observation and judgment as is the rough schooling of a knock-about practical life. While he has been dealing with books and abstract ideas, these men he has begun to teach have been handling concrete things. Many of them have travelled a good deal and seen many aspects of life hidden even from the first-class voyager through many lands. He will learn from them to look at matters from points of view that are to him startlingly new, and will, sooner or later, come to regard himself as one offering his contributions to the ' common stock of practical wisdom, rather than as one standing in the relation of teacher to pupils. Such, at least, has been the experience of the present writer.

But, for all this, the man who is educated in the conventional sense of the word, has, truly, unbounded opportunities of usefulness, if he will bear in mind these considerations and lay aside all "superior person" notions. For the man of books possesses many advantages over those whose life has led them almost entirely among things of immediate practical import; and there are round him, wherever he pitches his tent in East or South London, thousands of minds starving for the food he can give, hitherto denied them, or only doled out in scraps that make the hunger more sorely felt; and thousands more that may, by appropriate stimulus, be brought to feel and

satisfy a need of which they were before but dimly
conscious. It is not only what he can give directly; it
is the training in methods of study that he has received,
and his ability to point the way to the immense stores
of accumulated information that so often are within reach
but missed for lack of a little guidance, that make his
help so valuable.

As for the field itself, it is exceedingly varied. Just
as one finds, on exploration, that the region called vaguely,
in common parlance, " the East End," is really a congeries
of many large and distinct districts, each with a special
character of its own, in spite of the wearisome monotony
in external features, so one finds, also, of the people, that it
is not only a gross libel for Tennyson's Farmer to say,
" the poor in a lump is bad"; it is absurdly inaccurate to
say they are anything in a lump. It is only those persons,
possessed of one idea, who work in one rut, that meet only
one kind of poor people ; as, for example, some who confine themselves to sifting out applicants for charity, come
to believe that all poor folk are cadgers.

So the settler finds that he may use his powers in many
different ways of helping or education.

I. To begin with, there are a very great number of men
and women of a pre-Board School age. All those born
thirteen years before the passing of the Elementary Education Act—roughly, all those of more than thirty-five or forty
years of age—come within this term ; and it is not astonishing
that a considerable portion of these are not able to read
and write. But the expression must not be pressed too
strictly from a chronological point of view, for the passing
of the Act was naturally not followed by a perfect system
of gathering the children into the schools. The meshes

of education are still wide enough to let many slip through, and when fees had to be paid the number was much greater.

These grown men and women do not care to make use of the evening classes provided by the School Boards. They are out of place among the boys and girls not long out of the day schools, and are sensitive about displaying their ignorance before a number of possibly not too sympathetic young people of superior attainments. There is also a rigidity in these classes that is unavoidable where grants must be earned and a certain kind of discipline maintained, which makes them uncongenial to those who are heads of families and do not love to put themselves "under authority" overmuch.

The best way of helping such is to form classes of a freer social character, where they will meet only those in much the same position as themselves, and will have the least possible sense of going back to school again. The Friends have shown one most successful way of doing this in their early "Sunday Morning Adult Schools," which have been so widely imitated. In these the elementary subjects of reading, writing, and arithmetic are taken first, and afterwards the class turns to discussion of religious topics. From the simply educational point of view, of course, it is the discussion, not the subject, that is essential. Where teachers and members prefer it, the range may be over social, literary, or scientific topics. The main thing is to obviate the drudgery of elementary learning by an atmosphere of good fellowship and the introduction of what working-men dearly love—discussion on some matter of live human interest. Other matters must be modified to suit local exigencies.

II. Then there are those who have passed the school

D

age, the younger men and women who want to use their powers that have been trained, so far, in adding to the smattering of learning gained in their all-too-short a course. The Board's Continuation Classes are doing excellent work, but they do not by any means absorb all these. They are at present very largely composed of boys and girls who have only recently left school, for whose capabilities and natures the discipline and methods of school are still most appropriate; and their subjects are limited in scope by practical considerations. This makes them unsuitable for a great many who, without being in any sense unruly spirits, find the conditions in force to be restrictions that hamper rather than assist; who also desire to pursue lines of study not yet found in the curriculum.

To illustrate by a practical example. I was once returning with a party of East Enders who had been spending Whit-Monday at Oxford. Our compartment was occupied by young men, all being somewhere in the early twenties or even less. The conversation turned on their favourite fiction, and one young iron-worker quite simply mentioned, as the author he appreciated most—George Meredith. The rest, almost without exception, named other writers of quite great rank.

This is only one of many experiences that have convinced us who have lived in familiar intercourse with working people, that one of the saddest features of our social system is the enormous waste of intellect. One wonders at the tremendous force of brain power that would be at the service of the nation, if all these were given ample scope for development. As it is, countless numbers are discouraged and let their abilities run waste, being turned by social pressure away from their natural channels. Others plod on, but for want of that free association of mind with mind, that constitutes so valuable a part of University training, they make for themselves ruts, and are apt to become narrow in their appreciations. We meet constantly with men who have read with astonishing results as to the mastery of detail in their favourite authors, but who give one a second shock of surprise that, knowing so much, they should yet know so little.

It is just here the man of wider culture may make his personal efforts most valuable. By means of circles for study, rather than classes, he can introduce new authorities, elicit what each student has read, give helpful suggestions as to filling up the gaps of knowledge, and illuminate the points that rise for discussion out of his wider reading. It is here, too, that his own culture will be most helped, for those ideas which he has learned to hold in a merely traditional or academic manner—not unknown at our Universities—he will be compelled to re-examine from fresh points of view, as he is called upon to defend them. Nor is there any sphere of helpfulness in which a man can more readily win the trust and gratitude of those he is trying to aid. Even in the troublous regions of sociology and economics, in which, from the intimate relation they bear to the conditions of the worker's daily life, such strong feelings are mingled with intellectual concepts, difference of opinion will never alter friendship, if the opinion be urged without dogmatism, and with a transparent desire to ascertain the truth.

How wide is the range of such circles or classes may be seen by the reports of the different Settlements, notably that of the educational work at Toynbee Hall. Partly from being "the Mother of Settlements," and having had a longer experience than all others, partly from having laid great stress on the educational side from the beginning, and partly from its extremely favourable situation, which is so central and easily accessible, Toynbee Hall is far ahead of all other Settlements in this respect. It may be likened to a People's University. There are classes in the literature of classical (including Hebrew) and modern languages, in languages themselves; in different branches of natural science; in history; in economics; in ethics; in such technical subjects as shorthand, book-keeping, friendly society finance, drawing, ambulance, nursing, swimming, etc. There are also classes for men of the character indicated in the previous section, and afternoon classes for girls in subjects ranging from domestic economy to hygiene, through ordinary class subjects to such things as musical drill, wood-carving, and swimming.*

Other Settlements have laid more stress on other lines of work, and are, from their greater distance from Central London, not so well able to get a sufficient supply of able teachers. Still, a good deal of excellent work has been achieved which is likely to increase every year. The better part of the results cannot of course be put into figures or tangible form. We have to remember

> " All the world's coarse thumb
> And finger failed to plumb,
> So passed in making up the main account."

But even in the more sternly practical matter of making it easier for poor students to win certificates that will help them on in the struggle for a living, a goodly record

* See Appendix E.

could be compiled, which would appeal to the most
matter-of-fact persons. Speaking for our own Settlement,
Mansfield House, our students have gained certificates
in connection with the Society of Arts, London Matricula-
tion, and St John's Ambulance Society, all of which are
in their respective ways commercially valuable; I have
also by special request coached two men who were seeking appointment as Factory Inspectors, but cannot at the
moment speak as to the result.

It seems to me there are great possibilities to be
developed here. I have several times mentioned the
Continuation Classes under the School Boards, and indicated that there is no rivalry with these, but an endeavour
to be complementary. As a matter of fact, by complying
with certain structural requirements and putting the classes
under the supervision of H.M. Inspectors, it is possible
to receive the same financial aid and recognition by the
Education Department that the Board's classes receive.
Nor need this at all interfere with the greater freedom
I have laid stress upon. One has only to satisfy the
Inspector that education is really given, and that attend-
ances have been properly registered; there is no cast-iron
examination to be dreaded, and I understand that this
greater elasticity of method is no drawback, but a positive
merit in the eyes of H.M. Inspectors.

In the movement to develop a real teaching University
for London out of existing material, there is no reason why
University Settlements should not bear a useful, though
humble, part. In the endeavour to make a complete ladder
from the Board School to the University the need of kindly
hands to help the student up the rungs must not be forgotten, and it is to offer these that the Settlements exist.

III. Another organisation which may be both used and
helped by Settlements is the Society for the Extension of
University Teaching. I have made a separate section for
this, because, in this case, the teaching is supplied from
outside the ranks of the Settlement and its helpers. What
is left for these to do is to stimulate the necessary interest,
provide the local organisation, and sometimes lend the Hall
in which the lectures are to be given. Toynbee Hall has
no less than nine of these courses in its twelfth year's report.
Mansfield House supplied the original stimulus in its district,
and for some time provided premises and a secretary, and,
since the Corporation of West Ham made the lectures a
part of its Technical Education Scheme, it has had other
lectures in its own hall. The Warden of Browning Hall is
secretary for his district ; Bermondsey Settlement includes
among its residents the secretary of the London Society
itself ; Cambridge House, and the Passmore Edwards
Settlement, which have developed from Trinity Court
and University Hall respectively, will certainly carry on
the practice of their progenitors in this respect ; while Oxford
House has made a start this last year, with the aid of the
London County Council.

I can speak from personal experience of the keenness
with which the students at these lectures take up their
study, the pointed nature of their queries, for the most
part, and the continuance of the same students in the
successive courses ; while the examiners' reports testify to
the excellence of the work done.

IV. It has been assumed in all the previous sections that regular attendance is practicable. A very
large number, however, either cannot, or will not, set
aside a certain hour each week, and consequently can-

not receive the benefit of systematic study in one subject.

As regards those that cannot, this is mostly due to the irregular nature of their work. Of those in constant employment, many have to work in alternating periods of day and night shifts; others are liable to be called upon for overtime; while in the dock districts many callings, being dependent upon the arrival of ships, can hardly be said to have any regularity at all. Every day that a vessel remains in the docks is grudged. Dockers to unload, shipwrights to repair, and stevedores to load again, crowd upon each others' heels, working often night and day until the job is done; and, of course, where special cargoes are carried, such as grain or coal, the "cornies" or the "coalies" are under the same conditions. All this is discouraging to those who hold classes and those who wish to attend them, but needs must when Mammon drives, and the only thing to be done is to devise some way of meeting the circumstances.

Then one has to consider the great mass whose own natures are incapable of sustained effort, but who will gladly give an hour or so now and then for acquiring knowledge that is pleasantly put. For what I have said above as to the capabilities of some by no means applies to the great mass of East and South Londoners; these are for the most part what their circumstances make them.

The requirements of both these cases are met by single lectures. They must be held at some regular time and place, so as to be readily found when opportunity and inclination agree; but each must be complete in itself, so as to be perfectly intelligible without regard to anything said on an occasion when the listener was not there. If limelight views can be added, so much the better.

Most Settlements have tried these and found them a great success The best times are undoubtedly Saturday and Sunday evenings, for then the largest proportion of the population is likely to be free. Toynbee Hall undoubtedly takes the lead in the pre-eminence of its lecturers. Here, for example, are some of the names taken from the list of 1896-7—Rev. Canon Barnett; Sir Alfred C. Lyall, K.C.B., K.C.I.E., K.C.S.I.; Colonel C. Cooper King; Arthur Sidgwick, M.A.; J. Franck Bright, D.D.; Dr J. D. M'Clure; Leslie Stephen; W. H. Preece, C.B., F.R.S.; Frederic Harrison; Sir Charles Elliott, K.C.S.I.; Prof. J. W. Hales; Prof. A. V. Dicey; Prof. Victor Horsley, M.A., F.R.S.; Sir W. Martin Conway; Prof. Clifford Allbutt, F.R.S.; Major-Gen. Sir Francis Grenfell; Prof. Flinders Petrie; Sir Walter Besant; Augustine Birrell, Q.C., M.P.; Dr A. M. Fairbairn; Sir Herbert Maxwell, M.P.; Prof. J. E. Carpenter, etc., etc. Other Settlements, though at a great disadvantage from their remoter situations, are yet able to maintain a very high level in this respect, and it is a remarkably healthy sign that those who have won so deservedly high a reputation in the subjects they have made their own are willing, at considerable sacrifice of time and convenience, to give of their best so freely to those who are only able to offer their grateful and earnest attention in return.

As to this, however, it may be confidently said that there is no better audience than one of working men and women. None follow a lecture more closely, none are so hearty in their genuine applause, and, if it be a debatable matter, none so ready and frank in questions and criticism. This is the reason, I am convinced, why those who have something worth saying are so ready to say it without other reward. As to the benefits conferred, there is no room for question. Looking over the reports from the different Settlements, one notes that they range over every topic of human interest. At these lectures the dwellers in the dreary monotonous regions of Poorer London are taken into other lands by the vivid descriptions of travellers who have been there themselves, often aided by splendid lantern views; are initiated into the many-sided wonders of natural science; are introduced to the great men and women of all ages and all lands, and led to share their thoughts; are helped to appreciate the masterpieces of literature, art, and music; or are instructed in the facts which must be taken into account in the solution of those social problems in which they, of all people, are most vitally concerned. It is, indeed, a liberal education, and one wishes that the centres at which it is given could be indefinitely multiplied. In East London alone, including West Ham, there are at least a million and a quarter of people whose conditions tend inevitably to keep them ignorant and to narrow their outlook upon life, and this leaves South London and large tracts in other parts to be reckoned with also. When one runs over the list of centres such as have been described, and calculates the accommodation offered, the question rises with a sigh, " What are these among so many? "

V. In summing up the educational efforts of Settlements, a prominent place should be given to the Picture Exhibitions, introduced by Canon Barnett at Toynbee Hall. The example thus set has been followed by the Warden of Mansfield House, who has arranged three annual exhibitions on behalf of West Ham Corporation, and in

this last year by Bermondsey Settlement.   At these shows
the working folk are introduced to the works of many of
our foremost artists, and, as far as possible, guides are
provided who are able to give necessary explanations and
information.   The numbers of visitors at the three centres
show how keenly the exhibitions were appreciated :—
Toynbee Hall (nineteen days), 63,000 ; Canning Town and
Stratford (four weeks), 120,000 ; Bermondsey (one week),
11,675.

VI. I now come to a most important field in which the
settler may spend himself on behalf of education, one which
might well have a chapter to itself—viz. School Board work.
The machinery and the cost of public elementary education
are supplied, as they should be, by the community, but
money and organisation are of little worth without the
right men to use them.   For the administration of the
Education Act two sets of persons are required—members
of School Boards, whose duty is to care for the needs of
their entire district, and on whom all the financial responsibility rests ; and members of local Boards of Managers,
with special groups of schools under their care, who are
entrusted with such duties as visitation of schools, reporting
upon particular needs, primary selection of teachers, etc.
The great bulk of the metropolitan area is under the
London Board, which is of such size and importance that
it attracts men and women of more than local influence
and reputation, though my own personal belief is that
Boards of normal size controlling the separate districts
would do much better work, and that the reasons for a
united municipal London do not exist in educational
affairs.   West Ham, however, has a separate Board, and
there are districts distinctly metropolitan in character or

rapidly becoming so—*e.g.* Hornsey and Tottenham—which would be greatly benefited by Settlements in their midst and settlement members on their School Boards.

For the settler has at least three important qualifications for this post. He—or she—is in the first place educated himself, which, with all due respect, cannot be said of all those elected to supervise the education of others. Secondly, being a settler, he has a detachment of interest which sets him free to make this education his first object. For it must be sorrowfully recorded that election is too frequently sought on other grounds. Some are put forward mainly to keep down the rates; others on one side or the other of the great ecclesiastical strife; others with a pure Labour policy; while some appear to run with an eye to the advertisement of themselves and their business. Except for the last, no doubt much can be said for these. We need good business men to control the finances and check waste, always provided that the economy is not of that shortsighted kind that is of all things most wasteful. We need, while theological controversies are still allowed to intrude into the education of our children, a due balance of denominational interests. We need *bona fide* working-men to keep an eye on the conditions of labour for those directly or indirectly employed by the Board. But we need, above all, those who lay the greatest stress on their primary function—education. Nor is there any reason why the settler should not be well qualified to act in these other directions also.

Thirdly, the settler, if worth his salt, has a considerable knowledge of the actual conditions of the children's home-life, and is in touch with the thoughts and desires of the parents themselves, good and bad. This cannot fail to be of immense service in the practical details of his work. For the Boards are mainly administrative, not legislative, and the chief business is done in committees. It is here that particulars are thrashed out, and the complexities of practical matters are considered. Having been closely connected with West Ham School Board as member or as chairman of managers for nearly six years, I have had some experience of this. Suppose it is a question of Continuation Classes in his district; the settler knows pretty well what is the demand for them, and what should be their character. Or when sitting at Attendance Committee with grim magisterial functions, he knows whether the excuses are likely to be true, will sometimes be acquainted with the actual circumstances. Conversely, many cases with which he can most fittingly deal as member of a settlement, become known to him, first, as member of the Board; and in such questions as cheap or free dinners, boot supply, and others that are outside the legal scope of the Board, but are intimately related to its practical action, the settler should be of great service.

Pretty much the same may be said of the settler as School Manager. Here it is his business to make himself at home in the schools, to become the friend both of teachers and scholars, to smooth away friction, to make helpful suggestions, to go thoroughly into complaints and requests that are sent up to the managers from the schools, so that decisions may be made with knowledge. There is also a considerable activity in schools that goes beyond the legal requirements. Many teachers devote a good deal of energy and time to such things as clubs, concerts, etc., which add wonderfully to the life and *esprit de corps* of the school. The manager can do much to help this spirit where it exists and to stimulate it where it does not. In fact, there is much more than enough to take all the time that he (or she) can devote to it. Lastly, outside the actual holding of office, Settlements can be very useful allies of School Boards in what may be described as filling up the gaps.

In the first place, while the leading men are keen on education, there are still a large number of poor folk who are in daily life in practical antagonism to the School Board, personified in their visiting officer, who is always spoken of as if he were the entire Board in himself. The hard circumstances of their lot are principally responsible for this. It is extremely difficult for them to judge of the relative importance of Johnnie's being given a better start in life, or of being allowed to earn a few coppers as an errand boy; and it must go very much against the grain to let Nell go to school, when it would be so much more convenient to have her at home looking after the baby—or as is too often the case, the babies. The poor, having to live daily from hand to mouth, do not look far ahead; moreover, looking ahead seldom discloses any cheerful prospect. Settlements can do much to strengthen the belief in the value of education for the children, and make these poor people ready to undergo still greater sacrifices for it than they already do. What these sacrifices are only those who have received the *entrée* into their life can know.

But there is a more definite way of helping that has been discovered. In all poor districts there are a most distressing number of children who are physically unfit to attend school. In West Ham, for example, we find any number of cripples, who could not possibly mix with the boisterous throng that rush with whoop and yell round the playgrounds, nor climb the steep stairs that have become so familiar a feature of our "three-decker" schools; in most cases they could not get to the schools at all. The Women's Settlement in Canning Town have taken these helpless little ones under their wing, and opened a morning school for them. The children, or such of them as require it, are collected by means of a donkey-carriage; then school "goes on from 9.30 to 12, and consists of singing, drilling (!), handwork of various kinds, reading, arithmetic, and simple object-lessons." The results have given ample encouragement. In many cases proper instruments have been supplied and have given great relief; while all will sympathise with the closing words of the report :—"The children show marked improvement, not only in acquisition of the 'learned arts' (!) but in general intelligence and joy of life; and in this we specially rejoice, for it is indeed a good thing to bring brightness and happiness to children whose lot should naturally be joyous, who yet travel such a weary road."

WILL REASON.

SETTLEMENTS AND THE ADMINIS-
TRATION OF THE POOR LAW

THE task has been assigned to me of dealing with the relations of University Settlements to the Administration of the Poor Law. It is not easy to treat of this subject, because many burning controversies are concerned with Poor Law Administration, and these are involved with very difficult economic and moral problems, which try the most competent social thinkers and administrators. Of all such particular controversies this paper must keep entirely clear. The vexed questions of Outdoor Relief, of the Unemployed, or of the best methods of dealing with Pauper Children, cannot here be discussed.

But one preparatory word must be said. If Settlements have any particular call to take part in Poor Law Administration, it is in order to promote those humane objects which the wisest and best Poor Law reformers set before themselves. But those objects are not easily adjusted to the leading principle of the reformed Poor Law that life' under Poor Law authorities should be made less desirable than ordinary life. The authors of the Poor Law revolution of 1834 had to deal with a pauperised nation. This state of things had been brought about by the combined influence of a vicious system of relief, an unparalleled strain upon the national resources, the sudden introduction of machinery into manufacturing processes, and the unorganised condition of labour. The reformers set themselves to brand pauperism

63

as a disgrace and well-nigh a crime. They accepted the
principle that the destitute should not be allowed to
starve, but they treated destitution as so entirely attributable to the conduct of the destitute person, that continued
existence should be made as undesirable as possible to him.
They succeeded so well that they largely eradicated the
✓ tendency to pauperism, and created a disposition which,
in many cases, though extreme supporters of charity
organisation doctrines may deny it, prefers death to
submission to the workhouse test.   There is no question
that, taking all the facts into consideration, the reformers
did the greatest service, not only to the country as a whole,
but, above all, to the progress of the labouring classes.

But the new ideals, whether they aim at discriminating
treatment of the aged poor, at the improvement of medical
and nursing efficiency in Poor Law Infirmaries or Hospitals,
at securing the best elementary education for the children
of the State, or at the general increase of ordinary amenities
of life under the control of the Guardians of the Poor, do
unmistakably show that, the danger of a pauperised nation
having passed away, more complex considerations than
prevailed in 1834 are making themselves felt; and it is
not easy to see how far these may lead.   Certain it is that
if recourse to the Poor Law in old age, or in sickness, is to
be avoided by great multitudes of our deserving London
poor, it can only be either by a great increase in wages, or
by an enormous increase in the volume and a great improvement in the organisation of private charity.   The former
solution is, probably, impossible until a corresponding improvement takes place in the economic condition of labour,
not only throughout Great Britain, but elsewhere.   The
latter, if possible, would be open, so it seems to some of

us, to as many objections as can be urged against Poor Law Relief. Why shall not the Christian principles and sympathies of the community act through the Poor Law and its administration, as well as alongside it in the constitution of private charity? The work of Settlements, at least in connection with the Poor Law, must proceed upon this presupposition.

The Settlements have already contributed much service to Boards of Guardians. The influence of Canon Barnett and of Mrs Barnett, not only in local administration, but on the public discussion of Poor Law problems, is too well known to need explanation. It is, perhaps, not in strictness attributable to Toynbee Hall, for its origin is prior to that of Toynbee Hall, and would have existed had that Settlement never came into existence. Mr T. Handcock Lunn, a resident of Toynbee Hall, was for some years an active member of the Stepney Board of Guardians, and in that capacity did much to secure the discussion of problems connected with Outdoor Relief. Oxford House, though not directly represented on the Bethnal Green Board of Guardians, has taken a practical interest in Poor Law work; and residents of St Margaret's House have regularly visited the infirm wards of the workhouses and infirmary, besides taking part in carrying on the work of the "Workhouse Girls' Aid" Committee. The Women's University Settlement, under Miss Sewell, has co-operated with the St Saviour's Board of Guardians in various charitable enterprises. Mansfield House, Canning Town, has Miss Kerrison as its representative on the West Ham Board of Guardians; and Miss Cheetham, the head of the Settlement for Women Workers in Canning Town, has been a Guardian for the last five years, and is chairman of Plaistow House,

E

a branch of the West Ham Workhouse. Through their representatives a powerful influence has been exerted to secure improved nursing for the sick and infirm, improved classification, and increased recreation for the inmates of the workhouses, better education for the children, and discrimination in the administration of outdoor relief. The Bermondsey Settlement has taken a considerable share of Poor Law work in the St Olave's parish. I have been a Guardian for the last six years, and have been chairman of the Rotherhithe Infirmary for more than five. During that time I have been able to promote the establishment of a training school for nurses, to form a committee of ladies to visit the infirm wards of one of our workhouses to entertain the inmates, and generally to assist in the more humane treatment of the inmates of our institutions. Five years ago, by the influence of the Settlement, two lady Guardians were for the first time elected, one of them being Miss Simmons, the head of the Bermondsey Settlement Women's House, who has been again returned as Guardian this year. She and I together established a Workhouse Girls' Aid Committee, which meets regularly at the Settlement. Our lady residents also carry on the Brabazon Society at one of our workhouses, and at the infirmary. Recently I became a manager of the South Metropolitan District Schools, and in that capacity presided over an inquiry which led to the re-organisation of an Herne Bay Convalescent Home, and over another inquiry, which led to the introduction of many educational and sanitary improvements into Sutton schools. This account is necessarily incomplete, but enough has been said to show that the Settlements have already made a very important contribution to the improvement of Poor Law Administration.

Coming to the general question, it need hardly be said that Settlements can provide no panacea for Poor Law ills. The influence of Settlements will almost entirely depend upon the unostentatious way in which they carry out their aims. There is perhaps some danger lest, as the value of their work becomes more widely recognised, they should turn neighbourhoods against them by a certain tone of conscious superiority and a rash avowal of a purpose to set everything straight. But there are several high qualifications for service in administering the Poor Law, which Settlements may fairly be supposed to possess.

In the first place, their residents may be supposed to be actuated by true consecration to social service. They will contribute to Boards of Guardians neither stingy and selfish administrators whose only object is to save the rates, nor noisy demagogues whose great desire is to win popularity with the multitude. As they seek the coming of the Kingdom of God generally, so their object as Guardians will be the assertion of its principles, as they understand them, in dealing with the suffering, helpless, and sometimes vicious people who are dependent on the community for support. And to this high aim they may be expected to add trained intelligence, with both the leisure and the knowledge to follow out carefully the consequences of various policies offered to them, having always a careful eye for the probable effects upon the character both of individuals and of the community of any proposed line of action. Character will be with them the supreme concern, and they will criticise each proposal with regard to its effect in preserving or so far as possible restoring character in those over whom they take charge. And, once more, Settlements are associations of men and women animated by the same spirit, and ready to assist in carrying out great tasks. The Settlement Guardian can avail himself of the trained force of comrades with whom he is united to help in carrying out his work.

But these three qualifications—high consecration, trained and careful intelligence, and the power to secure the co-operation of like-minded friends, are just those which become rarest in the poor and overcrowded districts in which Settlements exist. Denuded of the educated, the prosperous, and the leisured, administration tends to pass into the hands of men with lower aims, or at least less competent ; and even where neither of these things is true, scarcely any have the power to bring capable and sympathetic workers into the field to assist them in their task. Yet of all departments of local administration the Board of Guardians is the one where this state of things is most disastrous, and therefore there can scarcely be a field of service where the distinctive advantages of Settlement workers can be of greater benefit to the common weal.

It will be well to indicate some of the special matters in which the presence of Settlement Guardians should make itself felt.

Speaking first of the *Infirm Wards of the Workhouse,* there is, above all, the great human problem. There are aged men and women spending together the closing years of their life, for whom it is necessary to secure, not only healthful, religious, and moral influences, but rational interests ; some degree of freedom, above all, from the wearisome monotony of routine, and some sense that they are not beyond all concern of the community, but are still the objects of sympathetic thought and care. It is hardly necessary to enumerate the methods and agencies by which these ends may be secured. But they are most important, not only for the inmates themselves, but as expressing and educating that humane spirit which it is most necessary to cultivate in the public mind.

Then again there is *the Infirmary*, in which all such work as is needful for the workhouse should be carried on, so far as sickness permits, and where, in addition, it is necessary to secure a steady increase in the efficiency of nursing, and improvement in the *personnel* of the nursing staff. More than can be said depends upon the tone of the administration, if this great end is to be attained.

Of most critical importance is the management of *the Poor Law Schools*, or of any other system of dealing with the children of the State. Upon two objects all high-minded Guardians are set, namely, first of all to give to these children increased educational advantages, so arranged as to be the best remedy possible for the inherited drawbacks of mind, body, and surroundings from which the children suffer ; and secondly, to secure such domestic arrangements for the children as will reduce to a *minimum* their loss in being deprived of the happy home which ordinary children enjoy. Under any circumstances that loss must be serious and real, and mischief is done when any new method of dealing with these children is represented as free from inevitable drawbacks. Barrack schools have great evils of their own, but so may cottage homes or boarding-out arrangements easily have. Vigilance, wisdom, and sympathy of administration is nearly everything. Better what is called "institution life," despite its evils, with thoughtful and tender oversight, than cottage homes or boarding-out, if laxity or satisfaction with cant phrases is allowed to prevail. Here, indeed, is scope for the most enlightened educationist, especially when the problems created by the physical, mental, and moral drawbacks of these children are taken fully into account.

Again, there are the *Able-bodied Paupers*, representing every kind of unfitness and of misfortune. Here the many-sided aspects of the unemployed difficulty may be studied in individual cases, and much detailed knowledge acquired, without which general speculation is lacking in adequate data.

And once more, there is the distribution of *Outdoor Relief*, a subject for careful study and prudent dealing. All will admit at least this, that outdoor relief will be in the highest degree demoralising unless it is administered with the highest motives and the most circumspect consideration.

I have but indicated the problems which must be dealt with, and I repeat that the way in which they are handled affects not only the individuals under the control of the Guardians, but the morale of the community to which the different Poor Law institutions belong. Settlements should make Poor Law work the object of their concern ; firstly, because they can find, and, in many districts they alone, the men and women who will redeem administration from self-seeking and harshness, or weakness and stupidity ; secondly, because Poor Law problems admit to the very heart of those social evils which Settlements are seeking to cure ; and, therefore, because by understanding them, Settlement workers may be enabled patiently to bear their part in those general movements of reform by which ultimately pauperism may be done away.

J. SCOTT LIDGETT.

SETTLEMENTS AND RECREATIONS*

IN the minds of many excellent people the word "recreation" has a somewhat frivolous sound. It seems intelligible that men of strong religious or political views should go on "missions" to make converts; that they should throw themselves earnestly into the promotion of education, thrift, the right distribution of charity, and other matters of serious import; but why spend time and money in helping working people to play?

The most effective answer to this would be a six months' residence under the conditions that dominate the lives of millions of our fellow-Londoners. As this is not practicable in more than a few cases, I must do my best to indicate by the feeble medium of words the main features of these conditions.

A traveller from Fenchurch Street or Liverpool Street to Stratford, let us say, by the Great Eastern overhead trains, sees stretching out for miles all round him a dreary monotonous area of narrow streets made up of dingy barrack-like houses. For the most part these are small; he can look down on the roofs, and note the ingenious device of raising the front wall above the tiles by some

---

* A good part of this article is taken from the writings of the late head of Oxford House, by his kind permission (see Preface). I have also to thank his publishers, Messrs Gardner, Darton & Co., for allowing such copious extracts to be made from "Work in Great Cities." W. R.

courses of brick, so as to make the house appear from the street to be larger than it really is. Scattered throughout this area are great ugly factories, which improve the landscape as little as the foul odours, of which they are so liberal, add to the delights of breathing. The church spires alone give any sense of relief. That is the general effect, and depressing enough it is. One feels almost grateful to the London fog for making it impossible to gaze too far in any one direction.

Now let the traveller get out at one of the stations, and pursue his researches on foot through any of the districts of which this area is made up:—Whitechapel, Stepney, St George's in the East, Shadwell, Limehouse, Mile End, Bow, Bromley, Poplar, the Isle of Dogs, Stratford, Canning Town, etc., each of which is a very fair-sized town in itself. The places do not improve on closer inspection, and if he can get inside the dwellings the sense of discomfort will increase. Most of what should be the "homes" of the people are constricted tenements of one, two, or three rooms, of such small dimensions that the proverbial cat, if swung by her tail, would suffer damage to more than her whiskers. They are for the most part ill-lighted, and the state of repair is never much to boast of. In these small inconvenient tenements the workman and his family have to make their "home"; and East End families are, to put it gently, *not* in proportion to the accommodation. The same features belong to South London life, save that, perhaps, the huge tenement houses are to be found here in greater proportion.

So much for a bare suggestion of the conditions, wonderfully different from those of most of the readers of this book. But is human nature in Deptford, Bermondsey or

Bethnal Green as strikingly different from that in Hampstead, Kensington or Clapham? Not at all. In all, man is a social being, desiring converse with his fellows; in all, his constitution demands the alternation of work and play, of strain and relaxation, of expenditure of effort and renewal of power—in a word, that continual *re-creation* that is necessary to restore the elasticity of life. The difference is not in the need but in the means of satisfying it.

How, for instance, can a man invite a few of his "pals" to spend a social evening at his house, when he has no house but a tenement that will not hold himself, his missus and the kids, without grave discomfort, and the one room must often serve as kitchen, wash-house, sitting-room, nursery, and bedroom, if not workroom as well? Even with the better off who have three whole rooms to themselves, the sitting-room is much too small for anything like social purposes. It is wonderful what a steady man and a clever managing wife can do with such places, but there are limits the best can never pass, and we have to deal in these matters with the great mass, who cannot rise superior to their upbringing and surroundings.

Now contrast this, not with any kind of mansion, but with the suburban villa, where a snug meal waits the home-coming of the city man, and the children, after their welcome kiss, are packed off to bed or play-room; where pictures are on the walls and books on the shelves; where arm-chair and slippers are ready for the tired back and feet, with innumerable little luxuries that are taken as a matter of course; where half-a-dozen friends can come in for a smoke and chat, or the piano is ready in the drawing-room for a musical evening; where there is perhaps a bit of garden at the back, or a glass-house in which to spend spare hours in the summer.

All these things are *recreative*, and are taken without thought of extravagance. If they do not minister to your life, why do you have them? If they do, if without them you would lose your force, become worn out, what of those who are compelled to go without?

As a matter of fact, there are in poorer London any number of places where men may meet with their fellows, in good light, genial warmth, and with elbow room; places that are attractive by their superior size, their striking decorations, and the strong glare that is thrown by their windows and outside lamps across the dull and murky street. But there are drawbacks to these places. They are called public-houses, gin-palaces, beer-shops, and a man who frequents them overmuch gets a light pocket, a heavy head, and a damaged character. I do not want to lay stress on the bad side of these places; we are all sufficiently familiar with that. What I do wish to emphasise is the point, that with all their faults they fulfil a most necessary function in social life, and that the only genuine reform must take heed of this. A residence of over six years in the East End has convinced me that if it were possible to close all the public-houses in London at a stroke, we should speedily have an uncontrollable revolution. By serving as centres of social life on the one hand, and on the other by drugging the great mass of undisciplined malcontents into apathy towards their wretched conditions, they prevent this. Whether the remedy is worse than the disease is a doubtful point; but the true line of reform is by supplying healthful social conditions, until we have succeeded in making the homes what they should be. The places of intercourse are of prime import-ance ; and the problem is to provide such as will be free from the noxious action of intoxicants, and at the same time will afford the discipline of character that is necessary to all permanent reform.

This is why all the Settlements, without exception, have made this matter of social recreation one of their primary concerns, and have taken up the club question ; not all, of course, to the same extent. Oxford House in Bethnal stands pre-eminent in this respect, but there is not one that has not either started clubs of its own or associated itself with those already in existence, as in the case of Toynbee Hall and the Club and Institute Union. We are here concerned, however, with the special Settlement clubs.

(I.) **Boys' Clubs.**—These may be taken first, since " the child is father to the man," and it is undoubtedly with the young that the most effective progress can be achieved.

In starting these clubs, the great thing to be remembered is, that they must be such as the boys will be at home in. One may have very nice ideas as to what they ought to like, but unless they have what they do actually like, the rooms will remain empty.

" In other words, it comes to this. I assume that you are going down into your districts to attack the real problem, and not some fancy problem, which you think ought to exist. If you are, then 'take the human animal as you find him, and touch him at any point where he can be touched.' Let your heart go out to these lads, so generous, so loyal, and so true when you know them ; love them—that is the main thing, and then, how to win them, 'love will find out the way.'"*

* "Work in Great Cities."

A goody-goody club, with many rules, is predestined to failure, while one of a more rough-and-tumble order gives just the material that is to be worked upon. Of course there will be no drink and no gambling, nor will foul language be allowed to pass unchallenged—I mean really foul, not merely ornamental language. But, if the promoters are wise, there will be no attempt to force religion on the lads. There will be ample opportunity to bring whatever form of Christianity the promoters may favour to bear upon their lives in a natural way, but the worst possible thing, both for the success of the club and the genuineness of the religion itself, is to make it compulsory. As Canon (now Bishop) Ingram has said:

"On Sunday, have a Bible-class connected with the club; but, if you take my advice, you will not make attendance at it a test for coming to the club. I know that in saying this I am going against the practice of many good workers, but it touches a question about which you will have to make up your mind for all clubs. Is it for Jacob or Esau? If it is for the peaceful Jacob, who is already in the choir, or just promoted from your Sunday school, to whom you merely want to give a little amusement in addition to his performance of his religious duties, then make any rules you like, so long as they don't make him a hypocrite; but if it is for the jolly but lawless Esau— who has never been inside a church in his life, who escaped early from Sunday school, if he ever went—I doubt the expediency of a test club, unless your rooms are so small that you can only take a small number, and definitely prefer to pick the boys who wish at once to be religious."*

There is, however, an existing cleavage that does

* "Work in Great Cities."

somewhat divide boys into unmixable classes. There are
social distinctions in poorer districts, though, to their
credit be it said, they are more nearly allied to distinctions
of character than are the social grades with which we are
more familiar.   So that, where possible, it is a good thing *t*
to have two clubs; one for the more tractable set with
better home influence, and the other for those who would
not feel at all comfortable in anything like a model club.
Oxford House has done this : we find not only the Webbe
Institute, but also the Repton Club, "which was started
some three years ago with the object of touching a lower
class of boys than those dealt with by the Webbe Institute "
(Oxford House Report for 1896).   This is the sort of boy
that delights in fighting, in gathering in gangs at the street
corners, in showing their superiority to those in the
conventional garb of respectability, sometimes in outbursts
of what our Australian cousins call "larrikinism."   It
requires a special genius to deal with these, or such of
them as are not really vicious but only rowdy; a true
perception of the difference between downright evil and
what is merely objectionable to a more cultivated taste.
The directors of the Repton Club seem to have been very
successful in this.

Of course, in such clubs physical recreation is the great
thing.   Boxing, cricket, football, harriers, etc., are strong
features; they provide a healthy outlet for animal spirits
with a discipline that street corner horseplay most decidedly
lacks.   But the Repton has also classes in reading, writing,
and drawing, a library, and a monthly church service, all of
which are reported as flourishing.

As to the comparatively sedate kind of club typified by
the Webbe Institute, where shirt collars are more numerous

than knotted scarves, and the hair is worn at the normal length, the same sports are keenly pursued, while the more intellectual pastimes, such as chess, etc., have greater scope, and the classes have a wider range. An excellent feature of some clubs is a workshop where handicrafts are taught and practised with very good results.

All these clubs are partly governed by committees elected by the members themselves, and this is one of the best things about them, since it develops an *esprit de corps* and a self-discipline which are invaluable in the moulding of social character.

Here, too, one may most fittingly refer to the summer camps, for these are mostly in connection with the clubs. In these, for a week or a fortnight, the members get a glimpse of what is to them another world. The crowded, noisy streets, the squalid courts and ugly houses, the close, used-up atmosphere, and the artificial excitements of the town give place to the spaciousness of sky and sea or countryside, the beauty of cliff and down, of field and hedgerow, of woodland and clear-running streams, the pure sunlight and fresh breezes, and a healthy, open-air life. In these, also, they learn to know each other better, and are certainly better known by those in charge of them. This camp idea may be indefinitely extended ; in fact, Browning Hall (Walworth) has successfully held a camp for men, women, and children together at Court Farm, Whyteleafe, Surrey. "The men slept on the straw in a large barn, while equally simple and primitive sleeping accommodation for the women and children was supplied at an outhouse on the other side of the farm. The whole party took meals together, and spent the day in strolls together, in long rambles through the charming Surrey Highlands, or in

restful enjoyment of the wide view from the hill-top. This
year the time was extended from ten to fourteen days, and
the number of the party was much larger. On Bank
Holiday there were as many as 126 in camp, and there
were never fewer than 30 " (Browning Hall Report for
1896).

II. Men's Clubs.—Much that has been said of Boys'
Clubs applies to these; the chief difference being that
grown men are, of course, much more able to manage
their own concerns. At the same time, it is necessary to
have certain safeguards in the constitution, for the Settlement has its own ideals, and cannot afford to find rooms,
etc. for a club that may conceivably so change in membership as to run counter to these. One has to steer, as the
Bishop of Stepney says, " between the Scylla of despotism
and the Charybdis of anarchy." The ex-head of Oxford
House speaks from " experience in working one club of
800 working-men, and another of 300, and also in watching
the working of the sixty different clubs which form our
federation, and which comprise nearly 8000 men.

" Here, again, you must at once make up your mind
whether you are going to cater for Jacob or Esau; if for
Jacob, then make any rules you like; there ought not to
be the slightest difficulty in working a quiet club for your
church working-men. They have already got the very thing
to which you hope some day to lead Esau—they have got
'religion,' the safeguard of righteousness and the bond of
peace. The clubs I speak of are for Esau, and, as a first
step to making him religious, have no religious test; let
him be as free from being 'buttonholed' in your club to
join anything against his will as a bishop is free from being
'buttonholed' in the Athenæum to join the Land League.

Have no political test either, of course; it is a *social* club you want; it is a union of men as men, to raise the life of man. Begin small, and educate a nucleus, then have a committee, just as with the boys. Safeguard your principles of no drink and no political test by a council with a power of veto ; put in a third rule that it must be carried on in a way consistent with its connection with the church ; keep the original property in your own hands, and have whatever the club itself buys entered on a separate inventory, and having taken these preliminary precautions, launch it on its way a free, self-governing thing." *

Oxford House has associated itself definitely with St Matthew's Parish, Bethnal Green. But if "Settlement" be read for "church" these words apply to all cases, whatever the religion of the promoters, or if they prefer "ethics" to religion the case is stronger still, if that is possible.

Just as it is only those who know the conditions of life in poorer London who can understand the need for these clubs, so it is only those who are closely associated with their working who can appreciate the results. I have referred to the tremendous hold the public-house has on our people ; that hold it has chiefly because it supplies, and has for generations supplied, just the social elements which are the main features of our clubs, with the additional attraction of strong drink. That the Settlement clubs, without this attraction, have succeeded in gaining so many members shows that they are on the right tack.

"In other words, your club must be an effective cut-out of the public-houses which flare at every corner; there is no good wasting your breath in abusing publicans: it is

* "Work in Great Cities."

useless, besides being usually quite unfair. Devote your energies to cutting them out. Let me quote an incident. I was visiting in the London Hospital, and found myself sitting by the side of a broken-legged publican. When he heard who I was, he began asking about the welfare of several of our club members. I asked him how he knew them. 'Oh,' he said, 'they were regular customers of mine before they joined your club; I had a public-house close down your way.' 'Are you still there?' I asked him. 'No, sir, I've moved a little farther off.'" *

Unfortunately it cannot often be claimed that a publican has had to remove farther off, but I am sure that all who have devoted their time and care to these clubs will confirm the experience that many a man's life has been steadied, and his home consequently improved, by simple membership in a Settlement club, without "buttonholing" of any kind.

The Federation of Working-Men's Clubs, referred to above, is also the work of Oxford House. The members of this Federation have the right of entry into any club belonging to it, wherever they may happen to be. There are seventy of these clubs in East, West, and South London, all of them of the kind indicated, while a similar Federation for boys numbers about forty clubs. Competitions of many kinds are continually in progress between club teams or individual members; and, after ten years' work, the promoters are able to report that "they have at last begun to respond to the many years of personal work which have been put into them. The men's clubs especially take more interest in one another, pay inter-club visits, back up competitions and sports, with a greater zest and

* "Work in Great Cities."

interest than ever, and are also responding to Mr Eyre's unceasing efforts to stimulate interest in matters of education and social service "* (Oxford House Report for 1896).

As to general results, "I should feel inclined to put first and foremost the astonishing education in self-government which a club, worked in such a way as I have described, gives to its members, and especially to its committee. The unselfish and unpaid work demanded of them, the grip of a new ideal to work for beyond the immediate necessities of daily life, the development of powers of organisation and management which long have been dormant for want of use, end by turning out, after some years, men whom you would readily trust with your life or your honour, and who would be well fitted, if opportunity offered, for posts of high responsibility in municipal and civil life.

"Then, secondly, we may note, as an undoubted effect of club life of this satisfying sort, the raising of the ordinary age of marriage among the younger members of the clubs. As the 'club parson,' who is generally invited by the bride and bridegroom—and allowed by the unfailing courtesy of the surrounding clergy—to bring to a happy termination an engagement of which he has long been in the secret, I have special opportunities for testing this, and I am never now asked to tie the irrevocable knot until the bridegroom is at least twenty-five; whereas, if I come across a boy who has 'dropped out' between the boys' club and the men's club, or for some other reason has 'turned up the club,' I almost invariably find that he has married at nineteen or twenty."†

* See Appendix F.
† "Universities and Social Settlements."

These, with the other results that have been noted in passing, the improvement in physique by the sports of cricket, football, cycling, running, swimming, and gymnastics that are always associated with these clubs, the broadening of mind by intercourse with fellow - members of different political, religious, and social views, the education by classes, lectures, etc. which is open to them, the steadying of character, and the raising of home-ideals, and the opportunities of social service that are constantly presented and frequently taken, must make all critics, if there be any, see much more in this "recreation" than at first was apparent.

III. So far, clubs for men and boys have engrossed our attention, but much is being done in this direction for the girls by members of Women's Settlements. The need is no less, for one of the most heart-sickening sights of poorer London is the multitude of girls who have to find their place of recreation in the streets; sometimes even the most seasoned settler is appalled at the outbursts of coarse laughter and rough jesting proceeding from a bevy of the gentler sex (!). Yet a closer acquaintance with their surroundings turns the aversion into pity, and a closer knowledge of themselves often converts this again into admiration and respect. "Judge not by appearances, but judge righteous judgment," is a lesson constantly forced home on those who take up their residence in the East End, though to the very last one is caught tripping. Somehow, offences against our taste and opinions strike deeper than we always care to own, and govern our judgment in spite of ourselves.

All the same, there is more need of some civilising force among these damsels of the large feathers and mighty "bang." (A bang, it may be explained, consists of the front hair brought over the forehead and cut short just above the eyebrows.) They are wild, shy creatures ; shy, that is, of all attempts to catch them. But a good many clubs have been formed for them by Settlement Workers, and others already established have been greatly helped.

Of course it must not be supposed that all girls in these districts are of this kind. It is always the worst that first catches the eye. Casual observers will condemn a whole district as drunken because they have seen half-a-dozen drunken men ; and one bad plumber will spoil the reputation of the whole trade. Just as the boys were shown to differ, so do the girls, and their clubs are similarly of different grades. But in their actual management they may be classed together. There is needlework of course, and cooking, but they are not purely domestic. Woodcarving and basket-work find favour, then there are classes in all kinds of educational subjects, singing, musical drill, gymnastics, etc. The games are of a less boisterous kind, and the open-air sports are conspicuous by their absence. If I might be permitted a suggestion, I should say that a good hockey club would prove a valuable branch of this kind of work ; it is played by girls in high schools, and the outfit is not costly : indoor gymnastics are good, but open-air sport is better.

Somehow the girls cannot grasp the principles of self-government as readily as the boys—it would be unfair to contrast them with the men—and this characteristic throws a great deal more hard work and responsibility on the organisers. In the Factory Girls' Club of the Women's Settlement at Canning Town the experiment of a committee of the girls themselves has recently been tried, and is favourably reported on. Perhaps it might be hinted that a more daring policy in this direction would bring about greater success than is anticipated by those in charge, but one hesitates to offer advice to those who doubtless understand the position better than we "mere males" can hope to.

A splendid feature of the work in the rougher girls' clubs is the Bank Holiday excursion. For those who stay in the London streets this means drinking, fighting, and often something worse. But their friends of the Settlements carry off as many as they are able to some quiet place in the country or seaside, *where there is no public-house*, and tire themselves out in the constant effort to provide interest and enjoyment, never leaving them until they reach home, too late to "get a drink." During the next day or two comparison of experiences with fellow-members of the club who did not go, clinches the conviction that they have really had a far better time, with no such after effects as black eyes, aching heads, and empty pockets. Slowly they begin to adopt truer judgments of life, that before were impossible to them, since they did not possess the materials for judgment. And it is quite certain that the girls who have been through these clubs will make much better mothers, and have much higher aims for their own girls, than those who have known only the factory, the street, and the public-house.

IV. Outside of club life, Settlements may do much for healthy recreation. Clubs are of course confined to their own members, but the smallness of available space, and the present scarcity of workers, makes it impossible to extend this membership indefinitely. There remains a large number who cannot for various reasons receive all the benefits of associated and systematic recreation. Whatever is done for them must be more of the nature of simple entertainment, and this must not be despised. The man who brings good healthy laughter to the lips of those who live constantly "on the seamy side" has done a thing, if not to be proud of, at least to rejoice in.

There are, of course, many places of amusement in East and South London, chiefly the music-halls. Now I would not at all like to be considered an enemy of these; on the contrary, I should like to see a much greater number of them. Nor do I uphold those criticisms which take it for granted that the entertainment there given is of a vicious kind. My own experience of them is not large, but such as it is, it has rather proved them to be at least as free from objection on the score of morality as many more "respectable" places. My criticism of them is rather that they are not amusing enough, and that they are too often connected with a public-house, or have drink within their own precincts. Now, apart from all question of these places and their control, there is evidently a big field for the provision of good, clean, and easily accessible entertainment, both to lighten the lives of those who do not care to frequent the ordinary music-hall, and to win away as many as possible from the opposing delights of the drinking shops.

Naturally, poor folk love ballad music more than severely classical productions, but it is astonishing what keen critics of good execution many of them are. I have come to the conclusion that it is not lack of appreciation that makes them welcome barrel organs and indifferent performers on the cornet, or pay their money to listen to fifth-rate singers at the halls, but simply that they are glad to get whatever they can. Certainly, many of the working-men's bands reach a high pitch of excellence, and, so far as my judgment goes, a really good performance almost always gets its appropriate meed of applause.

Now Settlements, having many friends of larger culture, can persuade these to come down at intervals, and give a really good concert on Saturday night. It is worth the trouble, to watch the lines smoothed out of the careworn faces, and note the childlike power of forgetting trouble for a time. But it must not be forgotten that it is pure amusement, not "edification," that is here needed; the humorous song or recitation must not be left out, and if a dramatic sketch can be supplied, so much the better.

But Settlements do well not to rely on this outside help altogether; they must have in their own ranks those who can fill up a vacant evening. An orchestral society, a brass band, a dramatic society, a glee society, a well-managed minstrel troupe are all exceedingly useful, both for the members themselves, and for the service they can render. It is surprising what promising material can be found among the members of the clubs and others attached to the Settlement. Some one with musical ability, tact, and perseverance, will be sure to succeed in training a company that may face comparisons boldly.

Then there are special social gatherings in connection with the many Settlement societies that almost insist on forming themselves when once the work has got into full swing. Complaint is sometimes made against churches that people may come together Sunday after Sunday and know nothing of each other — the same is equally possible in poor districts, and needs as much guarding against. In the Settlement reception-rooms, however, these informal "socials" serve at once to break down the barriers of strangeness and reserve, and at the same time to add another pleasant evening to the all too meagre list.

I cannot close without mentioning an experiment now being tried by the Warden of Mansfield House, although I have hesitated whether to put it here or in the article on education; the two are so closely related. This is a Lending Picture Collection; the pictures and prints are to be lent out for certain periods to be hung on the walls of the workmen's tiny houses, to bring them some gleams of beauty. They may be then exchanged for others, and so these messengers of pure, pleasant, and artistic taste will speak in many a dreary home. It is an experiment which might well be copied in all parts, and those who have not been able to help in any other way might be of great service here.

Pictures, books, good music, clear laughter, heart fellowship—are not these true aids to life? Is it not worth while to bring them within reach of the docker, the coal-heaver, the artisan, and the common labourer; nay, right down into the "doss-house," where the broken ones of Society get their precarious lodging night by night? For never will the evil spirits be permanently cast out until the empty house is tenanted by such as these; no reform was ever achieved by mere destruction and prohibition; the hovel must be replaced by a healthy home; the "boosing-shop" by a centre of true fellowship; mischievous books by clean literature; coarse ribaldry by pure fun. And let those who are apt to set such store by what they call the "spiritual," as to despise these things, remember that man is to live "by *every* word that proceedeth out of the mouth of God."   WILL REASON.

WOMEN'S SETTLEMENTS IN ENGLAND

IT is impossible in one short paper to give a picture of the work of all the Women's Settlements in England, or even to make a fair statement of their principles, or describe their methods; it seems better, therefore, after enumerating them, to sketch their work, and to consider shortly, what are the main questions that they all must consider, and whether Settlements, as such, have any vital characteristics.

In the year 1887, not long after the foundation of Toynbee Hall, some of the students of the Women's Colleges at Cambridge and at Oxford joined in the establishment of the Women's University Settlement in Southwark, leading the way in the movement which has since spread so quickly. This first Women's Settlement was, and still is, mainly supported by college women, including now many members of the London University and of the Royal Holloway College; and the majority of the executive committee is chosen by the colleges, not in general meeting, but by separate elections. Residents are, however, not necessarily from the colleges. In 1889 the Association was registered under the Companies' Acts. After renting a house in Nelson Square for some years, the committee was able to purchase three adjoining houses, including the original one, and to throw them into one for the use of the residents, of whom there are now sixteen. Religious work (in the accepted use of the term) has not been undertaken, and the management is entirely unsectarian.

Two years later, in 1889, Mayfield House was opened at Bethnal Green, by the Cheltenham Ladies' College, joining forces until 1892 with the Ladies' Branch of the Oxford House. Both were on Church of England lines, though not confining themselves entirely to parochial work. The latter, in 1893, was transferred to a new residence, St Margaret's House, still in Bethnal Green, and in 1896 enlarged its quarters by adding University House close by. The Cheltenham College Mission, in 1897, decided to move into Hoxton, and to build a new house there for sixteen residents.

The next oldest Women's Settlement is that of the Women Workers at Canning Town, founded in 1891. Its management is independent, but it works in co-operation with Mansfield House. Residents of all creeds are admitted, and the Settlement works in connection with the Congregational and other churches of the neighbourhood.

The Women's House at Rotherhithe, under the same committee as the Bermondsey Settlement for men, was started in 1892. It undertakes religious and social work in close connection with that of the men.

Two other houses, the College of Women Workers on Blackheath Hill, commonly called the Grey Ladies, and the North London Ladies' Settlement, Holloway Road, both founded in 1893, are usually classed among the Settlements, though they can hardly be so called in the strictest sense of the word, as the houses of residence are not placed in a neighbourhood chosen as the field of operations, and residents are sent out to various parishes at greater or less distance. Both are exclusively attached to the Church of England, and work only under the direction of the clergy. In both, the residents wear a uniform.

There are four other Settlements in London which should be mentioned : the Robert Browning Hall, Walworth, where men and women undertake social, philanthropic, and religious work together; the Lady Margaret Hall Settlement in Lambeth, opened in 1897, supported mainly by Lady Margaret Hall, Oxford; St Mildred's House, Millwall, Isle of Dogs, a Church of England House, also started in 1897; and the Stratford Settlement, opened in January 1898. These last two are affiliated to St Margaret's House, Bethnal Green.

Already the great provincial towns are following the lead of the capital. The University Settlement at Higher Ardwick, Manchester, was formally constituted in 1896, after experiments during the previous year. It is definitely connected with Owens College, and, like that college, combines the work of men and women. Each have their own house of residence, but they are under a common government, by a mixed committee elected in general meeting. It has been arranged that the Settlement shall work in close connection with the already existing Art Museum at Ancoats.

In Liverpool, also, the Victoria Women's Settlement, under an independent committee of managers, was started in the beginning of this year.

To give a description of the work carried on by all these centres, would be a monotonous task, involving much repetition. It would be hardly possible, and certainly not desirable, for every Settlement to initiate original schemes for the amelioration of evils which are so almost universal in the poorer parts of large towns. Experimental philanthropy, valuable as it is, is likely to yield its best results only in the hands of those who thoroughly understand, from their personal knowledge of it, the working of existing machinery; and it is probably to the credit of the founders of Settlements that the lines of work laid down by them were the highways of experience rather than the bye-paths of theory. To give local help, which was so scanty before, to existing organisations, whether the parish or the special society, has been the first aim of most, perhaps of all Settlements; such novelties as have been attempted, are quite subordinate. From this point of view the similarity between them is great, almost dull. Nearly all take part in school management, in boys' and girls' clubs, in the Childrens' Country Holiday Fund, in the case of invalid children; most help the Charity Organisation Committee of their district, and provide for district nursing: perhaps all make some endeavour to encourage thrift, and to advance education. But the relative importance of these common objects differs in each, and some two or three feel it of great importance to keep in view what are now often called "Charity Organisation principles."

In the details of their work a few distinctive points stand out from the rest. Canning Town supports medical sharing-out clubs, a medical mission, and a hospital with two resident lady doctors and several nurses. These ventures sprang from the special needs of the district, and are not very likely to be imitated elsewhere. The Women's University Settlement at Southwark has a sick benefit society, and helps in the management of a provident dispensary for women and children. It may perhaps be said that this Settlement devotes more attention than any other to the encouragement of thrift, by school banks, by district collections, and by carefully collecting parents' contributions towards expenses incurred on behalf of their ·children.

The Bermondsey Women's Settlement supports two district-nurses; they have taken up the idea of a country holiday fund for women, and make a special point of teaching the children to play organised games.

Canning Town has a workroom for needlewomen, preference being given to the old and others who cannot easily get work; and this is not very far from being self-supporting.

Of the Manchester Settlement it is rather early to speak, but in the first year at least, the work was very largely educational, and of the nature of University Extension.

· The Southwark Settlement works a mixed evening school, the Acland Club, under the London School Board, and inspected by the Education Department, which has now been established for several years and has achieved a fair fair measure of success.

Both Southwark and Canning Town definitely recognise the secondary value of Settlements as a training place for workers elsewhere, and the former has obtained endowed scholarships from the Pfeiffer trustees, and undertakes also to train a limited number of students, who can pay their own expenses, for a year or longer, in different branches of social and philanthropic work.

One distinction, deeper, perhaps, than a mere difference of detail—and this not in its religious, but in its constitutional aspect—is the point of dependence, or independence, of government. Those Settlements which share in the

usual work of a parish, under the direction of, and responsible to the parish clergy, gain in certain directions, but
give up, to some extent, the choice of their own principles
and the shaping of their own methods, and with them the
security of being able to maintain a consistent attitude.
Two or three of the women's houses, again, are branches of
men's Settlements, independent of them neither in management nor in work, but closely co-operating with them, and,
at least, ultimately responsible to the committee, or to the
head of the men's branch.

It is not uncommon to speak of the "Settlement idea"
as if it were a new one, especially distinctive of Settlements,
and of "the work of Settlements," as if that again were
something by itself; but what is the Settlement idea, and
what the work of Settlements?

The more closely we examine them, the more difficult it
is to answer these questions. The "idea" common to all
Settlements is that persons of various callings and standards
should, in some measure, share a common life, that rich
and poor, educated and uneducated, cultured and uncultured,
should meet, and know each other, and help each other.

This, of course, is no new idea, but a very old one, carried
out more or less successfully in every village and small town
where the population is mixed, and social duties are recognised; adopted, practically, by all the churches who send
men of education and means to live amongst the poor,
and also by various philanthropic agencies to a greater
or less degree.

If it be argued that the Settlement idea is one of a more
real fellowship between class and class than is reached
under ordinary conditions, it can only be answered that

existing Settlements have not succeeded in realising this ideal any better than other people, and that it is doubtful whether they will. It would seem, on the whole, more likely that, under the somewhat abnormal conditions of life in a Settlement, the difficulty would be rather accentuated than diminished.

Then as to "Settlement Work," there is again nothing new; no existing Settlement has struck out an entirely new method, or one that must, from its nature, be peculiar to Settlements.

It would, perhaps, therefore, seem best to recognise that Settlements have no ideas or methods peculiar to themselves, but that they are rather an adaptation of accepted methods to special conditions of society. To put it simply, the Settlement is an effort to reproduce, in large towns and cities, where the population tends to sort itself according to its means, the more natural conditions in which all classes live more or less together, and can, if they choose, and without any trouble, know a great deal about one another. The idea, if idea it can be called, is to do consciously, and with a definite purpose, where population is dense, that which is done unconsciously, and without effort, almost everywhere else.

Given in a Settlement and in the educated and cultured portion of a mixed society an equal zeal for social service and equal ability to perform it, there may be no great difference in the results obtained, though the Settlement will probably be always a weaker force than its analogue, both numerically, and from its lack of traditions, of local influence, and of natural bonds to the place in which it settles, as well as from the resulting constant change in its *personnel*, and from the comparative narrowness of its interests.

To set against these disadvantages is the advantage that the residents in a Settlement have all voluntarily chosen their sphere of influence, and are actuated by a common and avowed desire to embrace sympathies and interests outside their own class.

That a Settlement is an unfortunate necessity born of a disordered condition of society, and only useful in certain places, will perhaps be admitted; and the problem of Settlements may be granted to consist in determining how far they can reproduce a natural condition of society, by turning to the best account the advantages, and neutralising the drawbacks of their position.

These considerations lead to the point of trying to determine what questions a Settlement, as such, has to decide for itself in laying down the principles in accordance with which it is to live. One of the first of these questions must surely be that of locality. A deep underlying bond of classes is the possession of a common local life. We all know the extraordinarily strong attraction of our own town or village; the place we belong to, the people belonging to the same place as we do, appeal to us in a way nothing else can. To know our neighbours, to be touched by local grievances, interested, not by sympathy, but by right, in local schemes, should be the aim of any Settlement worthy of its name, but must be beyond reach for any which does not, in a thickly populated district, limit its endeavours to a fixed area, and that not a very large one. This advantage all clergy enjoy through the organisation of parishes, and no public work could be efficient had not each body its own well-marked sphere.

Nor can a Settlement be expected to identify itself with local interests, and gain local confidence unless its residents individually become settlers. Some may be birds of passage—probably it is well that they should—and may bring freshness and new vitality to the more stationary workers; but some continuity of residence is all-important. It is not enough that the houses should remain, sending ever fresh workers into the field; only proved steadiness of work and tried capacity and persevering friendship can inspire trust in the fellow-worker at the committee, in the teacher at the school, in the parent at the home. Nor can the locality in its varied aspects be learned by the visitor of a few months, or of even a couple of years. How can experience be accumulated, how can experiments be safely devised or intelligently watched, unless the threads of the work be held in hands which have guided some of its past, and are in no hurry to forsake it in the future?

Even more important, perhaps, than a geographical limit, is the necessity for common principles of action, without which the so-called Settlement cannot but degenerate into a mere boarding-house, where the only bond of union among the residents is their common participation in "good works." The *reductio ad absurdum* might be reached in such a case as one resident working heart and soul for the Charity Organisation Society among the same people to whom another was distributing free dinners and coal-tickets.

It is better to do nothing than to pull two different ways. This is easily stated, and would probably be generally admitted as reasonable, but it involves another axiom which does not seem to be universally recognised. If a Settlement adopts certain principles, it must devise some method for insuring that they are carried out consistently

G

through all branches of work. The simplest way, probably, is to appoint a resident head, whose views are carefully ascertained to be in accordance with those of the committee, and to give her sufficient powers. Other methods of course may be chosen, but in some way it seems quite essential, not only to profess principles, but to secure that all action shall be in accordance with them.

Given the necessity for common principles and means for carrying them out, the next point for an intending Settlement would be to decide upon a general line or lines of effort. What these should be cannot be discussed here; it is enough to suggest that underlying all other sorts of work is the question of relief, which will turn up, and must be faced. However great the desire may be to help the people, otherwise than by direct gifts, this matter of relief is ever in the background of nearly all social endeavours in the present condition of our large poor populations. It confronts us in the school as well as in the home, in the very savings-bank as well as in the C.O.S. office; and unless fixed principles of administering and of withholding relief are adopted, and resolutely acted up to, very little of the rest of the work undertaken will prosper.

It follows from this that in matters of relief, above all, it is important to make sure of co-operation with other relieving agencies in the district, to ensure efficiency and prevent waste and cheating, with the moral degradation which so quickly follows successful cheating and undeserved gifts. To be in a position to co-operate with other institutions, including the clergy, a Settlement must have won its way to their respect and confidence. This cannot come suddenly at the beginning, but is sure to come as soon as it is deserved, in any neighbourhood where the harvest is plentiful but the labourers few. And it is in such neighbourhoods as these that Settlements establish themselves. To be friendly without losing independence, to be critical without being hostile, useful but not interfering, able to work with and develop the best institutions, without being dominated by any—this is a task which may employ the best energies of a Settlement, and which implies an attitude of mind which no one, not the most ambitious, is likely to scorn as too easy of attainment.

If one main object of Settlements is to bring back a few of the "leisured class" to neighbourhoods from which they have fled, it should be pointed out that they form an invaluable centre to which many outside workers can come who cannot give the whole of their time to such work. The mere facility for getting a meal or a bed does not count for nothing in the vastness of London to one whose home is miles away, and the advantages of focussing much effort upon a district are easy to understand. The hands of the residents are strengthened, so that it is possible to undertake more work than could otherwise be thought of; "understudies" can be held in readiness for an emergency; those who come in and out connect the residents with the outside world and help to prevent too great absorption in their special work; and they benefit in their turn by the experience and special knowledge of the resident workers with whom they come in contact. Those Settlements which enjoy the advantage of many efficient outworkers can appreciate it even more than those whose demand for such help is far larger than their supply.

The question of training is an important one. Both resident and non-resident workers can hardly avoid becoming trained in a greater or less degree, if they stay long enough, by the mere process of steadily doing a bit of work until they see what it means, what is behind it, to what it might lead, how it is only part of much larger schemes, how little, and at the same time how important, it is as a link in the whole. But this is very partial, and for "professional" workers, as they may be called, much more regular teaching is desirable and possible. In this way Settlements may, if they will, do much for the furtherance of their objects by definitely setting before themselves, as one of their main objects, the education of the workers of the future.

It is a great responsibility to undertake; it doubles the danger of working upon wrong principles, and should never be lightly taken in hand; but it doubles also the good which may follow from work thoughtfully begun and earnestly carried on: it is an opportunity which ought not to be lightly thrown away.

It may be remarked that much of what has been said of women's Settlements applies equally to men's, and this is true. The ideal of both must be much the same, and careful examination will show that the apparently well-marked differences between them are superficial rather than fundamental. Ideally, no doubt, the best work will be done where men and women combine their forces.

MARGARET A. SEWELL.
E. G. POWELL.

WORKING GIRLS' CLUBS

THERE was a time when I thought of working girls as a class. Now I am more inclined to think of young ladies as a class, and of working girls as individuals.

There is a refreshing reality about the working girl. She says what she means. You know when you have "got" her. She refuses to be bored for the sake of appearances.

A friend of mine was telling the girls a story one night at our club. The story was a little bit over the heads of the audience. One of the girls slipped away to see if she could find something more exciting going on outside. She came back—put her head through the door—"Come on, girls!" A moment more, and the whole audience vanished.

The working girl, however, does not object to a "jawing," if you can strike straight home. If you are right, she will own up. If you are wrong, she will tell you of it.

One Sunday the writer of "Life in West London" was giving us an address from the text "Whatsoever things are pure—whatsoever things are lovely—think on these things" —a talk on the influence of a pure imagination. And the verdict, free and open, was—"He don't know nothing about nothing." For the girls thought he must be ignorant of the conditions of their lives, or he could not have spoken of fair vision and pure imagination as things within their reach. They have found out since then that life may be for them even a thing divinely beautiful.

The working girl is a born philosopher. She can put up with every kind of luck. She can live day after day when work is slack on a cup of tea in the morning with one piece of bread and butter, and can come smiling to musical drill, and you will never guess it; she will stand to her work through the long hot days of summer and never complain, as she will suffer discomfort, hardship, or pain, as a matter of course.

I knew of a girl who kept her family all through the winter. She was the only one in work, and her work was scrubbing floors; and all the while she had a sprained thumb and came to the club in the evening with her right hand in a sling.

Faithful she is too. Loyal and true to the core is the heart of the working girl to those she loves.

Her ideas of sticking to a "pal" are rooted. It is a distressing fact that a girl will sometimes deliberately throw herself away, and tread in the hard way of the transgressors, because her friend has chosen to walk in that path. If she sticks to her she may save her, if she forsakes her she is sure her friend will go altogether to the bad. The argument that she may lose her own soul in a bootless attempt has no weight with her. If it is to be, it will be, she says with pagan acquiescence to fate. The working girl has not yet realised the supreme importance of getting her own soul saved! So when she has a pal, she will stick to her through thick and thin, she will make nothing of gifts and services; she will refuse pleasures offered to her alone, and through good or evil report she will fulfil to the utmost the demands of friendship. She has the same dogged loyalty with regard to her own family, and will lie freely, rather than "show the game up," when her mother gets drunk or her father ill-treats her.

Of course you have to understand her. And to understand people is, generally, to love them. There are so many things that have to be rightly judged. Dulness and apathy are not attractive; but when you find out that they spring from semi-starvation or want of sleep, you can be very patient. Many a girl who works hard all day can never get to rest early, because she has to wait till all the family go to bed. She does not know what it is to have a solitary or quiet half-hour. She lives in a chronic condition of nervous exhaustion.

On the other hand, wildness and unruliness and boisterous spirits may be the direct outcome of a despair with which no young heart ever ought to be acquainted. Coarse gesture, or noisy laughter that is not merriment, may be repulsive, but when you know that a girl lives in a street where you would hardly venture after dark, and remember that as a little child she used to be left out at all hours of the night, while her mother went off on the drink, you can only wonder that she has kept any place at all in her soul for purity and goodness.

While you feel for the girl who has grown up in the atmosphere of the slum, living her real life alone,—the girl who, with no inspiration from the outside, has yet remained heroically pure and good,—a reverence which gives a new faith in the divine humanity that dwells amongst us, I know many who have achieved this conquest. I know, too, that to such as these the daily life of factory and home is an actual martyrdom, inconceivable to anyone who is not intimate with the under-side of an advanced civilisation.

Perhaps, before passing to a more general survey of the girls' club movement, which has extended so rapidly in our great cities and throughout the country, it might be well to give a brief account of the club I know best, having worked in it myself for seven or eight years.

When my friend Mary Neal started the club amongst the girls in the neighbourhood of Euston Road, W., and I came to share the work, it was with the first idea of making the club the home, where all who came would find welcome and sympathy and companionship as well as interest and amusement. We opened it nearly every night of the week from 8 to 10 o'clock. One evening every week was set apart for a singing class, another for musical drill, another for games, or sewing or cooking, the programme, of course, being varied to meet the tastes of the majority.

We wanted to put as much happiness as we could into the two hours spent together, and we hoped to build up in the club human relationships that would influence and uplift the rest of the life.

But we found that we could not close the doors on the world outside, or forget its facts in the charmed circle about the fireside. There were twenty-two hours every day to put against the two hours spent in the club. The conditions, not only of the home, but of the factory or workshop, had to be taken into account. It became our business to study the industrial question as it affected the girls' employments, the hours, the wages, and the conditions. And we had also to give them a conscious part to take in the battle that is being fought for the workers, and will not be won until it is loyally fought by the workers as well.

It was not easy at first to arouse their interest in these industrial questions, for here again the working girl is fatalistic. But when they saw that a real grievance could be reported to the proper authority, and could be set right without any retribution following to the girl who had been the first to speak, without anybody being able to trace the source of information, their interest grew, and they began to see how many matters could be set right by the workers themselves if they would only take a little trouble to understand the laws passed for their protection.   One object-lesson is more effective than any amount of exhortation or argument.

One evening in the week is kept free for lectures or for informal talks.   The simplest economic axioms, and the most ordinary commercial terms have to be constantly explained and illustrated.   As the interest is awakened the intelligence is quickened, and they begin to watch and compare, and draw conclusions from their own experience of life.

We occasionally meet in debate the members of the St Christopher's Boys' Club in Fitzroy Square, which has sprung up and developed beside us.   The debates have proved very interesting, and much sound wisdom has been given from both sides of the table.   The girls and boys appreciate this opportunity of discussing together.   One of the girls said in a vote of thanks: "We are glad you men are beginning to talk these things over with us; what is good for a man is good for a woman, I say.   But it's not very encouraging for a woman when you men come home from your Trade Union of an evening, and we show a little interest, and ask where you've been to, and you say, 'You shut up; that ain't none of *your* business!'"

The story of the industrial co-operative movement cannot

be too often told to show how largely it is in the power of a disciplined and self-controlled working-class to better their conditions, and the principles of co-operation cannot be too often put in practice in a small way in the club.

Perhaps the brightest bit of our history as a club is our co-operative summer holiday. The fortnight we have spent together every year in the country and by the sea has done more than anything else, perhaps, to weld the members together; and it has given us an insight into the lives of the girls, and a knowledge of their character that we could not have gained in any other way.

The country holiday evolved out of the idea with which we had first started—the idea of sharing our best pleasures with the girls. When we talked of the delights of our childhood, and brought back flowers and reports from a day's tramp, they were naturally not satisfied. The story only made them want to have the experience.

The first experience was certainly not a success. We often laugh over it now. One of the girls was over-worked and ill, and, after great efforts to scrape the money together (for in those days the club was very poor, and had fewer friends than it has now), we managed to send her away into the country of which she had heard so much. She wrote back to say how she was longing for the fortnight to be over—but "I am going to bear it for your sake."

But now, not only in the summer, but also at Easter, at Whitsuntide, and even at Christmas, we must arrange to get them away to "Mother Earth," or to "Father Sea," or they are not satisfied; and the love of trees and grassy places has become in some almost a passion.

We talk about all sorts of things when we get away together and have nothing else to do; and of course we dream all sorts of dreams, and make all sorts of plans. It was thus we dreamed of a workroom of our own, which has become now an established fact.

The idea was started as we talked, giving rein to our fancies, of a life lived together far away from the city, as we drew idyllic pictures of the co-operative dairy, or fruit-farm, or jam factory we would have some day.

We sighed, for it was only a dream after all; and the turmoil of the city and drudgery of the workshop were realities with which the next week would bring us face to face.

And then came the question. If our lives must be passed in the workshop, why should we not have a workshop of our own, and bring in conditions which should make work itself a happy part of life? This seemed a dream too.

But years after we had first talked of it, the dream came true.

These girls who, when they came to us, were children of fourteen and fifteen were children now no longer. Most of them had been engaged since they left school in the West End dress trade. The aggravation of the poverty problem in West London is the season trade. The dress trade is the worst in this respect; high pressure. of demand in summer, suspension in the winter, bringing all the evils of such fluctuation. I do not know which is worst, the driving over - work and worry of the season, or the anxiety and semi-starvation of the slack time. We saw in the girls, as years went on, the effect of this continual strain; their youth seemed likely to be all too short, and when your youth is over you are done for in the London labour market. We faced their future for them, and we felt that something further must be done.

Much public interest had been aroused by the publication of Mr Sherwell's "Study of Life in West London," where the conditions of the dress trade are specially dealt with ; and we felt that the hour had struck to initiate the experiment of a dressmaking business managed in the interests of the workers on practically co-operative lines. We felt that with such a business we should be able to answer the continual question put by women of means. "What is the use of talking to us about the conditions of working women unless you can suggest what can be done at once by individuals who want to get out of participation in the evil ? "

To answer this question we issued a circular on the 17th May 1897, drawing attention to a new business undertaking which was to be started upon principles which we believed to be sound commercially, and inherently just and fair, and a business in which the workers should enjoy conditions which would change their life of drudgery and uncertainty into one of glad service and security.

The following are some of the conditions :—The working hours eight a day (45 hours a week); the minimum wage fifteen shillings; the workrooms bright, comfortable, and well-ventilated; books, wage-sheets, etc., open to inspection, and accounts audited by chartered accountants.

We started with five girls in the workroom; as I write we are nearing the end of the first twelvemonth, and our working staff has increased steadily month by month, till to-day we are twenty; and still we must increase to meet the growing demand. We have not had any slack time at all since we opened. We have met with unlooked for response and great sympathy on all sides. The first year proves the experiment a financial success, and I think much more than a mere financial success. It has met the felt need of the present hour, and though it is such a small scheme at present, it may be the thin end of the wedge which will ultimately lift the intolerable burden from the shoulders of the working girl. For if one experiment succeed, others will certainly be tried, and new developments will be made. And we have called our business house (155 Gt. Portland Street) Maison Espérance, because we feel the great hope that lies in it for the future of working girls.

At present, I believe, this industrial extension in connection with a girls' club is unique. But I hope it will not remain solitary. I see no reason why other clubs should not carefully study the conditions of the trade special to their own locality, and consider how the welfare of the workers can be most effectively secured; and I see no reason why, if they cannot influence the employers in their locality, and bring them into line with their own ideas, they should not develop in that trade an industrial enterprise on co-operative lines. Such an enterprise would give the club a local standing, and an influence with local employers that nothing else could give. As an object-lesson to outsiders, as well as an education for the girls concerned in the business, and for all connected with it, it would be invaluable. But the subject is too far-reaching to come within the scope of this chapter.

Every club will have an individuality of its own, and will develop strongly on its own lines; but I want to take a glance of the movement as a whole, and rightly estimate its very great importance in this transition stage of our social development.

Let us see what the influence of the girls' club actually is on the lives of those working girls whom it touches;

and let us consider in what directions it might develop and become of yet greater influence and social significance.

I. **The club stands to the girls for "the home."**— Our cities have taken away "the home" from the workers, they have crowded out everything that links that word with sweet association or with sacred influence. This is obviously true in London, where 20 per cent. of the whole population live in overcrowded slums, and where even the well-to-do artisan has to pay a third of his income for decent living space.

The children's playground is the street, and when girls grow up and go to work, their evening recreation ground is the street, unless they can afford to go to some cheap place of amusement. Their room is wanted at home, and not their company.

It is here that the girls' club can come in to-day, and can do something to supply the working girl's need; for surely the girl of fifteen, sixteen, and seventeen years needs the happy shelter of home with its individual care and sympathetic companionship. Every girls' club can be that to its members. Every club I know has its "Mother," who is always at home there, and whose special work is the knowledge of the girls, individually, through sympathy, resource, and patience.

But, of course, the members need more than individual sympathy. They need the interest and mental stimulus and good comradeship of the happy family circle. They need to have their latent faculties developed, their imagination widened, their capacities for enjoyment encouraged; and many an educated girl coming into the club for even an hour a week is doing the part of the elder sister by giving of her very best to the girls, whether the gift be laughter or learning.

II. **The club stands to its members for the realisation of their womanhood.** — In our overcrowded cities we have crowded out womanhood. We have choked up the religion of life at its source. What the real meaning of the slum is few know or imagine. I doubt if many of us are great enough in heart to have it revealed. I know that moral miracles happen, that purity and virtue can survive in the most infected atmosphere, and can be the stronger for the resistance to evil ; but the average man is such as his environment makes him, and the average factory girl does not hold a higher standard than that she sees adopted by her neighbours. Even where the conditions of life are very much better, where the imagination and feeling are not vitiated, the working girl is generally quite untrained to any thoughtful apprehension of life. She grows up unguided, into irresponsible and unguarded womanhood, and unready to hold the keys of a future destiny—the woman's most sacred trust. And in the club a high standard is being lifted. It *must* be lifted, otherwise the club not only misses its opportunity, but is in danger of becoming a positive evil. It *can* be lifted, because there is nothing a girl's heart more quickly expands to than the idea of womanhood dignified in its consciousness of duty. There are endless opportunities and ways of teaching, and, on the whole, the more indirect and artistic the method, the better. Precept, too often repeated, becomes mere commonplace. The spirit of beauty and purity is vital, and must have vital expression. Song, story, human friendship, "Mother Nature," herself, are influences that go a great deal deeper than any moralising, and they will all strengthen the straight word that must at times be spoken.

_ III. **The club stands to its members for the first training ground for the social organisation of women.** —Women's Trade Unions have been hitherto a comparative failure, for women have never been trained in the discipline of associated interests, they have never yet had a chance of grasping the idea of duty that goes beyond the personal demand. But the working girl of to-day is unconsciously absorbing broader ideas that may help to change her attitude to life, as her interests and energies become absorbed in the club, and her latent faculties become active in working for its development. For the club is a voluntary association, the continuance of which depends on the concord of wills, and on the understanding that there is a common good and a general interest to which personal claims must give way. And as the whole club is ready to stand by its members who are in trouble or in difficulty, so the members learn that pride in their club that makes small sacrifices easy, and binds them together in mutual loyalty.

The possibilities of the further usefulness and influence of the working girls' clubs seem to be in three main directions—social, industrial, and educational; and I have described the social mission that the girls' club is achieving to-day. That is its first and most obvious usefulness; and its influence on the members' individual and social life must be guarded and strengthened, and the club itself must develop more and more to this end. But just in proportion as this individual and social influence is attained will be the possibility of yet further issues.

I believe the girls' club, or for that matter the boys' club, may greatly influence the adjustment of industrial questions in the near future. The club leaders have a unique opportunity of getting at the facts, they have sources of evidence which it is exceeding difficult for the factory inspector to touch. They know, too, what the workers want, which is often more than either the workers themselves or their rulers know. They know, too, what the employer wants—character and conscientiousness—and they can supply him with it; the good employer wanting good material to work good reforms with, will find his best ally in the good club leader. And it is open to the club that despairs of finding the right employer to plunge into the heart of the industrial system, and to organise on the lines of the enterprise I have alluded to the industrial life of its own members. And the possibilities of its educational usefulness tend towards its close alliance with our educational and municipal institutions. On every School Board or committee of management there ought to be at least one representative of the girls' clubs in the district; and we in the club ought to work side by side with the evening continuation schools and with other councils and boards of technical instruction. And in other ways we ought more and more to become the necessary link between the people, and the protection and provision that are theirs. We, who have the welfare of the working girl at heart, and understand her needs, must be prepared to represent her on the vestries, and keep her sufficiently in touch with sanitary and industrial authorities.

The aim in the clubs must be to make good citizens; and our present endeavour to represent the rights and

H

claims of the young, until they have entered into their citizenship. By an actual knowledge and experience gained in direct contact with the people, we are fitted to become their voice, and to give utterance to their claim upon society, for a life that is worth the living.

EMMELINE PETHICK.

SOCIAL SETTLEMENTS AND THE LABOUR MOVEMENT

IT is hardly possible at the present time to estimate at all accurately the nature and value of the contribution that Social Settlements are making to the solution of the labour problem. Such an estimate, it will be obvious, would require a mental detachment, and a critical and historical attitude that are altogether beyond the reach of a contemporary student of history, whose powers of observation and analysis are necessarily limited by conditions over which he has no control, and who has neither knowledge nor insight sufficient to enable him to discriminate with more than partial success between the many solvent and constructive forces that contribute to social progress. But it is comparatively easy to fix, at least approximately, the measure of their possible influence, and to state in broad outline the work that is within their reach.

The fact, for example, that they are, first and foremost, *district* Settlements, voluntarily charged with an honorable concern, if not with a definite and official responsibility, for clearly-defined and more or less homogeneous districts, suggests at once an invaluable form of service which they may render to the labour movement.

It needs no very intimate acquaintance with social and economic questions to become aware, first, of the singular and, from some points of view, pathetic sense of inevitableness with which the public still regards the general social problem; and, secondly—what probably is really responsible for this—a characteristic failure on the part of the average man or woman of intelligence to differentiate the various integrants of the problem. The mischief resulting from the latter habit — as seen, for example, in the paralysis of social faith and the stultification of remedial effort—is so serious, and the habit itself (in the light of information that is everywhere accessible to patient and expert investigation) so inexcusable, that it should at once be authoritatively pilloried.

Looked at in the aggregate—as has been our unfortunate custom—it may be admitted at once that what is called the social problem—by which is meant, primarily, the evils of poverty, unemployment, overcrowding, etc.—does seem hopeless and irremediable, but treated scientifically—*i.e.* by the progresses of segregation and differentiation, it at once takes lighter and less hopeless hues. No greater or more disastrous mistake, for example, could be made than to assume, as is popularly done, that the factors that create the problem of poverty in different districts are everywhere uniform in nature and operation. On the contrary, they vary in almost every locality, and are rarely, if ever, reducible to common forms. Poverty in Bradford, for example, is one thing, traceable, probably, in its main features, at least, to easily ascertainable causes; while poverty in Canning Town, or Whitechapel, or Soho, is a wholly other thing, brought about by a more or less complex set of entirely different causes. I am not here referring, of course, to first or ultimate causes, such, for instance, as would involve in their adjustment the reconsideration and reorganisation of our entire social and industrial systems, but to secondary or subordinate causes which vary in every district, but which are always more or less remediable. Obviously, therefore, the first essential in any effective discussion of the general social problem is full and reliable information concerning existing social facts, and this, singularly enough, is the one thing that hitherto has been completely lacking. Mr Charles Booth's *magnum opus* has recently supplied much of the deficiency, so far as London generally is concerned, and has made/ accessible for the first time a mass of information that will be invaluable in that complete and exhaustive segregation of the problem that must precede reform; but it is every way suggestive of our public and official attitude toward this question that that invaluable undertaking is a purely private enterprise, and one, moreover, that would have been impossible to any but a wealthy person.

Hitherto the public has been more concerned for hasty but well-intentioned philanthropic experiments, than for patient and expert investigation of the radical facts of the problem, and the comparative but inevitable failure of these has produced a mischievous pessimism that does not properly belong to the problem. But to remove this impression will be impossible without a change of attitude and method. To approach the question, as we have hitherto done, with certain *a priori* assumptions of inevitableness and irremediableness which we have never attempted to verify by actual investigations, is not only unscientific, but morally inexcusable, and this the modern progressive spirit is slowly but surely coming to realise.

But it needs to be insisted upon that the public at large does not yet realise how lamentably small and even precarious, despite all that has so far been achieved in this direction, is the stock of data upon which we at present depend in all our attempts to estimate the significance and proportions of the social problem. To attempt to divide the responsibility for this lack of knowledge would perhaps be difficult as well as unedifying, but it is time that the fact itself received the careful attention of all who are seriously concerned for social progress.

Facts, it should be remembered, challenge questions far more powerfully than theories, and the best service that the friends of social progress can render to the cause of reform to-day, is patiently and dispassionately to investigate and to disclose the actual facts of our existing social life.

In any case, until our information concerning sociological facts is more complete and perfect than it is, unhappily, at the present time, it is useless to look for those ultimate and far-reaching reforms to which the social student at the last analysis of the problem inevitably and irresistibly turns. It is not that the community is either callous or unjust. It is merely ignorant. It waits to be convinced; and conviction can only spring from knowledge. The first and most important business, therefore, that lies before the social worker is to organise the instruments of knowledge, and in this work Social Settlements might easily render invaluable help.

To begin with, they tend increasingly to attract to themselves as workers social and economic students, who, by force of sympathy and training, are well equipped for the work of investigation. Secondly, their clubs and other agencies bring them into sympathetic contact with large numbers of working-men, and make first-hand information easily accessible. Moreover, the general scheme of their work, with the concentration of interest that it involves, provides them with quite exceptional opportunities for studying the general conditions of life in particular districts, and, especially, the conditions of employment, wages, standard of living, enforcement of factory legislation, and the numerous other questions that are closely related to industrial progress. Our insensibility, hitherto, to the available sources of information, and especially to the facilities offered by existing philanthropic and other machinery for accurate sociological investigation, is one of the most depressing features of the past; and the attention of Settlement and other workers cannot too strongly be directed to the point that for the purposes of intimate and accurate investigation of sociological facts nothing more admirable could be devised than the machinery that already exists in almost every crowded district. In the great and increasing body of social workers everywhere there is a veritable mine of potential wealth which, carefully organised and wisely used, would be of invaluable auxiliary service to the social student, whose most strenuous investigations often do not bring him face to face with facts with which the ordinary social worker is daily familiar. If once the sources of information could be secured, the organisation of the information itself could easily follow. This is a work to which the best energies and enthusiasm of Settlement workers should be steadily directed. The appointment of small circles of earnest and skilled students in each of the Settlement districts, aided by the advantages that the existing Settlement machinery and other local agencies would undoubtedly give, might confidently be expected to yield important results in the shape of full and reliable information for which society at present actually waits, and which would be of quite incalculable value to the cause of industrial progress. The present writer would venture definitely to suggest that every Settlement should add to its existing agencies a carefully equipped and efficient Statistical and Investigation Bureau, and that systematic efforts should be made to ascertain and to classify the facts relating to—

(1) The housing of the people, overcrowding, etc., than which few more urgent questions exist, and in the absence of attention to which all attempts at social or industrial progress (to which it is closely related) will be vain.

(2) The question of Unemployment, both seasonal and chronic—a question that has become a veritable bread problem for tens and hundreds of thousands of our fellow-citizens, but concerning which, to the shame of our social and political arrangements be it said, we have little or no really reliable and authoritative information at present.

(3) Local industries, which should be studied as far as possible in their technical details, and especially as to the conditions of work, wages, seasonal fluctuations, etc., that prevail in them.

If carefully-equipped Bureaux of the kind suggested could be attached to University and other responsible Social Settlements, they might well be affiliated ultimately to the Labour Department of the Board of Trade, and be subsidised by State grants for the furtherance of their investigations. In any case, it cannot be doubted that they would do much to meet what at present is a serious social need.

II

One invaluable result of such systematic investigations would be, that much of the information obtained would equip the Settlement worker himself for important social service of a practical kind in his own district. No one to-day can go very far in the study of social and industrial problems, without realising that a very considerable proportion of the evils that at present darken social life are due to administrative, rather than to legislative deficiencies. Indeed, it is no exaggeration to say, that not a few of the gravest evils that confront the student of industrialism to-day could be materially remedied, if not entirely removed at once, if only our administrative resources were equal to our legislative enactments. For years past we have been crowding our statute books with measures which, however imperfect, have never been adequately enforced; and every session but adds to the confusion. It would be an incalculable gain to the cause of progress if for one whole session Parliament would pass a "self-denying ordinance" so far as new legislation is concerned, and devote itself exclusively to honest inquiry into the actual working results of already existing Acts. It would at least clear the ground and show us where we really stand, and be a wholesome, if not very palatable, revelation of the utter impotence of even the most august and representative Parliament to accomplish by itself more than mere paper reforms. The fact is, and the sooner we recognise it the better for the cause of progress, Parliament acting alone, and unsupported by public opinion, working through administrative efficiency, is powerless to effect reforms. The history of all social and industrial legislation affords full proof of this.

Few questions, for example, are of more vital importance in certain metropolitan, and also provincial districts,
where home or non - factory industries are carried on,
than the sanitary condition of the workshops, and it is
probable that there are few matters concerning which
our legislative arrangements are more perfect.   The
Public Health Act of 1891, for example, provides, among
other things, that any factory, workshop, or work-place
which is not a factory subject to the provisions of the
Factory and Workshop Acts (and "domestic" or tenement
workshops are not so subject *) may be dealt with sum-
marily as a nuisance if (*a*) it is not kept in a cleanly
state and free from effluvia arising from a drain, closet,
etc., or (*b*) is not properly ventilated, or (*c*) is so overcrowded while work is carried on as to be injurious or
dangerous to the health of those employed therein.

Now it will be clear that if these and similar provisions
were properly enforced, some of the most serious of the
evils connected with the conduct of home or non-factory
industries would at once disappear.   It would be unfair,
however, to lay the entire blame for the non-enforcement
of this Act upon the local sanitary authorities.   It is
true that they are legally responsible for its administration, and that, officially at least, they control the administrative machinery.   But a local authority, as a general
rule, simply reflects the prevailing public opinion of its
district, by which it is itself in the end controlled, and

* The section in the Factory and Workshop Act of 1895, relating
to "Tenement Factories," applies only to buildings in which steam,
gas, or other motive power is used, and in which one or more tenants
use such power for their own purposes in separate hired rooms (or
sets of rooms).

in advance of which it dare not greatly venture. A local authority, for example, may be fully aware that the administrative machinery at its disposal is altogether inadequate to meet the requirements of the district, but if it have not the strong support of public opinion behind it, it will probably leave things as they are. This may and does happen sometimes in the case of really progressive local bodies. It is easy to conjecture what is possible in the absence of the pressure of public opinion in the case of local authorities that have no progressive instincts.

In dealing with this problem of local administration elsewhere,* the present writer laid considerable stress upon the serious inadequacy of the present staff of sanitary officials, and the physical impossibility, under existing conditions, of coping with the work of inspection. It may be well to supplement the figures there given, which relate to 1894, with the figures for 1897, the latest date for which returns are available. In 1897 the total number of sanitary inspectors in London (including several temporary officials) was 248. That is to say, one to every 2,338 inhabited houses, or every 18,000 persons of the population—a ratio that is actually lower (by nearly one-third) than the ratio in the largest provincial towns! Now it will be obvious, even to the least initiated person, that a staff represented by these figures is altogether insufficient to meet the heavy demands of sanitary inspection in the metropolis, even in respect of dwelling-houses only; but when to these is added a further and onerous responsibility for the sanitary inspection and control of some thousands of workshops (as has

* *Life in West London.* 2nd edition. "The Problem of Reform."

been the case since 1891 *), the absurdity of our administrative arrangements at once appears.

How important and onerous the responsibility in respect of these workshops actually is, will be apparent when it is mentioned that in 1896 the inspector who is responsible for the inspection of workshops, etc. in one of the central metropolitan districts visited 500 workplaces, representing 1,358 visits, or less than three visits per workshop of those visited per year, and served orders requiring cleansing, etc. in no fewer than 247, or nearly one half.†

If we turn to other legislative arrangements for the regulation and control of industrial conditions, the same failure in administration meets us. In 1892, for example,

* The history of legislative procedure in respect of the inspection of domestic or tenement workshops offers a curious illustration of the vacillation that so often paralyses administrative effort, and hinders the practical work of reform. Up to 1872 the sanitary control of workshops lay in the hands of the local sanitary authorities. The unsatisfactoriness of that arrangement, however, led to its transfer at that date to the factory inspectors, by whom it was held until 1891, when it was re-transferred to the local sanitary authorities. It can hardly be questioned, however, that the present arrangement is eminently unsatisfactory, as, indeed, all arrangements involving a divided responsibility inevitably must be.

† The urgent importance of this question is shown by the following extracts from the most recently published Report of the Medical Officer of Health for London :—

Bethnal Green.—No periodical supervision of workshops has been undertaken, but trade premises have been dealt with when discovered in the ordinary course. All notices from H.M. factory inspectors have received attention, and insanitary conditions have been remedied.

Islington.—In this district it was stated that the work was of the most satisfactory character ; the female inspector made 1,251 inspections of workshops, containing 1,900 workrooms. It was found that in 27 there was overcrowding, in 10 the ventilation was bad, and in 50 there was uncleanliness. Other sanitary defects, "341 in number," were a Shop Hours' Act was passed, limiting the hours of young people employed in shops to seventy-four per week, and giving local authorities an *optional* power to appoint inspectors under the Act. In August 1896 (four years after the Act was passed) a return of the number of inspectors so appointed was published, and from this it appears that, taking the whole of England and Wales, the total number of inspectors appointed under the Act is 223, of whom only *five* devote the whole of their time to the work! The needs of London are supposed to be met by the appoint-

remedied. As many as 547 cards were distributed, showing the number of persons the rooms could accommodate.

Kensington.—A tabular statement in the report shows that 625 workshops and 1,184 workrooms therein are on the register. There were 2,372 inspections of workrooms; 24 were found to be overcrowded, 28 insufficiently ventilated, and 143 in a dirty condition. The medical officer of health states that with respect to workshops where men only are employed that nothing can be done comparable with the work which is done where women are employed. "It is time these establishments should be taken in hand, but it cannot be done in any effective way with the present limited and reduced staff of sanitary inspectors without letting other and more immediately pressing work fall into arrear."

Marylebone.—The number of visits to outworkers was 476. In 193 cases workrooms were measured and cards issued, in 263 cases the ventilation investigated, in 10 cases new places of business were reported on. There are 125 entries on the register, relating to over 2,000 employees, 1,883 of these being females engaged in dressmaking or allied work. On the first inspection the majority of workshops were overcrowded.

St George, Southwark.—There are 338 workshops on the register, 96 of which have been added during the past year. The registration has led to the removal of nuisances, such as filth, overcrowding, and bad ventilation. More pressing duties have militated against the enforcement of the requirements of the order under section 27 (1) of the Act of 1891. The appointment of a special inspector is recommended for the purposes of this order.

ment of one inspector (who, however, gives the whole of his time to the work), while the chief provincial boroughs are served as follows :—

	Inspectors giving *whole* time	Inspectors giving *part* time	Total No. of Inspectors appointed
Birmingham . .	0	29	29
Leicester . .	0	7	7
Oldham . .	0	7	7
Cardiff . .	1	5	6
Halifax . .	0	5	5
Bolton . .	0	4	4
Liverpool . .	0	3	3

The above represent the towns showing the *largest* returns. In many cases no appointment has been made.

An even more important illustration of this characteristic deficiency in our administrative arrangements appears when we consider the arrangements made for the enforcement of the Workshop and Factory Acts, than which, under present industrial conditions, nothing is more important to the ordinary worker.

Now, according to the latest figures,* the total number of registered factories and workshops in the United Kingdom is as follows :—

Registered Factories   83,873
Registered Workshops   .   .   .   110,234

Total   194,107

The entire staff appointed to administer the Acts in this enormous number of registered work-places is as under :—

* See the Annual Report of the Chief Inspector of Factories and Workshops, for the year ending 1896.

Chief Inspector	1
Superintending Inspectors	7
District Inspectors	44
Junior Inspectors	26
Assistant Inspectors	25
Assistant Examiners of Particulars . .	3
Lady Inspectors	5

Total 111

That is to say, adopting the principle of an equal division of labour, and assuming (what, of course, is not the case) that every member of the staff is available for the actual work of inspection, the average number of registered workshops and factories per inspector is 1,749.

If, however, we confine ourselves to London, the full seriousness of the situation is more readily apparent. The number of registered workshops and factories in the metropolitan area (which includes certain districts lying outside the county of London, but included for administrative purposes in the metropolitan districts) is 32,060. Of that number, 5,671 are in the East Metropolitan District, which comprises that part of the metropolis north of the river and east of the Mile End Road; 8,278 are in the Central district, which has for its boundaries, on the south the river, on the east Whitechapel, on the west the Farringdon Road, and running northwards by the "Angel" to the North London Railway, and thence to Willesden Junction; 9,602 are in the West Metropolitan District, which comprises the remaining portion of the metropolis north of the river; and 8,509 in the Southern District, which includes the whole of the metropolis south of the Thames.

Now the absurdity of the present situation will be seen

at once, when it is remarked that the entire staff appointed
to meet this demand consists of *eighteen* persons—namely,
four district inspectors, four junior inspectors, and ten assist-
ant inspectors.   The absurdity of the existing arrangements
will even more plainly appear if we narrow still further the
area of observation, and take as an illustration the district
assigned for administrative purposes to one official.   The
particular district to be considered is chosen partly because
it happens to include an area of which the present writer
has made a special study, but also because it is one where
the existing industrial conditions make the work of inspection peculiarly difficult and important.   To ascertain the
extent of the district in question, the reader should take a
map of London, and, starting at Blackfriars Bridge, trace
a line in a northerly direction along Ludgate Circus,
Farringdon Road, Rosebery Avenue, City Road, Old
Street, Kingsland Road, to the North London Railway.
Thence westward along the North London Railway to
Maida Vale, thence southwards by Maida Vale, Edgware
Road, Park Lane, Piccadilly, Trafalgar Square and Northumberland Avenue, to the river; and thence eastwards
along the river to Blackfriars Bridge.   The number of
registered workshops in this district—which, let me repeat,
is the area assigned to *one* official—is, roughly speaking,
3,150.   In addition to this area, moreover, the official in
question is responsible for an extra-metropolitan district
stretching from Uxbridge to High Wycombe and Aylesbury,
and including another 300 workshops !   It would be difficult,
indeed, to find a more complete and conclusive illustration
of the shameful inadequacy of our present adminstrative
arrangements.

It is impossible, therefore, in face of such figures to resist the conclusion that what is imperatively needed in any attempt at immediately practicable reforms is not so much fresh legislation as better and more adequate administrative arrangements. In a word, the adjustment of administrative machinery to existing legislative powers.

But how is this to be effected? Partly no doubt, by a large increase in the staff of inspectors—an administrative necessity to which, it must be admitted, public opinion is by no means awakened at present, but chiefly, as we would suggest, by a wise development of the idea of voluntary social service. It is just here, surely, that Social Settlements in London and elsewhere have a great opportunity and a great responsibility. To them, more perhaps than to other philanthropic agencies, belongs both naturally, and by the force of favouring circumstances, the responsibility of enforcing the claims, and of developing the highest possibilities of voluntary social service, and of meeting, at least to the point of their highest ability, the perhaps inevitable, but, at all events, very real deficiencies in our official administrative arrangements. In any case, it is in this direction that social service is most needed to-day, and along these lines that it will find the most entirely satisfactory and fruitful scope for its energies.

III

Much of what has already been suggested would be made easier of accomplishment by sympathetic co-operation on the part of Settlement workers with the representatives of labour in the Settlement districts, and by efforts to promote the election of suitable labour representatives on municipal and other public bodies in artisan districts.

The ordinary representative of labour may not possess,

I

and certainly would not claim to possess, exceptional wisdom or virtue in respect of general political and municipal questions, but he undoubtedly does possess a special and unrivalled knowledge of questions and facts that vitally affect the lives of the poor, and the lack of which must always make really effective legislation impossible.

From the practical point of view, therefore (which is obviously the point of view of highest political expediency, as well as, in this case, of justice), the duty of Settlements to help to secure a proper representation of labour in their districts would seem to be clear ; and, put upon these broad grounds of practical expediency and justice, their action in this direction should be secure against suggestions of social or political bias.

Then, again, they may still further help the labour movement by giving shelter and practical sympathy to trade unions, friendly societies, and the numerous other organisations that aim at the social and political development of the working-classes, and their equipment for ultimate self-government.

Moreover—and this is too important to be lost sight of—the Settlements have themselves a direct responsibility for the educational development of the workers, to fail in which will be to fail in one of the highest of their proper aims. They need to become centres where not only the dismal daily needs of the poor shall be sympathetically studied and made articulate, and where the just claims of labour shall be recognised and enforced, but centres also of helpful educational influence where definite help and guidance shall be given to minds unaccustomed to independent thought, and unfamiliar with the ways of knowledge. Their scheme of work should certainly include liberal opportunities for the study of political and economic questions by means of lectures, discussions, and regularly constituted classes. It is to be admitted that the demand for such systematic study is not at present very great, especially among those who would gain most from the pursuit of it. But this, all things considered, is hardly matter for surprise or discouragement, and is perhaps to be attributed, in part at least, to faults in the methods by which such studies have hitherto been conducted, as well as to obvious historic causes.

But from the point of view of the future, the importance of such educational work cannot be over-estimated. "The worst thing in the world," as Goethe well said, "is ignorance in motion," and the labour movement, if not the only movement concerning which it is necessary to remember this, is from the necessities of the case, one of the most important, involving as it must do, according to the lines of its development, either great social progress, or equally great social disaster. The student of history does not need to be reminded that it is the too frequent habit of impetuous inspirations to overlook the lessons of history, and to deny, in their haste for mechanical reforms, the worth of all that is past and most of what is present,—a method that is not only unscientific but also wantonly destructive; and it is from thèse and similar mistakes that the labour movement may be saved by its friends. We cannot too well remember that no movement can be other than mischievous that is based upon ignorance, especially when that ignorance happens to be ignorance of history.

IV

But it will probably be in less direct and formal ways that Settlements will most powerfully serve the social and

labour movements.   Their connection with such movements is an inevitable one, inasmuch as those movements
are related, as parts to a whole, to that sum-total of life
and experience which all organisations that act under a
religious, and especially Christian, inspiration claim as the
rightful portion of the individual man or woman everywhere.   It is because social and labour questions *are*
related to life, and through life to the goal of life—man's
moral and religious destiny—that they cannot be omitted
from any scheme of effort that aims at the realisation of
the Christian ideal.

But to admit this is also to recognise the limits within
which these questions range themselves and become important, and also to indicate the difference in the feeling
and attitude of the Settlement worker towards them as
compared with the ordinary political or economic student.
The standpoint of the latter is necessarily scientific and
practical, whereas that of the former is distinctively ethical
and religious.   That is to say, the Settlement worker, by
the force and character of the inspiration which gives him
his initial interest in these questions, is concerned with
them .primarily and pre-eminently for their moral rather
than for their political or economic importance.   To him
the social or labour movement is not represented adequately
and completely by any suggested scheme of constructive
politics.   Its real and vital significance for him lies in
its suggestion of a spiritual idea, a new human relationship,
the co-operation of all classes of society in a fellowship
of sympathy and service that shall give heed to the interests
of all while preserving the freedom of each: that it has
made us see that the true worth of a man consists not
in his economic value as an industrial unit, but rather

in his moral and intellectual and spiritual value as a necessary factor in the whole life and destiny of the nation. This, disclosing—as it has done—new potentialities and new qualities, has created new needs and a wider outlook, and it is to meet these that the efforts of the Settlement worker are primarily directed.

It is possible to conceive of social and economic re-arrangements which, *taken by themselves*, and not as the outgrowths of changed spiritual relationship, swould hinder rather than further the cause of progress. Mechanical, or material, reconstructions follow spiritual re-births. That, at least, would seem to be the lesson of history, and the most important social service that the Settlement worker, equally with other friends of progress, can render, is to help to clear the public mind (and his own) of cant and of all unmeaning shibboleths, and, above all, to avoid that which is the besetting danger of all intense inspirations—the spirit of an eager and often ungenerous partisanship. The social worker, it must be remembered, holds a brief not for a class, but for a principle of justice and right dealing, in the light of which he is called upon to examine facts, and to give help and sympathy.

The moral necessities of the case will often compel him to take sides, and to take sides fearlessly, in particular controversies or disputes, but he must not choose his side impulsively, nor by an invariable principle of partisanship, or his influence will assuredly be minimised, and his social usefulness in its larger possibilities destroyed.

The labour movement, it is not too much to say, has too often been seriously weakened and hindered by the well-intentioned but hasty and ill-considered partisanship of those from whom should have come strong and impartial counsel; and thus not only the workers, but also that large section of the public that is always and only concerned for facts, and for the rights of particular disputes, have lost an authoritative guidance that is always urgently needed.

The narrow and foolish sectarianism that speaks of Democracy as if it represented only a *class*, and the interests of a class, is as morally mischievous as it is *de facto* untrue, and this it should be the aim of the social worker to make clear.

The true business of the Settlement worker, it must be repeated, is not with class prejudices (which, speaking generally, are more matters of ignorance than of ill-will), nor with class aspirations, as such, but with the examination and disclosure of facts by means of which public opinion may be assisted and formed. What he needs, therefore, above all things, is a balanced judgment and well-placed sympathies : in a word, a scrupulous honesty that seeks only the things that are eternally true and eternally just. Labour and capital both exist for moral ends ; the moral end is, indeed, the ultimate idea involved in all thought and work and life. Hence the supreme need now and always is to let all forms of social work aim at spiritual education.

In any case, we do well to assure ourselves at the outset, that nothing will be gained on either side by eager and inconsiderate partisanship, or by indiscriminate denunciation and abuse. Anathema, as a method of propagandism, is always foolish and ineffectual. No class is free from prejudices, nor is either, as yet, fully alive to its social duties. If the friends of progress will take care to be just, and will be even moderately patient, the rest will certainly follow. Programmes and schemes may fail and prove abortive, but the *idea* that is behind the social movement, will, nevertheless, live and steadily assert itself. Give it time, and no true idea ever fails to secure its proper realisation, only it must have time. It is in the very nature of great spiritual truths which bear directly upon life and social conduct to arouse at first resentment and distrust. A new idea—an ultimate spiritual truth— is always at first a *sword*: and of this the social worker has special need to remind himself when the signs (as sometimes lately) are of reaction rather than of progress. It is well then to remember that it is often in the completeness, sometimes indeed in the very violence, of reaction that the eternal truth in an idea slowly disentangles itself, and is set free from misjudgment and error. Not once, but often, has it happened that in the very moment of apparent defeat ideas have claimed their conquest.

It is not too much to believe even now (despite certain disquieting tendencies to which no student of the labour movement can be indifferent) that passion and strife are behind us, and that before us is the day of fuller knowledge and of stronger confidence and trust. To ignore the intense social aim of our age is to miss its most characteristic sign. In the minds of men everywhere, underneath suspicion and distrust, there are treasures of right-mindedness and passionate sympathy that will before long be awakened, and then the day of true progress will have come. It is certain that many of those who now are most impatient and suspicious of the new ideas will be found in the end to have been among those who were the most accessible to them.

The world is awake, and the Spirit of God is brooding

over the forces of sympathy and divine pity that are working slowly, and sometimes ignorantly, in human hearts and human lives.   The end is not yet, but, nevertheless, surely, irresistibly, "after long ages" it may be, we shall sight the goal, and men will be reconciled to truth and to each other.   For this the social worker has to live and work and wait, striving to become as those

> "In whom persuasion and belief
> Have ripened into faith, and faith become
> A passionate intuition."

The late Dr Edwin Hatch summed up in a few memorable and pregnant words, the whole situation as it concerns us individually and collectively to-day.   "To you and me and men like ourselves," he says, "is committed in these anxious days, that which is at once an awful responsibility and a splendid destiny—to transform this modern world into a Christian society, to change the socialism which is based on the assumption of clashing interests into the socialism which is based on the sense of spiritual union, and to gather together the scattered forces of a divided Christendom into a confederation in which the organisation will be of less account than fellowship with one Spirit and faith in one Lord — into a communion wide as human life and deep as human need."

That may be accepted and urged as the motive and aim of all Settlement work.   The interest of Settlements in the labour movement is a necessary part of their interest in all the movements that make for truer, and fuller, and deeper life ; and there, as elsewhere, their supreme work is to spread knowledge and to kindle faith—to "beat the twilight into flakes of fire."   ARTHUR SHERWELL.

AMERICAN SETTLEMENTS

ALTHOUGH there are in America over seventy so-called Settlements, it is necessary to discriminate carefully between those which embody the Settlement idea and those which have simply adopted the name without the substance. A Bibliography of Settlements in America, which has recently been published, says : " Through stages of experiment, opposition, and misunderstanding, the movement has come to be dangerously popular. The method is being apotheosised at the expense of the simple spirit, and many of the so-called Settlements are very far from the highest ideal. Yet to the Settlement social work owes a very large share of impulse and method, and the list of Settlements which follows will serve to show how largely its suggestions have been accepted by churches and missions, and how it has spread with all its vital vigour to numerous large social centres on both sides of the Atlantic, and even unto Japan."

Not more than twenty or thirty of these institutions, at the most, are Settlements, in our acceptance of the term. In many cases there are no residents, and many again are simply evangelistic missions which do not recognise the neighbourhood idea as of prime importance. The Americans are very quick to seize upon names that are useful and popular, and I fear that the term will soon become so common that "Settlement" will at last come to mean any mission attached to a church. If we were to re-christen all

our college and school missions in the same way we should
have a large number of "Settlements" in London. It is
useful to point this out, lest it should be thought that
England, which gave birth to the idea, had allowed itself
to be out-distanced in the development.

Another point that is worth noticing at the outset is that
the establishment of Settlements in America seems to be left
very largely to women. The men are so much engaged in
commercial pursuits, and the aggregation of huge fortunes,
that they have no time for altruistic effort or philanthropic
endeavour. As a consequence, with the exception of about
three Settlements in New York, two in Boston, and two in
Chicago, women lead everywhere. It is greatly to their
credit that they have so nobly taken upon their shoulders
the task of socialising education and culture. In a note-
book of thought and reflections, which dates from his
earliest years, a well-known Italian reformer and statesman
has written this maxim: "In whatever country in the
world, in whatever social condition thou art placed, it is
with the oppressed thou must live, for one-half of ideas and
feelings are lacking in those who live only with the great
and happy." The spirit of this maxim has been caught by
scores of refined and educated college-women in America,
and it is perhaps the most hopeful sign for our transatlantic
cousins that *women* are everywhere throwing themselves into
social and philanthropic work. I trust and believe that it
is more than a passing phase; for, after watching their
development during the past six years, I feel convinced
that they have gone beyond the stage of experiment.

This great interest in the life of the common people has
not come before it is needed. I do not pretend to speak
with authority on the subject, but the evidence seems to

place it beyond doubt that the conditions which are attached to the life of the poor in East London are beginning to have their counterpart in the great crowded city centres in America. The struggle for existence in the principal towns like New York and Chicago is almost as keen as that which confronts us in London. The problem is rendered the more complex in the United States by the racial question, and the differences in politics and religion resulting therefrom. We in England have a good many problems to face, but nothing, as it seems to me, that approaches this in magnitude. For this reason I lay great stress on the importance of the Settlement in creating the neighbourhood spirit, becoming a nucleus around which men, women, and children of different nationalities may gather, and learn the meaning of citizenship. Out of the neighbourhood feeling will grow the social consciousness, and slowly but surely the Settlement will become the voice through which the civic conscience makes itself heard. When we regard the great need there is for municipal reform on non-political lines in the American cities, this development of the Settlement creed is surely worth emphasising.

The oldest Settlement in America is the New York University Settlement in Delancy Street. It was established by Dr Stanton Coit in May 1887, and was then called "The Neighbourhood Guild." Dr Coit was succeeded by Charles C. Stover, and the present head is James B. Reynolds, who spent a considerable number of years in Europe and England, studying social and especially Settlement work. It is interesting to note that Reynolds was chairman of the committee which nominated and ran Seth Low, President of Columbia College, for the mayoralty of Greater New York. I had an opportunity of meeting him, with his committee, just before the election, and although at the time matters seemed to be in a state of chaos, it was freely prophesied that the Republican and Democratic organisations would unite to keep out a good Government candidate. This Settlement has a kindergarten school, several athletic and social clubs for lads, meeting once or twice a week, and a few classes. Lectures are also given every winter on social and economic questions. There is a good library of nearly three thousand volumes, and concerts are provided regularly during the winter session. Annual art and picture exhibitions are held, which remain open for six weeks, and are visited by about 50,000 people during that time. Conferences concerning sanitation, education, and the problem of the unemployed, naturally find their best meeting-place to be the Settlement, and a good deal has been done to call the attention of the thoughtful and sympathetic public to the evils of sweating. Several of the residents take an active interest in public school education, filling the office corresponding to that of manager in our board schools. When I was last in New York there were five or six men in residence, and plans for a more commodious building were being discussed.

The next in historical order, and perhaps the best known of all American Settlements, is Hull House, situated at 335 South Halsted Street, in the nineteenth ward of Chicago. It was established in September 1889 by Miss Jane Addams and Miss Helen G. Starr, who, on their own account, took a house which was already called by the name adopted by the Settlement. Miss Jane Addams is the daughter of the Hon. John H. Addams, State Senator of Northern

Illinois. She is still at the head of Hull House, and by her tact and devotion, her organising power and indomitable courage, has developed the Settlement work with a rapidity that is almost phenomenal. She is an excellent speaker, and an even better writer; with the result that throughout the United States she is in great request, taking very much the same place there that the Warden of Toynbee Hall occupies in England. From the slender beginnings of two settlers has grown the institution which now includes about twenty-five women. A good deal of the work has been done by non-resident men, and there are seven in residence, but only one man has yet been found to devote his whole time to the work. This is George B. Hooker, who is well known both at Toynbee Hall and Mansfield House. To give an adequate account of Hull House would demand an entire paper to the exclusion of all else. It began, as Settlements always seem to begin in America, with children's clubs and a kindergarten school. Then there came into existence the "Working People's Social Science Club," formed through the activity of an English working-man for the discussion of social problems. Afterwards, there followed a Hull House Men's Club, and at present about thirty of these clubs meet regularly at Hull House, uniting in a congress once a quarter. In the same manner the Hull House Women's Club, started at first in a social way, has done valuable service in street and alley inspection, and is, indeed, a kind of women's co-operative guild. College Extension courses appeared very early on the scene, some time, as a matter of fact, before the University Extension movement began in Chicago; some 250 students are now enrolled. A corollary and supplement to this is the Summer School, which has now been held for over five years at Rochford College. The students pay twelve shillings a week, which covers board, residence, and all fees, with complete use of the buildings. Would it not be a magnificent thing if Holloway College, let us say, could be used in similar fashion during the summer vacation? With regard to both art and music, I can testify that the Settlement has reached a very high standard; their efforts have met with a larger measure of success than would perhaps be possible in East London. The free concerts on Sunday afternoons are first-rate in character, and the same may be said of the musical instruction generally.

One of the most interesting features of Hull House is its connection with the labour movement. It has consistently applied the principles it professes, and has supported every judicious attempt on the part of the workers to better their position; therefore it is on excellent terms with the labour organisations. One very great result of this was the Factory Inspection Law, passed in the spring of 1893 by the Legislature of Illinois. The resident who practically initiated and drew up the measure, was appointed, after its enactment, Inspector of Factories in the State of Illinois. The pressing need for such a public policy may be seen by visiting the sweating-shops that flourish in great numbers around Hull House. It is most unfortunate that the portion of this Bill which limited women's labour to eight hours, should have been declared unconstitutional. Some of the women's unions regularly hold their meetings at the House—two were organised there; and in four cases men and women on strike against reductions in their wages have met there while the strike lasted. In one case a trade dispute was successfully arbitrated by Miss Addams, the abuses of which the employées complained being removed.

On behalf of the Department of Labour at Washington, a "slum investigation" was made by the Settlement, resulting in the publication of "Hull House Maps and Papers"; the maps themselves indicating wages and nationalities. The book compares very favourably with Charles Booth's work of a similar kind in London, though, of course, the scope and area of the investigations are much more restricted. The nationality map of the Hull House district shows no less than sixteen different nationalities: this fact alone should convince the unprejudiced mind that there is a far more difficult problem before the American cities than that which confronts us in England. In East London we find the crux of the situation to be in the unmanageable size of the poverty-stricken districts. In Canning Town the endeavour to assimilate in a neighbourhood that has not yet reached "saturation point" the constantly increasing stream of immigrants, the ebbing tide of older East London, and the flowing tide of agricultural Essex and the provinces, taxes our powers to the utmost. There is a yet greater task before Chicago, New York, and Boston; a task which, were it not for the influence of the public schools, might fill the bravest heart with despair. While in a little restaurant in New York I overheard a German mother exhorting her son to put away his books and retire for the night. "Don't speak to me in German!" he answered. "I'm an American boy." Unfilial and unpatriotic as that answer may have seemed to the mother, it is valuable as showing that the public school is slowly but surely doing its work of assimilation; and, from what I have seen, I think I may add that it is being well backed up by the Settlement. Here, for example, are two extracts from the report of the New York Settlement.

"The mothers' teas were given nearly every fortnight through the winter months. The directors of the clubs called at the houses, invited the mothers, and entertained them here. We are always particularly glad to know the mothers, for they often find life very difficult in this strange land where the children grow up with the American ideas so little understood by the parents. We hear the complaint from people of every nationality that the children do not obey, and that they are harder to manage here than they were in Europe, and we use all our influence with the children and young people to strengthen the position of the mothers."

"Many of us have received a part of our education in the public schools, and we are, naturally, much interested in the schools of New York, since we believe them to be the greatest agents of social reform in our city. The head worker has been one of the inspectors for the fifth district, and the delight the children have expressed in having some-one they know come to visit their schools has been almost pathetic. It is our earnest wish that the Settlement may be able to help strengthen the schools, for we believe that with the cause of public education is bound up the future of society. So closely has our Settlement been identified with work for the coming generation that the parents are occasionally apologetic about intruding upon our attention in other matters. One father said, 'I know it is the children you care about; but I want to tell you what is happening in our house, and perhaps you will be interested.'"

One or two other features in the work of Hull House

ought not to be overlooked. "The Jane Club," so called after the president, is a co-operative boarding-house for factory girls and young working-women. It began with seven members, and now has over fifty. From the outset it has been *self-governing*. The boarders do such share of the housework as does not interfere with their daily work at the various factories. The cost is three dollars a week, which covers everything. It should be understood that *comradeship* rather than thrift is the first object.

In connection with the work among children there is a free kindergarten, a day-nursery, where for five cents a day a mother can leave her child, a children's playground, a children's dining-room, and — the last acquisition — a children's building, which is set apart for their especial convenience.

Besides these, the Settlement has a co-operative association, a gymnasium, a coffee-house and restaurant, a New England kitchen, with a mid-day delivery of food at the factories, a temporary lodging-house, a labour bureau, and a public dispensary, with a resident physician. One of the residents of Hull House is a member of the State Board of Charities, and has been active in the movement to organise all the charities of Chicago.

The influence of Hull House is not confined to its own particular organisations, but is brought strongly to bear upon all kinds of works that are making for the material and moral progress of the people. It led the way in trying to get clean streets. "If I cannot clean the ward myself, I will make others keep it clean," said Miss Addams, after she had tried unsuccessfully to get the contract for garbage-collecting, and she certainly has been a terror to the careless or dishonest contractor. Other

K

examples of this activity have been already given (see pp. 33, 36, 37). To those good folk who appear to regard men and women as disembodied spirits this may seem no great matter, but to my mind it is a most important advance on all former positions. For one thing, it definitely links Settlement activity to the work of municipal reform, not merely from the outside, but from within — a much more drastic mode of procedure. I have not the slightest fear for the future of a Settlement working on these lines; further than that, I venture to prophesy that it is only a question of time before all Settlements worthy of the name have representatives holding official positions on the various local and public bodies of their cities. These are the oldest and most widely-reaching institutions, and must, therefore, be the next point of attack.

I have dwelt at length on Hull House, because it has most of the societies which are found in other different Settlements ; and is thus not only a type of all, but may, without invidiousness, be pronounced the most interesting example, which has been followed by many others in planning their lines of work.

The best known Settlement in Boston is that which, started as Andover House, is now called South End House : it is situated at 6 Rollins Street. At its head is Mr Robert Woods, who spent considerably over a year at Toynbee Hall, and visited Mansfield House, at that time in its early years. Few have ever done more to bring to a focus the progressive forces of any one city, and nearly every movement for the good of the people in Boston has benefited by his generous co-operation and counsel. In close co-operation with South End House is Denison House, over which Miss Helen Dudley presides. Both are engaged in various branches of social investigation and public work, the results of which are full of promise for the future. Mr A. F. Sanborn of South End House has made some extremely interesting and useful studies in the former of these departments, as the articles under his name in the *Forum* bear witness. These Settlements are in close touch with the American Federation of Labour, Associated Charities, the Municipal League, the Better Dwelling Societies, the Emergency and Hygiene Association, and other similar institutions. "The House is of increasing use as a kind of neutral ground at the boundary line that separates the working-classes from the other classes of the community. Here the business man and the professional man can meet the trade union man with perfect freedom from restraint on both sides. Every time such a meeting has occurred at the House, there has been an increase of mutual understanding and respect" — "Fifth Annual Report."

Denison House, with rooms for thirteen residents, was the third Settlement established under the auspices of the College Settlements Association, which is the only practical undertaking in which the college women of America are *collectively* engaged.* It is interesting to note the suggestions the workers of Denison House have formulated.

1. "The working-people want what we can give; not of course all of them. A small proportion in any class care for the intellectual life; naturally a less proportion

* The Association itself owes a great debt to the work of three women : Miss Vida Scudder, Mrs Spahr, and Mrs Thayer, but at least eleven colleges are represented on the Governing Board.

of those absorbed in toil. But many are ready and eager to advance beyond the subjects covered by a common school education, and will show sacrifice and patience to do so.

2. "You cannot make scholars out of people whose chief nerve force is given to manual work all day long. You must take them as they are, ignorant and immature.

3. "The lack of training is compensated for to a certain degree by unspoiled intuitions, and a poetic sensitiveness in artistic and literary lines, rare in more highly-trained students. If you cannot turn out scholars you can make happier women.

4. "A little culture, with all the joy and enlargement it brings, can be gained—let us boldly say, it is worth gaining—without any basis of education.

5. "The subjects most profitable for working-women to study are not, as a rule, utilitarian subjects, but those which enrich the imagination."

The College Settlement in Rivington Street, New York, and the Philadelphia Settlement in St Mary Street, are the other two founded by the College Settlements Association. They have both of late lost the services of their chief workers, Dr Elizabeth Robbins and Miss Katherine B. Davis, their places being now filled by Miss Mary Kingsbury and Miss Annie Davies. I have already quoted two paragraphs from the report of the New York Settlement; a third from Dr Robbins' pen will further illustrate their position.

"The unusual distress of the winter forced us to realise anew that industrial questions are the great questions of the day. We have had a chance to urge this belief in public and private, in church and synagogue, in school and college.

We find on all sides great ignorance of the facts which seem to us most important. The rich often show pity for the poor, but they seem far from having a real under-standing of the industrial problems. As the Settlements grow older we shall probably see more clearly what can be done to right the present terrible wrongs, and to bring about those social changes for which so many are longing, and we shall be in a position to share whatever light we may receive with both rich and poor."

The Philadelphia Settlement has co-operated so effectively with public bodies that the City Council has enlarged their garden and transformed it into a park, pulling down the worst of the surrounding tenements, and has established a branch free library in a building provided by the Settle-ment. In the same way the kindergarten work was taken over by the Board of Education. In a canvass made of the seventh ward in connection with the Civic Club, at an election, the Settlement lent its aid; it is not a little disturbing to the mind of an Englishman to find, on the authority of Miss Davis, who paid the visit, that the financial secretary of the Seventh Ward Republican Execu-tive Committee was an illiterate coloured man, noted for his drinking propensities and living in a house of bad reputation. It might be added that the "Judge of Elec-tions" in that division had to come out of jail to discharge his official duties.

Another Settlement, run by men, which has achieved a great success during the last few years, is that called Chicago Commons, at 140 North Union Street. Its head is Professor Graham Taylor, who is in the theological department of the University of Chicago, and is himself a man of remarkable power. The sacrifice he has made, both financially and socially, in going with his wife and children to live at the Settlement in the seventeenth ward, amongst a population of Scandinavians, Poles, and Italians, has been rewarded by an astonishing rapidity of growth in the work of the Settlement, which has done valuable work in the direction of municipal and political reform, besides in its various clubs and classes. Chicago Commons has a large number of residents, both men and women, and has distinguished itself by its economic conferences, now held jointly with Hull House. Its little paper, *The Commons*, has become almost the recognised organ of American Settlements ; a result due to the fact that the editor, Mr John P. Gavitt, is a journalist of no mean ability and experience. Lack of space will not allow me to do more than mention the Chicago University Settlement, situated near the Stock Yards, and presided over by Miss M'Dowell; Prospect Union, Cambridge, Mass., in connection with Harvard University ; Whittier House, New Jersey, of which Miss Cornelia Bradford is the head ; East Side House, in New York, where Mr George Gordon is the chief resident ; Westminster House, Buffalo, which is under the control of Miss Emily Holmes: all these are doing most excellent work, and enlarging their borders and sphere of operations with considerable rapidity. The Settlements in the United States are justifying their existence. They are their own best defence. The spirit which animates the workers and residents is the true one. As Sir John Gorst says, "The charity which consists in subscriptions at bazaars and public meetings cannot satisfy their desire. They long to come into personal contact with human suffering, to bind up the wounds with their own hands, to pour in oil and wine from their own stores,

to give up their own beast and go on foot themselves, and
to welcome the afflicted to their own society and abode.
Gifts of money cannot cure the misery of the poor—it is
fortunate if they do not aggravate them; duty to your
neighbour cannot be done by deputy: the life of devotion
to the good of the human race at large demands personal
service." Neither the racial nor the religious difficulty
effectually bars the progress of the Settlement in America,
and there seems to be no doubt but that it is rapidly
becoming one of the chief reforming and ameliorative
agencies of that country.

PERCY ALDEN.

APPENDIX A

THE POOR MAN'S LAWYER

THE origination of this widely-copied institution is claimed by Mansfield House. A college friend of the Warden, then a barrister, desired to help the Settlement when it was first started, and thought that his knowledge of the law might be helpful to some poor people who could not afford the aid of a lawyer in the ordinary way. Accordingly this was one of the first institutions of the infant Settlement, and the experience that has been gained in the seven years and more that have elapsed, has shown that even the originators had but a small conception of the extraordinary amount of trouble and difficulty that might be lifted from the lives of the poor without interference with the practice of those who look to the law as a means of livelihood. For while the total number of cases per annum has to be figured in thousands, the number that reach the courts may be easily counted on the fingers; moreover, it is significant that so far from the local practitioners objecting, one of the Mansfield House lawyers has his practice within the Borough of West Ham, in which the Settlement is situated. The extracts below are from the last reports of Mansfield House and Browning Hall. The former was written by a helper who acted for a time as secretary to the lawyers, of whom there are now four, three solicitors and a barrister.

I. "In at least one branch of our work at Canning Town, neither the weather nor the season of the year makes the slightest difference. On Tuesday nights, wet or dry, cold or hot, the committee-rooms and staircases are thronged with Poor Man's Lawyer clients. This is at once an evidence of useful work, and a sign that sad elements in society still persist in disturbing human life. As an unprofessional spectator, there have been times when I have not known to which of three sentiments to yield myself—sorrow for the poor people who get into such strange muddles, amusement at their efforts to justify themselves, or admiration for the skill with which the lawyers get to the bottom of things. The three sentiments alternate during the course of an evening's sitting.

Sometimes the people hardly know what they want, at other times they know only too well. In those pathetic cases of domestic difference and incompatibility, what they want is often evident from the look of their faces. One can tell their story before they open their lips. Perhaps I ought not to say it as an outsider, but I have felt at times that the law of England fails to help just where help is most needed.

Our clients have numbered over 2000 this year. They have come from different parts of London, though they are mostly drawn from the neighbourhood of Canning Town. The appreciation in which the Poor Man's Lawyer is held may be estimated from the fact that only last month a man walked from a town forty-two miles distant for the sole object of taking advice on his supposed claim to a large estate under a will made in 1770. This is a typical class of inquiry in this region of destitution. We have had during the course of the year as many as 112 cases of wills and division of intestacies.

Many of the cases could be dealt with by anyone having a comparatively small knowledge of the law; 50 per cent.

come under the law of landlord and tenant, as regards
weekly tenancies; and the jurisdiction of magistrates as
regards the domestic relations of husband and wife. The
Summary Jurisdiction (Married Women's) Act, 1895, may
almost be said to be the Magna Charta of the oppressed
womenkind of the district.

A considerable proportion of the cases, however, require
very delicate professional handling; such, for instance, as
disputes between employers and workmen, touching wages
and compensation for accidents and similar matters (of
which we have had about 200 during the year). In many
cases the respectfully-worded letters of the committee are
sufficient to bring a previously unapproachable employer
or insurance company to swift and favourable terms. Two
cases of this kind will illustrate the gain which the people
derive from consulting the Poor Man's Lawyer:—

One poor fellow injured his foot terribly by slipping into
a copper of molten lead, which was not properly protected.
He was, consequently, incapacitated for work for months.
At the end of a few weeks he was asked to sign a paper in
receipt for the wages paid up to then, and to repudiate all
further claim upon his employers. He consulted the Poor
Man's Lawyer, and we wrote a respectful letter urging a
claim on two doctor's certificates for a more substantial
amount. Ten pounds, in addition to wages which had
already been paid, was offered in settlement, which we
urged our client to refuse, advising him to threaten proceedings if a larger amount was not offered. The end of
it was that he received in all £25, and a promise of work.

The other case was that of a man who had insured
against accidents in a small Company. He had the misfortune to sprain his ankle, and sent in his claim, according
to the terms of the policy, for 15s. a week for the eight

weeks he was incapacitated. No notice was taken of the claim. Letter after letter was sent, and two calls were made at the office of the company. At last, after several attempts, their agent got the man's signature for a five-pound note, which we had steadily urged him to refuse, as it was a pound short of the amount due. He wanted the money badly, and naturally thought that five pounds was better than none at all. This shows how some of these companies try to '*do*' the people. Our lawyers endeavour to prevent this, and succeed in many cases.

As usual, we have had some humorous cases. One impressed me very much. A woman consulted us as to the liability of her landlord for a scalded foot which she had received through the boiling over of a kettle. A would-be client had a quarrel with the Queen and the Pope. He had written to the Home Secretary and the Pope, but had received no answer. He consulted us in order to know what he ought to do. Another woman complained that her neighbour said she had spots on her face. She asked whether, supposing a medical certificate to the contrary could be obtained, she could prosecute for defamation of character.

The vast majority of cases are serious and sad enough. The fact that during the year we have had 180 cases of quarrels between husband and wife, including desertion and divorce, tells its own tale. I have known a case of a husband and wife sitting opposite each other in the waiting-room. Each knows quite well what the other has come for; and there, in such close company, they may have to sit for an hour until their turns come, and then they may follow immediately after each other.

It should be remembered that we do not prosecute, we

only advise. This is often misunderstood; and people come expecting that we should carry their case through for them, and, consequently, they are sometimes disappointed. If we advise prosecution, we usually refer intending litigants to local or other practitioners, where legal aid is necessary, with the assurance that there is, at any rate, a case on which to proceed. Under circumstances of desperate need, however, we do take up a case; but even then usually a compromise is effected before action is entered upon."— "Mansfield House Report, 1897."

II. "Increasing numbers of poor persons flock to the consulting-rooms every Tuesday night, amounting in the year to some one thousand clients. The lawyers now seldom rise until after a two-hours' sitting, during which their sympathy has been deeply aroused, and their minds fully occupied. The stories unfolded to them are by turns piteous, romantic, thrilling, humorous, and tragic.

Any legislator who spent an evening with the Poor Man's Lawyer and his clients would receive a deep and salutary lesson in the inadequacy of the existing means of administering the law in the just interests of the poor. Prominent among such instances may be. mentioned the many cases of bad husbands; the husbands whose brutality just stops short of what the magistrate would recognise as an 'aggravated assault'; and yet more frequently the husband who deserts his wife.

Next to matrimonial difficulties the most frequent source of trouble is that arising between employers and employed. Seldom an evening passes without advice being sought in consequence of accidents; but in nine cases out of ten there has been no neglect on the part of the master, and the applicant goes sorrowfully away with his broken or mangled limb.

Street accident cases are numerous; but compensation for these can rarely be obtained. Our lawyers have no fund to defray the cost of litigation. The party liable is most often a wealthy corporation or public body, or large employer of labour, with an insurance company at his back; and take no notice until a writ or summons has been issued, and it is known that a plaintiff is backed and financed by a solicitor. So many a poor client, merely because he is poor, fails to obtain redress for his injuries.

Whether a workman has had a proper notice of discharge from his employer is a question that is frequently raised, and one that is usually complicated with many difficulties. Often the amount claimed is not worth the expense of recovery, and the kindly advice of our lawyers has induced many a poor client to forego his legal but valueless right.

Many cases of hardship come up, in which bad and unscrupulous masters withhold or retain characters due to their servants. Questions relating to bad lodgers and how to get rid of them come next in point of frequency. On the other hand, many a poor lodger under threat of immediate ejection, and consequently in great consternation, is comforted and soothed by hearing that he cannot be turned out until after the proper notices from the police court have been served on him. Wills are a very prolific source of inquiry. Printed forms of wills filled up unintelligently are responsible for many a hopeless muddle. Many wills are submitted to our lawyers to make sure that they are correctly worded; and they have often drafted a small will for an old woman leaving her 'little all' to the most deserving as against the most nearly related friend. Supposed claims to property are frequently presented for consideration, but the meagre grounds and the lack of funds generally justify the lawyers in dissuading from any attempts to recover. They find ample reason for warning people against advertisers who promise for a certain fee to investigate whether there is 'unclaimed money in the family somewhere.' In many cases it seems nothing more than a trick to obtain money from the ignorant. Endless disputes arise over the sale and purchase of small businesses among the poor.

The following cases out of many will illustrate the service this institution is rendering :—

A widow woman complained that although her sister had died possessed of property valued at £250, neither she nor either of her sisters (all three people in humble life) could get any account from a well-to-do brother, who had obtained letters of administration and possessed himself of the estate. An investigation showed that the complaint was well founded, and that an attempt was being made to deprive these women of their rights. Proceedings were advised and were vigorously prosecuted, with the result that an account was ordered, the estate properly administered, and each received her proper share. Upon receiving the money each gave a donation to the Settlement funds, by way of thankoffering.

In another case, a sailor lad was injured whilst loading cargo at a north country port, owing to the negligence of the shipper's labourers. He was treated by a doctor abroad, and was then sent home by the consul. Under the care of the Dreadnought doctors he recovered ; and application to the shippers of the cargo—a highly respectable firm—resulted in a substantial sum of money being obtained for him."—"Browning Hall Report, 1897."

APPENDIX B

A SETTLEMENT HOSPITAL

THE Canning Town Women's Settlement is, we believe, the only one with an hospital of its own, as well as a medical mission, though the latter is also a feature of Browning Hall. Some extracts from the last report of the Canning Town Settlement will illustrate the working of this institution.

"In spite of the many agencies at work for the bettering of the working-class, a district like this shows that poverty with its attendant miseries still exists to a heart-rending extent. Consequently there is much need for gratuitous medical aid, for although it may be possible to 'make ends meet' in times of health, it is practically impossible to do so when sickness with all its demands visits one of these destitute homes. Two days a week, Monday and Friday, are spent at the dispensary in giving free advice to those women and their children who are unable to pay for the services of a doctor. The number attended in this way last year was 5584. The majority of these, I am sure, were 'necessitous poor,' although here, as in every dispensary, it is difficult—do what we will—to escape from imposition. The rest of the week is spent by those on the out-patient staff in visiting in their own homes such patients as are too ill to come out for advice, and in dressing surgical cases at the dispensary.

The number of surgical dressings last year was 1835; the number of visits paid by the out-patient doctor 1894;

and visits paid by the nurses 1723. This home-visiting continues to be one of the most interesting, though at the same time one of the saddest parts of the work, for East-end life is seen in its true colours.

It is impossible to emphasise sufficiently the amount of anxiety the medical officers are saved, by having the hospital to fall back upon for serious or difficult cases. No really serious case of illness is now in the patient's own home, if she will consent to come into hospital, and if we have a bed to spare. . . .

The number of patients admitted into hospital last year —our third working year—was 125; and I do not think that any of us knew many idle days—I might even venture to say many idle moments, for work is usually at high pressure. If it is not some specially serious case which needs constant attention and watching, it is a question of meeting the wants of the whole thirteen patients, or some point in the organisation of the work which takes both time and thought, for the hospital is now the centre of activity of the whole medical department of the Women's Settlement. Of the 125 cases admitted, 53 recovered, 43 were much improved, 2 were admitted for diagnosis only, 1 was unrelieved, 8 were discharged for various reasons, 10 were transferred to other hospitals, and there were 8 deaths."—"Medical Officer's Report, 1897."

L

APPENDIX C

FROM MANSFIELD HOUSE REPORT, 1897

THE "WAVE" LODGING-HOUSE

WE are glad to say that the "Wave" still grows in popularity; it has, indeed, been a successful year from many points of view, and we have no hesitation in saying that the success is very largely due to the good management of Mr Truscott and his wife. At the present time there are 116 beds in the main house, but often it has been necessary to make up additional beds in the kitchen and reading-room. The largest number of beds occupied on one night was 127, while on very few occasions the number has been down to 100, but never below.

There are two classes of beds ; the ordinary lodger pays 4d., and sleeps in a ward with about 40 other men, but those who are able to afford the luxury of a sixpenny bed sleep in a room with only three others. Of course we get a very varied class of men. We have had with us some who have been masters of vessels ; some, again, who have been in time past in a good business, and on one occasion we had an M.A. of Balliol staying with us. But the great majority are casual labourers, and are very desirous of getting work. . . . One often wishes that the people who talk about the unemployed not being willing to work could spend a week at the "Wave." In August it was heard that there was work to be had at Tilbury Docks, twenty-three miles away. When I went down at 11.30 P.M. seven men, with scarcely ninepence between them, started off for Tilbury. They walked all night, arriving there at 5.30 A.M., and were fortunate enough to secure employment. So, after spending the night in walking, they began at once to grapple with their day's toil.

The permanent element in the house is a growing one; to encourage this, a free bed is offered on Sunday night to all who have spent the preceding six at the "Wave." During the year, 4000 beds have been given in this way, the largest number on any one night being 95. The men who are permanent take a great pride in the place, and often put out a helping hand to strangers. Truscott gives a good instance of this; he says, "An old man came to me one day and said he wanted a bath; I saw in a moment that his joints were pretty stiff with rheumatism, and asked one of the men to help him. It was a good thing I did, for when the old chap once got into the water, the man who was helping had to get assistance to lift him out. Later in the day the bather found out his attendant, and asked him to accept 2d. for his help. 'No, no, no!' said he, 'if a young fellow can't help an old chap like you without being paid for it, it's a pretty hard world.'" "This," said Truscott, "was splendid, because the young man owed me 2d. for his bed for the previous night, and would not be able to pay me until he was working again." Truscott says, "We put all kinds of men on their feet here." A coloured man turned up one night starving; he was taken in and made comfortable. The men soon found that this dark friend was musical. Guy Pearse became interested in the man, and found he had written some really pretty music. He was fitted out with clothes, and supplied with a little money, and then, having got a ship, sailed for home, where he had once held a good position. Later, Truscott received the following letter from him :—

NORTH CAROLINA.

SIR,—Having got here safely home, I want from safety to thank you for aiding me when in peril. The circumstances surrounding me when I met you were the most unfortunate I've experienced. I have no word to express the extent of my gratitude ; please, therefore, accept my most sincere thanks.

Another letter Truscott received is interesting. In it the writer says—

" I made such a quiet disappearance from your place, that I presume you may often puzzle yourself as to my whereabouts. Yes ; my only reason for leaving you as I did was the fear that my attempt would be an ignominious failure ; as you are aware, all my previous attempts were futile."

He goes on to say that after arriving in Natal, he passed an examination as interpreter, and joined the Natal Police, and finishes his letter with—

"I very often think of your generousness towards me, especially extended to me when in absolute need. Yes ; I feel I cannot thank you often enough for the same ; and, bad as London is, I really don't know what it would be like if the generous-minded people I have from time to time met when in absolute need and distress were not in it."

Mrs Truscott likes to tell you of incidents in which the men have shown kindness towards each other. Two men came into the reading-room one day quite done up for want of food. The two rested and then went out to look for work, but one came back very soon, apparently unsuccessful, and, being exhausted, went to sleep. The other returned in an hour or two, and prepared for himself a plate of meat and potatoes which "Mother" (as the men called Mrs Truscott) says was scarcely enough for one. He was just about to demolish it when he caught sight of his sleeping friend. Then he made two plates of meat out of his one, awakened

his friend, and the two dined together. This was indeed
hospitality. "You know," Mrs Truscott goes on to say,
"there are many of our men whose stomachs are nearly
always empty; we know very little of the amount of service
that our men do each other." Truscott is full of interesting
stories about his lodgers. Here is one: "A Hungarian
sailor arrived here on his way home from America. He
was perfectly destitute; we kept him here until he received
money from home, when he was enabled to resume his
journey. On leaving, he bade me 'good-bye' and asked
me to accept the photograph of his wife and child, which
was the most valuable thing he possessed, and was the
one thing with which he had not parted during all his
wanderings."

The reputation of the "Wave" is world-wide, as the
following incident will show:—A few days ago a man
rushed in and dropped a roll of papers on the bar counter,
and as quickly departed. The roll was found to be six £5
Bank of England notes. No explanation had been given,
no name left; in fact, there was an air of mystery about
the whole proceeding. Three days later a seaman with his
bag came in, and said in his rough way, "I say, guv'nor,
you got my six notes all right?" They were handed over
directly the man was recognised as the owner, though the
risks of his banking methods were pointed out. He then
gave some account of himself, and explained that he had
heard about the "Wave" in New Zealand, and had
determined to leave the money there directly he received
it, chiefly because he wanted to send five of the notes to his
old mother in Scotland. He knew very well if he had kept it
himself it would soon have gone, as many seamen's fivers go.
Truscott's experiences as a banker are very numerous.
During the past year he has had more than £200 given

him to take care of, in sums ranging from £6 to £30 ; such is the confidence of the men in the "guv'nor."

It is not possible for the men ever to forget the kindness of "Mother." On many occasions when I have visited the "Wave" she has been at one of the hospitals seeing men who were ill. The following, which is taken from the April *Magazine*, is a type of many such cases :—"We cannot pass on without speaking of a dear old friend, 'Paddy,' who died in West Ham Hospital after a few days' illness. A great friend with all, and ever ready with a witty answer, he was always welcomed at the 'Wave.' But he could not keep from the drink ; it broke him down at last, and he is gone. On the morning he died, Mrs Truscott was with him in the Hospital, and, though unable to speak, he showed by the pressure of the hand what her presence meant to him."

Every Sunday night some one or more of the residents go down under the superintendence of Grafton Milne, to conduct a "free-and-easy" service in the reading-room ; it is in very truth "free and easy." On hot summer nights I have seen Guy Pearse sitting in his shirt-sleeves at the piano, singing and playing with heart and soul. I have seen the preacher also addressing the congregation in the same attire. Strange as it may seem, our men enjoy singing "Sacred Songs and Solos." On Monday evenings a concert is given in the same room. But the room is too small ; when the little place is filled with men the atmosphere is most oppressive. We badly want more beds and more room. Truscott regretfully informs us that he very often has to send men away because his beds are all occupied. He tells us that when a number are cooking their meals in the large kitchen, and as many as the reading-room will hold are crowded in, there is no room anywhere for anybody.

But it is natural that Mr Truscott should be discontented. The needs of the neighbourhood are great, and notwithstanding the endeavours of himself and his wife, and those who support them, what is done seems very small compared with what might be done to help the casual docker and labourer.

APPENDIX D

FROM BROWNING HALL REPORTS, 1896-97

HEATH COTTAGE AND ITS GUESTS

A VILLA-COTTAGE, planted on the summit of a salubrious hill far away in the country, is the home of three young ladies, who chose it, and whose father purchased it for them, that it might also be a home to many of their poorer sisters in crowded Walworth. There they entertain week by week or fortnight by fortnight a succession of women and girls, four at a time, selected by the Settlement. Those who are sent are treated as guests, and share meals and home life generally with their hostesses. They come back loud in their praises of the gracious hospitality shown them in the cottage. Excepting their railway fare, this charming sojourn in the country does not cost them anything. This happy arrangement has been the means of new health and life to many who, but for the kindness of the three sisters, would have had no breath of country air to revive their fading strength . . . . (1896).

The idyll of sisterly helpfulness of which Heath Cottage is the scene still pursues its gracious course. The miniature villa nobly fulfils the purpose for which the three kind sisters secured it. It is a spot of sunshine and of fragrance in the memory of many a straitened Walworth home. One of the hostesses writes: "We received nearly fifty guests last summer. We take exceeding great pleasure

168

in entertaining the people, they see mto make themselves so happy and contented during their stay. We have been particularly struck with the nice and courteous manner towards us, every one being so well-behaved and anxious to please and help us. I cannot remember one instance of even one of our few rules being broken. I should like here to say that I think it is the absence of many rules and restrictions that in a great measure has been the secret of our success. We feel that our guests have felt at home with us. We have been overwhelmed with thanks on their departure, and have in every case received a loving letter afterwards, which we keep as a memento of the visit. Many have sent us their photograph, and we have been particularly touched once or twice by receiving a charming little present. One man sent a canary, and a little girl who works in a tie factory sent us each two dainty little ties of her own making. We are much interested in hearing of the home life and different occupations of our guests, descriptions of which keep our breakfast and dinner table lively. We encourage our visitors to be out in the fresh air as much as possible, and during the finest weather we pack them baskets containing luncheon and tea, so that they can spend the whole day away. I believe the boiling of the gipsy kettle has afforded much merriment, and the sensation of a real picnic been much appreciated. Perhaps it is interesting to know that we keep a register of the names, ages, and occupations of our guests, and that our oldest guest was a lady of eighty-six, and our youngest a baby girl of three months." (1897.)

APPENDIX E.—FROM TOYNBEE LECTURES AND CLASSES,

ALL THESE CLASSES AND LECTURES MEET AT TOYNBEE

SUBJECT.	TEACHER.
Men's Continuation Classes—	
Arithmetic, Writing and Composition	F. H. Butcher - - - *Responsible Teacher.*
Drawing	J. W. Rice, *Assistant*
Citizenship	R. E. S. Hart, B.A.
Chemistry	J. W. Rice - -
Girls' Afternoon Classes—	
Dressmaking; Writing and Composition, Geography, Book-keeping, Needlework, Hygiene, Reading and Recitation, French, Class Singing, Musical Drill, Cooking, Swimming, - -	Mrs Lobb, Miss Quay, Miss Sargeant, & Special Teachers from the Technical Education Board of the L.C.C.
Ambulance Drill (for members only)	W. H. Winny, *Superintendent*
Ambulance Drill (at Millwall) - -	Sergt. J. A. S. Coleman -
Practical Nursing - - -	Special Lecturers - -
"First Aid to the Injured" (for Women)	Alfred Eddowes, M.D.
"First Aid to the Injured" (for Men) -	R. Hutchison, M.D. -
Life Saving (for Men), Land and Water Drill	W. W. Jones (Medallist L.S.S.) - - -
18TH CENTURY MUSIC—	
Works by Handel, Bach, Scarlatti, &c.	T. W. Bourne, M.A., *Conductor* - - -
Drawing and Shading from the Round -	Miss Mabel Bourne - -
Drawing and Shading from Casts - -	Roland Hall - - -
EUROPEAN HISTORY (1852 to 1897) - THE MAKING OF MODERN ENGLAND	S. R. Gardiner, D.C.L., LL.D. Edward Jenks, M.A. -
*History Reading Party - - -	R. E. S. Hart, B.A. -
SIR WALTER SCOTT - - - -	F. S. Boas, M.A. - -
"Scott" Reading Party - - -	*Under arrangement* - -
"The Pilgrim's Progress" - - -	Rev. Canon Barnett, M.A.
Hebrew Literature - - -	H. S. Lewis, M.A. - -
†Greek(*Elem.*)—Smith's *Initia Græca*, Pt. 1	E. W. Brooks, M.A. -
† „ (*Adv.*)—Homer: *Odyssey*, Bk. v. -	E. W. Brooks, M.A. -
Latin—Livy: Bk. xxiii. - - -	A. Chapman, M.A. - -

* Text-book: Fyffe's *Modern Europe*. † Beginners must

HALL EDUCATIONAL PLANS, 1897.
COMMENCING OCTOBER 4TH, 1897.
HALL UNLESS EXCEPTED IN THE NOTES COLUMN.

NOTES.	FEE FOR THE TERM.	DAY.	HOUR.	BEGINS.
			P.M.	
No Fee		Mon. Wed. Thur.	8.0	Oct. 7
		Mon.	9.0 -	Oct. 11
		Wed.	9.0 -	Oct. 13
	3d. per week or 2/6 per term.	Mon. Tues. Wed. Thur. Fri.	2 to 5	Oct. 11
T. Div. Amb. Brigade—	1/ per qtr.	Wed.	8.0 -	Sept. 1
	,, ,,	Fri.	8.0 -	Sept. 17
Toynbee Nursing Guild -	6d.	Tues.	8.0 -	Oct. 5
	2/-	Wed.	8.0 -	Oct. 13
	2/-	Thur.	8.0 -	Oct. 14
Water Practice at the Whitechapel Baths - -	6d. per an.	Tues.	8.0 -	Oct. 5
Toynbee Orchestral Soc.— *Class open to all approved by Conductor*	1/- or 5/-	Tues.	8.0 -	Sept. 14
2nd and 4th Tuesdays -	,, ,,	Tues.	11 A.M. -	Oct. 12
	,, ,,	Fri.	8.0 P.M.	Oct. 8
University Ext. Lectures	1/- or 5/-	Wed.	8.0 -	Oct. 6
University Ext. Lectures at Limehouse Town Hall	6d. or 5/-	Fri.	8.0 -	Oct. 8
For Dr Gardiner's Students	1/- or 5/-	Wed.	9.15 -	Oct. 13
University Ext. Lectures *In connection with above.*	1/- or 5/-	Mon.	8.0 -	Oct. 4
	,, ,,	—	—	—
	No Fee	Wed.	5.30 -	Oct. 6
Davidson's Hebrew Grammar used.	1/- or 5/-	Wed.	8.0 -	Oct. 6
	,, ,,	Wed.	8.30 -	Oct. 6
	,, ,,	Wed.	7.30 -	Oct. 6
	,, ,,	Fri.	7.30 -	Oct. 8

have some knowledge of either Latin or German.

SUBJECT.	TEACHER.
*Italian—Dante: *Inferno* - - -	T. Okey - - - -
* ,, —Dante: *Paradiso* - - -	T. Okey - - - -
*French—Diderot: *Selections (Lemaire)*	J. Macfarlane, M.A. -
* ,, —Moliere: *Le Bourgeois Gentilhomme*	Mrs Nevinson - - -
* ,, —Hamlet (*French translation*) -	Miss Meylan - - -
*German—Goethe: *Wahrheit u. Dichtung*	Miss Benecke - - -
,, —Elementary Class - - -	(*Under arrangement*) -
Elizabethan Literature (Dekker and Lyly)	Frederick Rogers, *Vice-President*.
Shakespeare - - - - - -	Rev. Ronald Bayne, M.A. *President*
Shakespeare—"Hamlet" - - -	J. C. Bailey, M.A. - -
,, —"The Taming of the Shrew"	A. C. Hayward - -
Browning: *Luria, Strafford, etc.* -	Hugh E. Egerton, M.A.
English Literature - - - -	G. L. Bruce, M.A. - -
,, ,, - - - - -	H. S. Lewis, M.A. - -
,, ,, - - - - -	Rev. J. Bullock, M.A. -
The Principles of Law - - -	W. Blake Odgers, Q.C., LL.D
†Social Questions of To-day - - -	C. H. Denyer, M.A. (Lond.).
HUMAN ANATOMY - - -	**P. C. Mitchell, M.A., F.Z.S.**
GEOLOGY—"The Earth" - -	**F. W. Rudler, M.A., F.G.S.**
THE WORLD'S GREAT EXPLORERS -	**H. Yule Oldham, M.A.**
Human Physiology - - - -	Miss K. M. Hall (*Curator, Nat. Hist. Mus., Whitechapel*)
Elementary Botany - - - -	Miss M. O. Mitchell -
Practical Botany - - - -	
Advanced Botany - - - -	George May - - -
Geology—Rocks and Fossils - -	Miss C. A. Raisin, B.Sc.
Practical Chemistry - - - -	Louis Stamm, B.A. - -
Practical Chemistry - - -	H. L. Eason - - -
Chemistry of Photography - - -	

* Students must have some previous knowledge of the language. † Text-books :

NOTES.	FEE FOR THE TERM.	DAY.	HOUR.	BEGINS.
			P.M.	
	1/- or 5/-	Wed.	6.45 -	Oct. 6
	,, ,,	Wed.	8.0 -	Oct. 6
	,, ,,	Wed.	8.15 -	Nov. 3
	,, ,,	Thur.	8.0 -	Oct. 7
Provisional Notice.	,, ,,	Fri.	7.30 -	Oct. 8
	,, ,,	Mon.	7.30 -	Oct. 4
Names to Hon. Sec., Education Committee.	,, ,,	—	—	—
Elizabethan Literary Soc.	6d. per Session	Fri.	8.0 -	--
New Mems. will be welcomed				
Toynbee Shakespeare Soc.	1/- per Session	Thur.	8.0 -	Oct. 7
Open to members only.				
For men only.	1/- or 5/-	Wed.	8.0 -	Oct. 13
For Members of Sydney and Old Rutlanders Clubs.	No Fee	Sun.	11.30 A.M.	Oct. 31
	1/- or 5/-	Fri.	7.0 P.M.	Oct. 8
Membership by Election	No Fee	Thur.	8.0 -	Sept. 23
For Members of E.L. Jewish Communal League	,, ,,	Sat.	5.0 -	Oct. 9
	,, ,,	Mon.	8.15 -	Oct. 25
	No Fee.	Tues.	8.0 -	Oct. 26
	1/- or 5/-	Mon.	8.0 -	Oct. 4
University Ext. Lectures	1/- or 5/-	Fri.	8.0 -	Oct. 8
University Ext. Lectures St Stephen's Hall, Poplar	6d. or 5/-	Wed.	8.0 -	Oct. 6
University Ext. Lectures	1/- or 5/-	Mon.	8.0 -	Oct. 4
In connection with Mr Mitchell's Course	,, ,,	Wed.	7.30 -	Oct. 13
Under arrangement	,, ,,	Thur.	8.0 -	Oct. 7
	,, ,,	Thur.	7.30 -	Oct. 7
	,, ,,	Tues.	7.45 -	Oct. 5
	2/-	Mon.	8.0 -	Oct. 4
	2/-	Thur.	8.0 -	Oct. 7
Under arrangement	—	—	—	—

Marshall's *Economics of Industry*, Walker's *Brief Political Economy*.

APPENDIX F—FROM OXFORD HOUSE REPORT, 1897.
LIST OF FEDERATED CLUBS, WITH NAMES OF DELEGATES, &C.

EASTERN DIVISION.

NAME OF CLUB.	ADDRESS.	DELEGATE.	WHEN OPEN.
Stoke Newington District :			
1. Amethyst Institute -	110 Church Street, Stoke Newington, N.	A. K. LEWIS	Daily
2. Clay Hill Church Institute, W.M.C.	Clay Hill, Enfield, N. -	J. LAWRENCE	...
3. St Paul's -	Clevedon Street, Stoke Newington	A. RULE -	Daily
Hackney District :			
4. All Souls' -	141 Rushmore Road, Clapton Park	E. EMANS	,,
5. St Augustine -	Cadogan Terrace, Victoria Park Road, E.	E. P. WILLMOTT	,,
6. Eton Mission -	Gainsborough Road, Hackney Wick, E.	{ W. WHEELER, E. WATSON }	,,
7. Merchant Taylors' Mission	Shacklewell Lane, Dalston, N.	J. DYTER -	Tu., Th., Sat.
Shoreditch District :			
8. Trinity Club -	Shepherdess Walk, Sturt Street, Hoxton	JOHN R. SCOTT	Daily
9. St Mary's -	Mansfield Street, Haggerston	G. IVESON	,,
10. Tee-To-Tum -	Shoreditch, E. -	{ G. BREEDON, F. HARDING }	,,
11. St Saviour's -	56 Hyde Road, Hoxton	S. RENDALL	,,

Bethnal Green District:			
12. St Andrew's -	St Andrew's Street, Bethnal Green -	{ A. Buckey - { A. Tyler -	Daily
13. Oxford House -	Derbyshire Street, Bethnal Green -	{ T. Welch - { E. Robson -	,,
14. University -	Victoria Park Square, Bethnal Green	{ S. C. Markquick - { J. S. Easterbrook -	,,
Stratford District:			
15. G. E. R. Institute -	David Street, Stratford, E. -	{ E. Potter - { F. L. Holmes -	,,
16. Trinity Col. Mission -	Tenby Road, Stratford, E. -	G. Matthews -	,,
17. St Philip's W.M.C. -	Whitwell Road, Plaistow, E. -	J. B. Bensley -	,,
Whitechapel and Shadwell District:			
18. All Saints' -	North Place, Buxton Street, Mile End New Town	W. Maughan -	Tu., Wed., Th., Sat.
19. Aberdeen -	Johnson Street, Shadwell, E. -	J. Pengelly -	Daily
20. Christ Church -	Workman's Hall, Hanbury Street, Spitalfields	A. Catharine -	,,
21. St Paul's -	Schoolhouse, High Street, Shadwell, E. -	J. Daniels -	,,
22. Whitechapel Parish Club -	2 Church Lane, Whitechapel, E. -	R. J. A. Bennett -	Daily except Thursday.
Poplar and Stepney District:			
23. All Hallows -	Mission Rooms, Leven Road, Poplar -	J. I. Burke -	Tu., Th., Sat.
24. St Anne's Guild -	Dixon Street, Salmon's Lane, Limehouse -	R. J. Wells -	Daily
25. Christ Church, Oxford Mission (St Frideswides) -	Lodore Street, Poplar -	C. Ruse -	,,

NAME OF CLUB.	ADDRESS.	DELEGATE.	WHEN OPEN.
Poplar and Stepney District —continued			
26. Men's Union Club	Garden Street, Stepney	T. E. Williams	Daily
27. St Saviour's	Arcadia Street, Poplar	{ W. J. Franklin, W. G. Legge	Mon., Wed., Sat.
28. Tee-To-Tum	Medland Street, Ratcliff, E.	H. Roberts	Daily
Isle of Dogs District:			
29. St John's	Roserton Street, Cubitt Town, E.	E. T. Morris	Tu., Fri., Sat.
Victoria Docks District:			
30. Felsted Mission	225 Prince Regent's Lane, Victoria Docks	A. W. Akers	Daily
31. Mansfield House	Barking Road, Canning Town, E.	{ W. Boyce, T. Scoular	"
32. Tate Institute	Silvertown, E.	{ B. Harvey, W. Downie	"
Holborn District:			
33. Rose and Shamrock	8A Red Lion Square, W.C.	H. Munro-Ferguson	"

SOUTHERN DIVISION.

NAME OF CLUB.	ADDRESS.	DELEGATE.	WHEN OPEN.
Southwark District:			
34. All Hallows	Union Street, Southwark, S.E.	W. H. Stewart	Daily
35. Charterhouse Mission	40 Tabard Street, Borough, S.E.	E. E. Henderson	"
Camberwell District:			
36. Cheltenham College Mission	Nunhead, S.E.	J. Leatherbarrow	"
37. Lothian Institute	20 Elliott Road, Brixton, S.W.	...	...
38. Trinity and St George's	265 Albany Road, Camberwell, S.E.	{ W. Peakall, A. Porter	Daily

No.	Club	Address	Contact	
39.	Wellington College Mission	South Street, Walworth, S.E.	A. J. Thorpe / G. Varney	Daily
Streatham District:				
40.	British Workman	Upper Tulse Hill	W. Westlake / C. J. Goodwin	"
41.	Beaufoy Institute	10 Lambeth Walk, Lambeth Road	F. Briant	"
42.	Holy Trinity W.M.C.	Holy Trinity, Felix Street, Westminster Bridge Road, Lambeth	T. W. Garnish	"
43.	Bradfield Mission	Goldsmith Road, Hill Street, Peckham	E. Devereux	"
Battersea District:				
44.	Baroda W.M.C.	85 Lambeth Road, S.E.	G. H. Colville	"

WESTERN DIVISION.

No.	Club	Address	Contact	
King's Cross District:				
45.	St John's	136 York Road, King's Cross	J. G. Owens / W. Payton / C. Webb	Daily
46.	Christchurch	50 Cumberland Market, Regent's Park		"
47.	St Mary's	80 Chalton Street, Somers Town, N.W.	F. Viney	"
48.	St Thomas' Working-Men's Social Club	Elm Road, Camden Town, N.W.	W. J. Walker	"
Kilburn District:				
49.	St James'	58 Netherwood Street, Hampstead	Rev. A. N. Guest	"
Paddington District:				
50.	St Mary Magdalene	146 Clarendon Street, Harrow Road	— Sampson	"

M

NAME OF CLUB.	ADDRESS.	DELEGATE.	WHEN OPEN.
Notting Hill District:			
51. St James' -	43B Addison Road, Notting Hill -	I. Powell -	Daily
52. Harrow Mission -	191 Latimer Road, Notting Hill -	F. Burton -	,,
53. Rugby Mission -	218 Walmer Road, Notting Hill -	J. Davis -	,,
54. St Clement's -	Blechynden Street, W. -	....	...
55. St Stephen's Club and Institute -	234 Uxbridge Road, Shepherd's Bush	C. E. Wood -	,,
Kensington District:			
56. Anchor -	Johnson Street, Notting Hill Gate	{ J. B. Crossley / Mr Leishman -	,,
Marylebone District:			
57. Christchurch W.M.C. -	The Schools, Stafford Street, Lisson Grove, N.W.	W. M. Tombleson -	,,
58. Middlesex House Postal Institute	25A Chapel Street, Edgware Road, N.W.	S. L. Geaves -	,,
59. Portman Club for Working Lads	80 Church Street, Lisson Grove	W. H. Bonham Carter	,,
Westminster District:			
60. St Matthew's -	Strutton Grounds, Victoria Street, S.W.	A. H. Mure -	,,
61. St Gabriel's -	9 Sutherland Place, S.W. -	A. P. Fletcher -	,,
62. St Andrew's -	Ashley Place, Victoria Street, S.W. -	T. H. Robb -	,,
63. St Barnabas -	174 Ebury Street, Pimlico, S.W. -	J. Ball -	,,
64. St Mary's, Acton -	The Steyne -	F. Tucker -	Daily
65. Chiswick Working-Men's Church Club	213 Devonshire Road, Chiswick	G. H. Hamilton -	,,

DIRECTORY OF SETTLEMENTS

LONDON

TOYNBEE HALL, 28 Commercial Street, E. Founded 1885.

The "Mother of Settlements." It was founded as a memorial of Arnold Toynbee, and as a practical outcome of his teaching. Its main features are educational and social, and in the former respect it stands far above all other Settlements. Several of its residents have taken distinguished places in London's public service. It is completely unsectarian in the broadest sense of the term.

Warden, Rev. Canon S. A. BARNETT, M.A.

OXFORD HOUSE, Bethnal Green, E. Founded 1885.

"Oxford House, in Bethnal Green, is established in order that Oxford men may take part in the social and religious work of the Church in East London; that they may learn something of the life of the poor; may try to better the conditions of the working-classes as regards health and recreation, mental culture, and spiritual teaching; and may offer an example, as far as in them lies, of a simple and religious life."

Warden, Rev. BERNARD WILSON, M.A.

MANSFIELD HOUSE, Canning Town, E. Founded 1890.

Named after Mansfield College at Oxford, by the students of which it was practically founded. The distinguishing

179

feature of this Settlement is not so much any one line of activity as an all-round occupation with the different aspects of the life of the poor, social, economic, educational, and religious. Its members have taken a great share in the public life of West Ham, on the Town Council, School Board, and Board of Guardians. It originated the "Poor Man's Lawyer," while its Lodging-House for Working-Men is unique among Settlements. It is Congregational in origin and association, but in practice is unsectarian.

Warden, PERCY ALDEN, M.A.

BERMONDSEY SETTLEMENT, Farncombe Street, S.E.
Founded 1891.

Established under the auspices of the Wesleyan Methodist Conference. The work is many-sided, University Extension and other educational work receiving a great deal of attention. The warden is a Guardian of the Poor and a member of the London School Board. Much assistance is also given to the other institutions for helpfulness in the district.

Warden, Rev. J. SCOTT LIDGETT, M.A.

NEWMAN HOUSE, Kennington Park Road, S.E.
Founded 1891.

A Settlement for Catholic lay work. At present it is mostly engaged in such social activities as clubs, concerts, classes, etc.

Secretary, J. L. O'CONNELL.

CHALFONT HOUSE, 20 Queen Square, W.C.   Founded 1893.

"A hall of residence for young men, either friends or closely associated with the Society, who may be in London

for business or educational purposes, and to present opportunities for work of a social or religious character."

Warden, GEORGE NEWMAN, M.D.

BROWNING HALL, York Street, Walworth, S.E.
Founded 1894.

"We stand for the Labour Movement in religion.   We
stand for the endeavour to obtain for Labour not merely
more of the good things of life, but most of the best
thing in life.   Come and join us in the service of Him who
is the Lord of Labour and the soul of all social reform."
Several residents and helpers have obtained positions on
the local public bodies, and have done much useful work
in sanitation and other respects.   Congregational and
unsectarian.

Warden, F. HERBERT STEAD, M.A.

CAMBRIDGE HOUSE, Camberwell Road, S.E.
Founded 1897.

A development from "Trinity Court," established in
1889.   The larger scheme has been inaugurated for the
purpose of giving to the University of Cambridge a distinctive
Settlement similar to Oxford House.   Work in the past has
been mainly that of clubs, classes, etc., among boys, but a
considerable extension is looked for.

Warden, Rev. W. F. BAILEY, M.A.

PASSMORE EDWARDS SETTLEMENT,
St Pancras, N.W.   Founded 1897.

A development from University Hall (1891), the chief
object of which was stated to be " To provide a fresh rallying

point and enlarged means of common religious action for all those to whom Christianity, whether by inheritance or process of thought, has become a system of practical conduct, based on faith in God and on the inspiring memory of a great teacher, rather than a system of dogma based on a unique revelation. . . . The first aim of the new hall will be a religious one." Educational and social work are the chief features at present.

Warden, R. G. TATTON, M.A.

RUGBY HOUSE, 292 Lancaster Road, Notting Hill, W.
Founded 1889.

Although not on its present footing, this semi-Settlement was started as a club for boys in 1884, and was taken over by Rugby School in 1889. The work among lads is being developed into work among men as the boys grow to manhood. Though the house has four of five bedrooms for workers, they are only for occasional use, so that the house can hardly be styled a Settlement in the full sense of the term. The house is unsectarian.

Head Worker, I. A. DAVIES.

PEMBROKE COLLEGE MISSION, 207a East Street, Walworth, S.E.   Founded 1886.

This is really a mission station of the Church of England, and is worked as such ; but the fact that it originated in the general movement which gave rise to the Settlements proper, and is of a social and educational nature as well, has caused it to be included here.

Warden, Rev. C. F. ANDREWS, M.A.

Other school and college missions are : Charterhouse Mission, Christ Church Mission, Eton Mission, Gonville and Caius College Settlement, Harrow Mission, Trinity College Mission, and Wellington College Mission.

NORTH-EAST LONDON CHURCH SETTLEMENT,
Upper Edmonton. Founded 1897.

This Settlement is in course of formation. It is in close connection with the parish of St James, Edmonton. The work at present consists of lectures, classes, religious meetings, where social questions are discussed, etc.

Warden, Rev. LUCIUS G. FRY, M.A.

WOMEN'S SETTLEMENTS
WOMEN'S UNIVERSITY SETTLEMENT,
45 Nelson Square, Blackfriars Road, S.E. Founded 1887.

" To promote the welfare of the poorer people of the districts of London, and especially of the women and children, by devising and promoting schemes which tend to elevate them physically, intellectually, or morally, and by giving them additional opportunities for education and recreation." A very large proportion of the work done is in connection with agencies already constituted, and a special feature of the Settlement is the training of workers, in connection with which there are annual scholarships.

Warden, Miss SEWELL.

CHELTENHAM COLLEGE SETTLEMENT (late Mayfield House), St Hilda's, Old Nicholl Street, Shoreditch.
Founded 1889.

This Settlement was formerly working in connection with Oxford House, at Bethnal Green, but has recently moved to an independent sphere.

Head Worker, Mrs REYNOLDS.

ST MARGARET'S HOUSE, 4 Victoria Park Square, Bethnal Green, E.   Founded 1889.

The women's branch of Oxford House. " The movement, of which the two houses are the outcome, came from Oxford ; its inspiring force was the desire to share with the people of East London the two things to which Oxford has owed her greatness — her religious faith, and her development of the higher faculties—intellectual, physical, social—of her sons." Like Oxford House, it is a distinctively Church of England Settlement.

Head Worker, Miss HARINGTON.

CANNING TOWN WOMEN'S SETTLEMENT, Barking Road, E.   Founded 1892.

The Settlement is independent in management and finance, but works in close association with Mansfield House. A special feature of the work is the medical department, consisting of a Medical Mission Dispensary and a Hospital for Women and Children. The head worker has been for some years a member of the West Ham Board of Guardians.

Head Worker, Miss CHEETHAM.

BERMONDSEY SETTLEMENT (Women's House), 149 Lower Road, Rotherhithe, S.E.   Founded 1892.

This, as its name implies, is an integral part of the Bermondsey Settlement (Wesleyan), and its aim is to do the same for the women of the district as is done by the other branch for the men.

Head Worker, Miss SIMMONS.

COLLEGE OF WOMEN WORKERS (Grey Ladies),
Dartmouth Row, Blackheath, S.E.   Founded 1892.
Head Worker, Miss YEATMAN.

NORTH LONDON LADIES' SETTLEMENT,
York House, 87 Highbury, New Park, N.   Founded 1893.

This and the "Grey Ladies" are not strictly Settlements in the full sense, since the residents do not live in the districts in which they work, but go from the College or Settlement to work under the clergy of different parishes.

Head Worker, Miss MAGEE.

LADY MARGARET HALL SETTLEMENT,
129 Kennington Road, S.E.   Founded 1897.
Head Worker, Miss LANGRIDGE (Organising Secretary).

ST MILDRED'S HOUSE, Millwall, Isle of Dogs, E.
Founded 1897.

Affiliated to St Margaret's House, Bethnal Green.

Head Worker, Miss A. M. HARINGTON.

TRINITY SETTLEMENT, Stratford, E.   Founded 1897.

In connection with Trinity College Mission in Stratford, and also affiliated to St Margaret's House.

Head Worker, Miss YATMAN.

HOXTON SETTLEMENT, 280 Bleyton Street,
Nile Street, N.   Founded 1897.

This Settlement is of too recent foundation to have developed special features. It is started in the "hope of helping their poorer neighbours, and making a dreary atmosphere brighter by their presence."

Head Worker, Miss HONOR MORTEN.

MAURICE HOSTEL. Founded 1898.

Founded by the Christian Social Union, and controlled by a special committee of that body.   It is intended to have a men's house and a women's house, but at present the latter only is at work, in temporary premises.

Head Worker, Miss F. Eves, 45 Shepherdess Walk, City Road, E.C.

NEIGHBOURHOOD GUILDS

LEIGHTON HALL NEIGHBOURHOOD GUILD,
8 Leighton Crescent, Kentish Town, N.W.   Founded 1889.

ALLCROFT ROAD NEIGHBOURHOOD GUILD,
140 Allcroft Road, N.W.

The Neighbourhood Guild differs from the Settlement proper in that it is not an institution planted in a district, but starts with the idea "that, irrespective of religious belief or non-belief, all the people, men, women, and children, in any one street, or any small number of streets, in every working-class district of London shall be organised into a set of clubs, which are, by themselves, or in alliance with those of other neighbourhoods, to carry out, or induce others to carry out, all the reforms—domestic, industrial, educational, provident, or recreative—which the social ideal demands."—Dr Stanton Coit.

IN THE PROVINCES

BRISTOL
BROAD PLAIN HOUSE, St Philip's, Bristol.
Founded 1891.

The house has grown out of Mission work started in 1870 by Bristol Congregationalists.   In 1891 the present warden was appointed, working under a committee of Highbury Congregational Church, to develop the activity on Settlement lines. "Though the word Mission is not used, the idea is certainly there ; and we believe that through what are often called Settlement ways, the message we have to bring can best be brought."

Warden, G. H. LEONARD, M.A.

IPSWICH
IPSWICH SOCIAL SETTLEMENT, 133-5 Fore Street.
Founded 1896.

An application of the Settlement idea to the poorer districts of the smaller towns. At present the warden and the "nursing sister" are the only residents proper, but the intention is to provide for and obtain others. Meanwhile, it stands midway between the Settlement and the Neighbourhood Guild. Mr D. S. Crichton of Mansfield College was the first warden, and the work generally is modelled on Mansfield House lines.

Warden, D. MORRIESON PANTON, B.A.

LIVERPOOL
VICTORIA WOMEN'S SETTLEMENT, 322 Netherfield Road. Founded 1897.

As this Settlement has only recently started, it has not yet, of course, had time to develop special characteristics.

Head Workers, Miss E. M. SING and Miss HAMILTON, M.D.

MANCHESTER
LANCASHIRE COLLEGE SETTLEMENT, 34 River Street, Hulme. Founded 1895.

The outcome of social work on the part of the students

and friends of Lancashire College (Congregational). This Settlement is hardly yet fully constituted ; the warden has yet to take up his full office, and the promoters are planning a large and immediate extension. A great deal has, however, been done in the way of clubs, classes, and the usual Settlement activities, and a women's branch has been at work for some time.

Warden-elect, G. PARKER, B.A.
Secretary for Women's Work, Miss B. POCHIN.

UNIVERSITY SETTLEMENT, MANCHESTER.
Founded 1895.
Men's House, 17 Manor Street, Ardwick.
Women's House, 114 Higher Ardwick.

Owens College, through some of its old students, gave the impulse for this Settlement, and the work is "connected closely, though not exclusively, with Owens College." There are two houses of residence, one for men, and the other for women, independent in internal matters, but the direction of the whole work is in the hands of the warden. There is a close co-operation with an already existing institution— Ancoats Hall, otherwise known as the Manchester Art Museum—in educational and recreative work. The activity of the Settlement is of a very wide and varied character.

Warden, E. T. CAMPAGNAC, B.A.
Head of Women's House, Miss C. H. STOEHR.

SHEFFIELD

THE NEIGHBOURHOOD GUILDS ASSOCIATION,
Sheffield.   Founded 1897.

As its name implies, this is not a Settlement, but an attempt to carry out the same purpose by means of the same kind. The Association has two Guilds already in action, The Shalesmoor Guild, and The North Sheffield Settlement, and Neighbour Guild. The latter is at present chiefly occupied with work among women. The Association is entirely unsectarian.

Hon. Secretary, FRANK TILLYARD, B.A., 282 Granville Road.
Hon. Director of North Sheffield Settlement, Dr HELEN M. WILSON, 381 Glossop Road.

SCOTLAND

EDINBURGH

CHALMERS UNIVERSITY SETTLEMENT,
10 Ponton Street.   Founded 1887.

Mostly concerned with clubs and guilds for men and boys.

NEW COLLEGE SETTLEMENT, 48 Pleasance.
Founded 1889.

The emphasis is on religious work, but "we believe the more purely secular agencies maintained further this end.'

Warden, Rev. A. C. DAWSON, M.A.

UNIVERSITY HALL.   Founded 1887.

"University Hall was founded in the year 1887 by the private efforts of Professor Patrick Geddes, assisted by a committee of friends in the University who were personally interested in the institution of the system of Social Residence among students, graduates, and others, and has now along with other ventures, been handed over to the Town and Gown Association, Limited."

"We are, at any rate, not primarily a University Settlement at all; that is to say, we are not a body of people whose essential bond and purpose is that of bringing such *culture* as we may have in such *leisure* as we can spare, upon the *culture* of the working world and its *leisure*. . . . But instead of leisure, we are dealing with *occupation*; trying, therefore, to organise industry, urban and rustic, to organise capital accordingly, and, in the same way, we are trying to publish rather than to lecture. Our Museum, Summer Meeting, etc., seek primarily to arrange knowledge, not primarily to popularise; and so on."—Letter from Professor Geddes.

GLASGOW

TOYNBEE HOUSE, Cathedral Court, Rotten Row.
Founded 1886.

A movement in Settlement work through "family groups" of members of the association.

UNIVERSITY STUDENTS' SETTLEMENT,
10 Possil Road. Founded 1889.

Founded at the suggestion of the late Professor Henry Drummond. It is an extension of the former work of missionary and temperance societies in social directions, with a residence of about fifteen students.

Chief Worker, J. M'LEAN RAMSAY.

INDEX

191

A SELECTION OF

MESSRS. METHUEN'S

PUBLICATIONS

In this Catalogue the order is according to authors. An asterisk denotes that the book is in the press.

Colonial Editions are published of all Messrs. METHUEN'S Novels issued at a price above 2s. 6d., and similar editions are published of some works of General Literature. Colonial editions are only for circulation in the British Colonies and India.

All books marked net are not subject to discount, and cannot be bought at less than the published price. Books not marked net are subject to the discount which the bookseller allows.

Messrs. METHUEN'S books are kept in stock by all good booksellers. If there is any difficulty in seeing copies, Messrs. Methuen will be very glad to have early information, and specimen copies of any books will be sent on receipt of the published price *plus* postage for net books, and of the published price for ordinary books.

This Catalogue contains only a selection of the more important books published by Messrs. Methuen. A complete and illustrated catalogue of their publications may be obtained on application.

Andrewes (Lancelot). PRECES PRIVATAE. Translated and edited, with Notes, by F. E. BRIGHTMAN. *Cr. 8vo.* 6s.

Aristotle. THE ETHICS. Edited, with an Introduction and Notes, by JOHN BURNET. *Demy 8vo.* 10s. 6d. net.

Atkinson (C. T.). A HISTORY OF GERMANY, from 1715-1815. Illustrated. *Demy 8vo.* 12s. 6d. net.

Atkinson (T. D.). ENGLISH ARCHITECTURE. Illustrated. *Fcap. 8vo.* 3s. 6d. net.
A GLOSSARY OF TERMS USED IN ENGLISH ARCHITECTURE. Illustrated. *Second Edition. Fcap. 8vo.* 3s. 6d. net.

Bain (F. W.). A DIGIT OF THE MOON: A HINDOO LOVE STORY. *Ninth Edition. Fcap. 8vo.* 3s. 6d. net.
THE DESCENT OF THE SUN: A CYCLE OF BIRTH. *Fifth Edition. Fcap. 8vo.* 3s. 6d. net.
A HEIFER OF THE DAWN. *Seventh Edition. Fcap. 8vo.* 2s. 6d. net.
IN THE GREAT GOD'S HAIR. *Fifth Edition. Fcap. 8vo.* 2s. 6d. net.
A DRAUGHT OF THE BLUE. *Fourth Edition. Fcap. 8vo.* 2s. 6d. net.
AN ESSENCE OF THE DUSK. *Third Edition. Fcap. 8vo.* 2s. 6d. net.

AN INCARNATION OF THE SNOW. *Second Edition. Fcap. 8vo.* 3s. 6d. net.
A MINE OF FAULTS. *Second Edition. Fcap. 8vo.* 3s. 6d. net.
THE ASHES OF A GOD. *Fcap. 8vo.* 3s. 6d. net.

Balfour (Graham). THE LIFE OF ROBERT LOUIS STEVENSON. Illustrated. *Fifth Edition in one Volume. Cr. 8vo. Buckram,* 6s.

Baring-Gould (S.). THE LIFE OF NAPOLEON BONAPARTE. Illustrated. *Second Edition. Royal 8vo.* 10s. 6d. net.
THE TRAGEDY OF THE CÆSARS: A STUDY OF THE CHARACTERS OF THE CÆSARS OF THE JULIAN AND CLAUDIAN HOUSES. Illustrated. *Seventh Edition. Royal 8vo.* 10s. 6d. net.
A BOOK OF FAIRY TALES. Illustrated. *Second Edition. Cr. 8vo.* 6s. Also *Medium 8vo.* 6d.
OLD ENGLISH FAIRY TALES. Illustrated. *Third Edition. Cr. 8vo. Buckram.* 6s.
THE VICAR OF MORWENSTOW. With a Portrait. *Third Edition. Cr. 8vo.* 3s. 6d.
OLD COUNTRY LIFE. Illustrated. *Fifth Edition. Large Cr. 8vo.* 6s.
STRANGE SURVIVALS: SOME CHAPTERS IN THE HISTORY OF MAN. Illustrated. *Third Edition. Cr. 8vo.* 2s. 6d. net.

YORKSHIRE ODDITIES: INCIDENTS AND STRANGE EVENTS. *Fifth Edition.* *Cr. 8vo. 2s. 6d. net.*
A BOOK OF CORNWALL. Illustrated. *Third Edition. Cr. 8vo. 6s.*
A BOOK OF DARTMOOR. Illustrated. *Second Edition. Cr. 8vo. 6s.*
A BOOK OF DEVON. Illustrated. *Third Edition. Cr. 8vo. 6s.*
A BOOK OF NORTH WALES. Illustrated. *Cr. 8vo. 6s.*
A BOOK OF SOUTH WALES. Illustrated. *Cr. 8vo. 6s.*
A BOOK OF BRITTANY. Illustrated. *Second Edition. Cr. 8vo. 6s.*
A BOOK OF THE RHINE: From Cleve to Mainz. Illustrated. *Second Edition. Cr. 8vo. 6s.*
A BOOK OF THE RIVIERA. Illustrated. *Second Edition. Cr. 8vo. 6s.*
A BOOK OF THE PYRENEES. Illustrated. *Cr. 8vo. 6s.*

Baring-Gould (S.) and Sheppard (H. Fleetwood). A GARLAND OF COUNTRY SONG. English Folk Songs with their Traditional Melodies. *Demy 4to. 6s.*
SONGS OF THE WEST: Folk Songs of Devon and Cornwall. Collected from the Mouths of the People. New and Revised Edition, under the musical editorship of CECIL J. SHARP. *Large Imperial 8vo. 5s. net.*

Barker (E.). THE POLITICAL THOUGHT OF PLATO AND ARISTOTLE. *Demy 8vo. 10s. 6d. net.*

Bastable (C. F.). THE COMMERCE OF NATIONS. *Fifth Edition. Cr. 8vo. 2s. 6d.*

Batson (Mrs. Stephen). A CONCISE HANDBOOK OF GARDEN FLOWERS. *Fcap. 8vo. 3s. 6d.*

Beckett (Arthur). THE SPIRIT OF THE DOWNS: Impressions and Reminiscences of the Sussex Downs. Illustrated. *Second Edition. Demy 8vo. 10s. 6d. net.*

Beckford (Peter). THOUGHTS ON HUNTING. Edited by J. OTHO PAGET. Illustrated. *Third Edition. Demy 8vo. 6s.*

Belloc (H.). PARIS. Illustrated. *Second Edition, Revised. Cr. 8vo. 6s.*
HILLS AND THE SEA. *Fourth Edition. Fcap. 8vo. 5s.*
ON NOTHING AND KINDRED SUBJECTS. *Third Edition. Fcap. 8vo. 5s.*
ON EVERYTHING. *Third Edition. Fcap. 8vo. 5s.*
ON SOMETHING. *Second Edition. Fcap. 8vo. 5s.*
FIRST AND LAST. *Fcap. 8vo. 5s.*
MARIE ANTOINETTE. Illustrated. *Third Edition. Demy 8vo. 15s. net.*
THE PYRENEES. Illustrated. *Second Edition. Demy 8vo. 7s. 6d. net.*

Bennett (Arnold). THE HONEYMOON. *Second Edition. Fcap. 8vo. 2s. net.*

Bennett (W. H.). A PRIMER OF THE BIBLE. *Fifth Edition. Cr. 8vo. 2s. 6d.*

Bennett (W. H.) and Adeney (W. F.). A BIBLICAL INTRODUCTION. With a concise Bibliography. *Sixth Edition. Cr. 8vo. 7s. 6d.*

Benson (Archbishop). GOD'S BOARD. Communion Addresses. *Second Edition. Fcap. 8vo. 3s. 6d. net.*

Bensusan (Samuel L.). HOME LIFE IN SPAIN. Illustrated. *Second Edition. Demy 8vo. 10s. 6d. net.*

Betham-Edwards (Miss). HOME LIFE IN FRANCE. Illustrated. *Fifth Edition. Cr. 8vo. 6s.*

Bindley (T. Herbert). THE OECUMENICAL DOCUMENTS OF THE FAITH. With Introductions and Notes. *Second Edition. Cr. 8vo. 6s. net.*

Blake (William). ILLUSTRATIONS OF THE BOOK OF JOB. With a General Introduction by LAURENCE BINYON. Illustrated. *Quarto. 21s. net.*

Bloemfontein (Bishop of). ARA CŒLI: AN ESSAY IN MYSTICAL THEOLOGY. *Fourth Edition. Cr. 8vo. 3s. 6d. net.*
FAITH AND EXPERIENCE. *Second Edition. Cr. 8vo. 3s. 6d. net.*

Bowden (E. M.). THE IMITATION OF BUDDHA: Quotations from Buddhist Literature for each Day in the Year. *Sixth Edition. Cr. 16mo. 2s. 6d.*

Brabant (F. G.). RAMBLES IN SUSSEX. Illustrated. *Cr. 8vo. 6s.*

Bradley (A. G.). ROUND ABOUT WILTSHIRE. Illustrated. *Second Edition. Cr. 8vo. 6s.*
THE ROMANCE OF NORTHUMBERLAND. Illustrated. *Second Edition. Demy 8vo. 7s. 6d. net.*

Braid (James). ADVANCED GOLF. Illustrated. *Sixth Edition. Demy 8vo. 10s. 6d. net.*

Brailsford (H. N.). MACEDONIA: ITS RACES AND THEIR FUTURE. Illustrated. *Demy 8vo. 12s. 6d. net.*

Brodrick (Mary) and Morton (A. Anderson). A CONCISE DICTIONARY OF EGYPTIAN ARCHÆOLOGY. A Handbook for Students and Travellers. Illustrated. *Cr. 8vo. 3s. 6d.*

Browning (Robert). PARACELSUS. Edited with an Introduction, Notes, and Bibliography by MARGARET L. LEE and KATHARINE B. LOCOCK. *Fcap. 8vo. 3s. 6d. net.*

Buckton (A. M.). EAGER HEART: A Christmas Mystery-Play. *Tenth Edition. Cr. 8vo. 1s. net.*

Budge (E. A. Wallis). THE GODS OF THE EGYPTIANS. Illustrated. *Two Volumes. Royal 8vo. £3 3s. net.*

Bull (Paul). GOD AND OUR SOLDIERS. *Second Edition. Cr. 8vo. 6s.*

Burns (Robert). THE POEMS AND SONGS. Edited by ANDREW LANG and W. A. CRAIGIE. With Portrait. *Third Edition. Wide Demy 8vo. 6s.*

Busbey (Katherine G.). HOME LIFE IN AMERICA. Illustrated. *Second Edition. Demy 8vo. 10s. 6d. net.*

Butlin (F. M.). AMONG THE DANES. Illustrated. *Demy 8vo. 7s. 6d. net.*

Cain (Georges), WALKS IN PARIS. Translated by A. R. ALLINSON. Illustrated. *Demy 8vo. 7s. 6d. net.*

Calman (W. T.). THE LIFE OF CRUSTACEA. Illustrated. *Cr. 8vo. 6s.*

Carlyle (Thomas). THE FRENCH REVOLUTION. Edited by C. R. L. FLETCHER. *Three Volumes. Cr. 8vo. 18s.*
THE LETTERS AND SPEECHES OF OLIVER CROMWELL. With an Introduction by C. H. FIRTH, and Notes and Appendices by S. C. LOMAS. *Three Volumes. Demy 8vo. 18s. net.*

Celano (Brother Thomas of). THE LIVES OF S. FRANCIS OF ASSISI. Translated by A. G. FERRERS HOWELL. Illustrated. *Cr. 8vo. 5s. net.*

Chambers (Mrs. Lambert). LAWN TENNIS FOR LADIES. Illustrated. *Cr. 8vo. 2s. 6d. net.*

Chesterfield (Lord). THE LETTERS OF THE EARL OF CHESTERFIELD TO HIS SON. Edited, with an Introduction by C. STRACHEY, and Notes by A. CALTHROP. *Two Volumes. Cr. 8vo. 12s.*

Chesterton (G. K.). CHARLES DICKENS. With two Portraits in Photogravure. *Seventh Edition. Cr. 8vo. 6s.*
ALL THINGS CONSIDERED. *Sixth Edition. Fcap. 8vo. 5s.*
TREMENDOUS TRIFLES. *Fourth Edition. Fcap. 8vo. 5s.*
ALARMS AND DISCURSIONS. *Second Edition. Fcap. 8vo. 5s.*
THE BALLAD OF THE WHITE HORSE. *Third Edition. Fcap. 8vo. 5s.*

Clausen (George). SIX LECTURES ON PAINTING. Illustrated. *Third Edition. Large Post 8vo. 3s. 6d. net.*
AIMS AND IDEALS IN ART. Eight Lectures delivered to the Students of the Royal Academy of Arts. Illustrated. *Second Edition. Large Post 8vo. 5s. net.*

Clutton-Brock (A.) SHELLEY: THE MAN AND THE POET. Illustrated. *Demy 8vo. 7s. 6d. net.*

Cobb (W. F.). THE BOOK OF PSALMS: with an Introduction and Notes. *Demy 8vo. 10s. 6d. net.*

Collingwood (W. G.). THE LIFE OF JOHN RUSKIN. With Portrait. *Sixth Edition. Cr. 8vo. 2s. 6d. net.*

Conrad (Joseph). THE MIRROR OF THE SEA: Memories and Impressions. *Third Edition. Cr. 8vo. 6s.*

Coolidge (W. A. B.). THE ALPS. Illustrated. *Demy 8vo. 7s. 6d. net.*

Coulton (G. G.). CHAUCER AND HIS ENGLAND. Illustrated. *Second Edition. Demy 8vo. 10s. 6d. net.*

Cowper (William). THE POEMS. Edited with an Introduction and Notes by J. C. BAILEY. Illustrated. *Demy 8vo. 10s. 6d. net.*

Crispe (T. E.). REMINISCENCES OF A K.C. With 2 Portraits. *Second Edition. Demy 8vo. 10s. 6d. net.*

Crowley (Ralph H.). THE HYGIENE OF SCHOOL LIFE. Illustrated. *Cr. 8vo. 3s. 6d. net.*

Dante Alighieri. LA COMMEDIA DI DANTE. The Italian Text edited by PAGET TOYNBEE. *Cr. 8vo. 6s.*

Davey (Richard). THE PAGEANT OF LONDON. Illustrated. *In Two Volumes. Demy 8vo. 15s. net.*

Davis (H. W. C.). ENGLAND UNDER THE NORMANS AND ANGEVINS: 1066–1272. Illustrated. *Second Edition. Demy 8vo. 10s. 6d. net.*

Dawbarn (Charles.) FRANCE AND THE FRENCH. Illustrated. *Demy 8vo. 10s. 6d. net.*

Dearmer (Mabel). A CHILD'S LIFE OF CHRIST. Illustrated. *Large Cr. 8vo. 6s.*

Deffand (Madame Du). THE LETTERS OF MADAME DU DEFFAND TO HORACE WALPOLE. Edited, with Introduction, Notes, and Index, by Mrs. PAGET TOYNBEE. *In Three Volumes. Demy 8vo. £3 3s. net.*

Dickinson (G. L.). THE GREEK VIEW OF LIFE. *Seventh Edition. Crown 8vo. 2s. 6d. net.*

Ditchfield (P. H.). THE PARISH CLERK. Illustrated. *Third Edition. Demy 8vo. 7s. 6d. net.*
THE OLD-TIME PARSON. Illustrated. *Second Edition. Demy 8vo. 7s. 6d. net.*

Ditchfield (P. H.) and Roe (Fred).
VANISHING ENGLAND. The Book by
P. H. Ditchfield. Illustrated by FRED ROE.
Second Edition. Wide Demy 8vo. 15s. net.

Douglas (Hugh A.). VENICE ON FOOT.
With the Itinerary of the Grand Canal.
Illustrated. *Second Edition. Fcap. 8vo.*
5s. net.
VENICE AND HER TREASURES.
Illustrated. *Round corners. Fcap. 8vo.*
5s. net.

Dowden (J.). FURTHER STUDIES IN
THE PRAYER BOOK. *Cr. 8vo.* 6s.

Driver (S. R.). SERMONS ON
SUBJECTS CONNECTED WITH THE
OLD TESTAMENT. *Cr. 8vo.* 6s.

Dumas (Alexandre). THE CRIMES OF
THE BORGIAS AND OTHERS. With
an Introduction by R. S. GARNETT.
Illustrated. *Second Edition. Cr. 8vo.* 6s.
THE CRIMES OF URBAIN GRAN-
DIER AND OTHERS. Illustrated. *Cr.
8vo.* 6s.
THE CRIMES OF THE MARQUISE
DE BRINVILLIERS AND OTHERS.
Illustrated. *Cr. 8vo.* 6s.
THE CRIMES OF ALI PACHA AND
OTHERS. Illustrated. *Cr. 8vo.* 6s.
MY MEMOIRS. Translated by E. M.
WALLER. With an Introduction by ANDREW
LANG. With Frontispieces in Photogravure.
In six Volumes. *Cr. 8vo.* 6s. *each volume.*
VOL. I. 1802-1821. VOL. IV. 1830-1831.
VOL. II. 1822-1825. VOL. V. 1831-1832.
VOL. III. 1826-1830. VOL. VI. 1832-1833.
MY PETS. Newly translated by A. R.
ALLINSON. Illustrated. *Cr. 8vo.* 6s.

Duncan (F. M.). OUR INSECT
FRIENDS AND FOES. Illustrated.
Cr. 8vo. 6s.

Dunn-Pattison (R. P.). NAPOLEON'S
MARSHALS. Illustrated. *Demy 8vo.*
Second Edition. 12s. 6d. net.
THE BLACK PRINCE. Illustrated.
Second Edition. Demy 8vo. 7s. 6d. net.

Durham (The Earl of). THE REPORT
ON CANADA. With an Introductory
Note. *Demy 8vo.* 4s. 6d. net.

Dutt (W. A.). THE NORFOLK BROADS.
Illustrated. *Second Edition. Cr. 8vo.* 6s.
WILD LIFE IN EAST ANGLIA. Illustrated. *Second Edition. Demy 8vo.* 7s. 6d.
net.

Edwardes (Tickner). THE LORE OF
THE HONEY-BEE. Illustrated. *Third
Edition. Cr. 8vo.* 6s.
LIFT-LUCK ON SOUTHERN ROADS.
Illustrated. *Cr. 8vo.* 6s.
NEIGHBOURHOOD : A YEAR'S LIFE IN
AND ABOUT AN ENGLISH VILLAGE. Illus-
trated. *Cr. 8vo.* 6s.

Egerton (H. E.). A SHORT HISTORY
OF BRITISH COLONIAL POLICY.
Third Edition. Demy 8vo. 7s. 6d. net.

Exeter (Bishop of). REGNUM DEI.
(The Bampton Lectures of 1901.) *A Cheaper
Edition. Demy 8vo.* 7s. 6d. net.

Fairbrother (W. H.). THE PHILO-
SOPHY OF T. H. GREEN. *Second
Edition. Cr. 8vo.* 3s. 6d.

Fea (Allan). THE FLIGHT OF THE
KING. Illustrated. *Second and Revised
Edition. Demy 8vo.* 7s. 6d. net.
SECRET CHAMBERS AND HIDING-
PLACES. Illustrated. *Third and Revised
Edition. Demy 8vo.* 7s. 6d. net.
JAMES II. AND HIS WIVES. Illustrated.
Demy 8vo. 12s. 6d. net.

Firth (C. H.). CROMWELL'S ARMY :
A History of the English Soldier during the
Civil Wars, the Commonwealth, and the
Protectorate. Illustrated. *Second Edition.*
Cr. 8vo. 6s.

Fisher (H. A. L.). THE REPUBLICAN
TRADITION IN EUROPE. *Cr. 8vo.*
6s. net.

FitzGerald (Edward). THE RUBAI'YAT
OF OMAR KHAYYAM. Printed from
the Fifth and last Edition. With a Commentary by H. M. BATSON, and a Biographical Introduction by E. D. Ross. *Cr. 8vo.*
6s.

Fletcher (J. S.). A BOOK ABOUT
YORKSHIRE. Illustrated. *Demy 8vo.*
7s. 6d. net.

Flux (A. W.). ECONOMIC PRINCIPLES
Demy 8vo. 7s. 6d. net.

Fraser (J. F.). ROUND THE WORLD
ON A WHEEL. Illustrated. *Fifth
Edition. Cr. 8vo.* 6s.

Galton (Sir Francis). MEMORIES OF
MY LIFE. Illustrated. *Third Edition.
Demy 8vo.* 10s. 6d. net.

Gibbins (H. de B.). INDUSTRY IN
ENGLAND : HISTORICAL OUT-
LINES. With 5 Maps. *Sixth Edition.
Demy 8vo.* 10s. 6d.
THE INDUSTRIAL HISTORY OF
ENGLAND. Illustrated. *Eighteenth
and Revised Edition. Cr. 8vo.* 3s.
ENGLISH SOCIAL REFORMERS.
Second Edition. Cr. 8vo. 2s. 6d.

Gibbon (Edward). THE MEMOIRS OF
THE LIFE OF EDWARD GIBBON.
Edited by G. BIRKBECK HILL. *Cr. 8vo.* 6s.
THE DECLINE AND FALL OF THE
ROMAN EMPIRE. Edited, with Notes,
Appendices, and Maps, by J. B. BURY.
Illustrated. *In Seven Volumes. Demy
8vo. Each* 10s. 6d. net.

Gloag (M. R.) A BOOK OF ENGLISH GARDENS. Illustrated. *Demy 8vo.* 10s. 6d. net.

Glover (J. M.). JIMMY GLOVER—HIS BOOK. *Fourth Edition. Demy 8vo.* 12s. 6d. net.

Glover (T. R.). THE CONFLICT OF RELIGIONS IN THE EARLY ROMAN EMPIRE. *Fourth Edition. Demy 8vo.* 7s. 6d. net.

Godfrey (Elizabeth). A BOOK OF RE-MEMBRANCE. Being Lyrical Selections for every day in the Year. Arranged by E. Godfrey. *Second Edition. Fcap. 8vo.* 2s. 6d. net.

Godley (A. D.). OXFORD IN THE EIGHTEENTH CENTURY. Illustrated. *Second Edition. Demy 8vo.* 7s. 6d. net.
LYRA FRIVOLA. *Fourth Edition. Fcap. 8vo.* 2s. 6d.
VERSES TO ORDER. *Second Edition. Fcap. 8vo.* 2s. 6d.
SECOND STRINGS. *Fcap. 8vo.* 2s. 6d.

Gordon (Lina Duff) (Mrs. Aubrey Water-field). HOME LIFE IN ITALY: LETTERS FROM THE APENNINES. Illustrated. *Second Edition. Demy 8vo.* 10s. 6d. net.

Gostling (Frances M.). THE BRETONS AT HOME. Illustrated. *Third Edition. Cr. 8vo.* 6s.
AUVERGNE AND ITS PEOPLE. Illustrated. *Demy 8vo.* 10s. 6d. net.

Grahame (Kenneth). THE WIND IN THE WILLOWS. Illustrated. *Sixth Edition. Cr. 8vo.* 6s.

Grew (Edwin Sharpe). THE GROWTH OF A PLANET. Illustrated. *Cr. 8vo.* 6s.

Griffin (W. Hall) and Minchin (H. C.). THE LIFE OF ROBERT BROWNING. Illustrated. *Second Edition. Demy 8vo.* 12s. 6d. net.

Hale (J. R.). FAMOUS SEA FIGHTS: FROM SALAMIS TO TSU-SHIMA. Illustrated. *Cr. 8vo.* 6s. net.

Hall (Cyril). THE YOUNG CARPEN-TER. Illustrated. *Cr. 8vo.* 5s.

Hall (Hammond). THE YOUNG EN-GINEER: or MODERN ENGINES AND THEIR MODELS. Illustrated. *Second Edition. Cr. 8vo.* 5s.
THE YOUNG ELECTRICIAN. Illustrated. *Second Edition. Cr. 8vo.* 5s.

Hannay (D.). A SHORT HISTORY OF THE ROYAL NAVY. Vol. I., 1217–1688. Vol. II., 1689–1815. *Demy 8vo. Each* 7s. 6d. net.

Harper (Charles G.). THE AUTOCAR ROAD-BOOK. Four Volumes with Maps. *Cr. 8vo. Each* 7s. 6d. net.
Vol. I.—SOUTH OF THE THAMES.
Vol. II.—NORTH AND SOUTH WALES AND WEST MIDLANDS.

Hassall (Arthur). NAPOLEON. Illustrated. *Demy 8vo.* 7s. 6d. net.

Headley (F. W.). DARWINISM AND MODERN SOCIALISM. *Second Edition. Cr. 8vo.* 5s. net.

Henderson (B. W.). THE LIFE AND PRINCIPATE OF THE EMPEROR NERO. Illustrated. *New and cheaper issue. Demy 8vo.* 7s. 6d. net.

Henderson (M. Sturge). GEORGE MEREDITH; NOVELIST, POET, REFORMER. Illustrated. *Second Edition. Cr. 8vo.* 6s.

Henderson (T. F.) and Watt (Francis). SCOTLAND OF TO-DAY. Illustrated. *Second Edition. Cr. 8vo.* 6s.

Henley (W. E.). ENGLISH LYRICS. CHAUCER TO POE. *Second Edition. Cr. 8vo.* 2s. 6d. net.

Hill (George Francis). ONE HUNDRED MASTERPIECES OF SCULPTURE. Illustrated. *Demy 8vo.* 10s. 6d. net.

Hind (C. Lewis). DAYS IN CORNWALL. Illustrated. *Third Edition. Cr. 8vo.* 6s.

Hobhouse (L. T.). THE THEORY OF KNOWLEDGE. *Demy 8vo.* 10s. 6d. net.

Hodgson (Mrs. W.). HOW TO IDENTIFY OLD CHINESE PORCELAIN. Illustrated. *Third Edition. Post 8vo.* 6s.

Holdich (Sir T. H.). THE INDIAN BORDERLAND, 1880-1900. Illustrated. *Second Edition. Demy 8vo.* 10s. 6d. net.

Holdsworth (W. S.). A HISTORY OF ENGLISH LAW. *In Four Volumes.* Vols. I., II., III. *Demy 8vo. Each* 10s. 6d. net.

Holland (Clive). TYROL AND ITS PEOPLE. Illustrated. *Demy 8vo.* 10s. 6d. net.
THE BELGIANS AT HOME. Illustrated. *Demy 8vo.* 10s. 6d. net.

Horsburgh (E. L. S.). LORENZO THE MAGNIFICENT: AND FLORENCE IN HER GOLDEN AGE. Illustrated. *Second Edition. Demy 8vo.* 15s. net.
WATERLOO; A NARRATIVE AND A CRIT-ICISM. With Plans. *Second Edition. Cr. 8vo.* 5s.
THE LIFE OF SAVONAROLA. Illustrated. *Cr. 8vo.* 5s. net.

Hosie (Alexander). MANCHURIA. Illustrated. *Second Edition. Demy 8vo.* 7s. 6d. net.

Hudson (W. H.). A SHEPHERD'S LIFE: IMPRESSIONS OF THE SOUTH WILT-SHIRE DOWNS. Illustrated. *Third Edition. Demy 8vo.* 7s. 6d. net.

Hugon (Cécile). SOCIAL LIFE IN FRANCE IN THE XVII CENTURY. Illustrated. *Demy 8vo.* 10s. 6d. net.

Humphreys (John H.). PROPORTIONAL REPRESENTATION. *Cr. 8vo.* 5s. net.

Hutchinson (Horace G.). THE NEW FOREST. Illustrated. *Fourth Edition. Cr. 8vo.* 6s.

Hutton (Edward). THE CITIES OF SPAIN. Illustrated. *Fourth Edition. Cr. 8vo.* 6s.
THE CITIES OF UMBRIA. Illustrated. *Fourth Edition. Cr. 8vo.* 6s.
FLORENCE AND THE CITIES OF NORTHERN TUSCANY WITH GENOA. Illustrated. *Second Edition. Cr. 8vo.* 6s.
SIENA AND SOUTHERN TUSCANY. Illustrated. *Second Edition. Cr. 8vo.* 6s.
VENICE AND VENETIA. Illustrated. *Cr. 8vo.* 6s.
ROME. Illustrated. *Second Edition. Cr. 8vo.* 6s.
ENGLISH LOVE POEMS. Edited with an Introduction. *Fcap. 8vo.* 3s. 6d. net.
COUNTRY WALKS ABOUT FLORENCE. Illustrated. *Second Edition. Fcap. 8vo.* 5s. net.
IN UNKNOWN TUSCANY With Notes by WILLIAM HEYWOOD. Illustrated. *Second Edition. Demy 8vo.* 7s. 6d. net.
A BOOK OF THE WYE. Illustrated. *Demy 8vo.* 7s. 6d. net.

Ibsen (Henrik). BRAND. A Dramatic Poem, Translated by WILLIAM WILSON. *Fourth Edition. Cr. 8vo.* 3s. 6d.

Inge (W. R.). CHRISTIAN MYSTICISM. (The Bampton Lectures of 1899.) *Second and Cheaper Edition. Cr. 8vo.* 5s. net.

Innes (A. D.). A HISTORY OF THE BRITISH IN INDIA. With Maps and Plans. *Cr. 8vo.* 6s.
ENGLAND UNDER THE TUDORS. With Maps. *Third Edition. Demy 8vo.* 10s. 6d. net.

Innes (Mary). SCHOOLS OF PAINTING. Illustrated. *Second Edition. Cr. 8vo.* 5s. net.

Jenks (E.). AN OUTLINE OF ENGLISH LOCAL GOVERNMENT. *Second Edition.* Revised by R. C. K. ENSOR, *Cr. 8vo.* 2s. 6d. net.

Jerningham (Charles Edward). THE MAXIMS OF MARMADUKE. *Second Edition. Cr. 8vo.* 5s.

Jerrold (Walter). THE DANUBE. Illustrated. *Demy 8vo.* 10s. 6d. net.

Johnston (Sir H. H.). BRITISH CENTRAL AFRICA. Illustrated. *Third Edition. Cr. 4to.* 18s. net.
THE NEGRO IN THE NEW WORLD. Illustrated. *Demy 8vo.* 21s. net.

Julian (Lady) of Norwich. REVELATIONS OF DIVINE LOVE. Edited by GRACE WARRACK. *Fourth Edition. Cr. 8vo.* 3s. 6d.

Keats (John). THE POEMS. Edited with Introduction and Notes by E. de SÉLINCOURT. With a Frontispiece in Photogravure. *Third Edition. Demy 8vo.* 7s. 6d. net.

Keble (John). THE CHRISTIAN YEAR. With an Introduction and Notes by W. LOCK. Illustrated. *Third Edition. Fcap. 8vo.* 3s. 6d.

Kempis (Thomas à). THE IMITATION OF CHRIST. With an Introduction by DEAN FARRAR. Illustrated. *Third Edition. Fcap. 8vo.* 3s. 6d.; padded morocco, 5s.

Kipling (Rudyard). BARRACK-ROOM BALLADS. 105th Thousand. *Thirtieth Edition. Cr. 8vo.* 6s. Also *Fcap. 8vo, Leather.* 5s. net.
THE SEVEN SEAS. 86th Thousand. *Eighteenth Edition. Cr. 8vo.* 6s. Also *Fcap. 8vo, Leather.* 5s. net.
THE FIVE NATIONS. 72nd Thousand. *Eighth Edition. Cr. 8vo.* 6s. Also *Fcap. 8vo, Leather.* 5s. net.
DEPARTMENTAL DITTIES. *Twentieth Edition. Cr. 8vo.* 6s. Also *Fcap. 8vo, Leather.* 5s. net.

Knox (Winifred F.). THE COURT OF A SAINT. Illustrated. *Demy 8vo.* 10s. 6d. net.

*Lamb (Charles and Mary). THE WORKS. Edited with an Introduction and Notes by E. V. LUCAS. *A New and Revised Edition in Six Volumes.* With Frontispiece. *Fcap 8vo.* 5s. each. The volumes are :—
I. MISCELLANEOUS PROSE. II. ELIA AND THE LAST ESSAYS OF ELIA. III. BOOKS FOR CHILDREN. IV. PLAYS AND POEMS. V. and VI. LETTERS.

Lane-Poole (Stanley). A HISTORY OF EGYPT IN THE MIDDLE AGES. Illustrated. *Cr. 8vo.* 6s.

Lankester (Sir Ray). SCIENCE FROM AN EASY CHAIR. Illustrated. *Fifth Edition. Cr. 8vo.* 6s.

Le Braz (Anatole). THE LAND OF PARDONS. Translated by FRANCES M. GOSTLING. Illustrated. *Third Edition. Cr. 8vo.* 6s.

Lindsay (Mabel M.). ANNI DOMINI: A GOSPEL STUDY. With Maps. *Two Volumes. Super Royal 8vo. 10s. net.*

Lock (Walter). ST. PAUL, THE MASTER-BUILDER. *Third Edition. Cr. 8vo. 3s. 6d.*
THE BIBLE AND CHRISTIAN LIFE. *Cr. 8vo. 6s.*

Lodge (Sir Oliver). THE SUBSTANCE OF FAITH, ALLIED WITH SCIENCE: A Catechism for Parents and Teachers. *Eleventh Edition. Cr. 8vo. 2s. net.*
MAN AND THE UNIVERSE: A STUDY OF THE INFLUENCE OF THE ADVANCE IN SCIENTIFIC KNOWLEDGE UPON OUR UNDERSTANDING OF CHRISTIANITY. *Ninth Edition. Demy 8vo. 5s. net.*
THE SURVIVAL OF MAN. A STUDY IN UNRECOGNISED HUMAN FACULTY. *Fifth Edition. Wide Crown 8vo. 5s. net.*
REASON AND BELIEF. *Fifth Edition. Cr. 8vo. 3s. 6d. net.*

Lorimer (George Horace). LETTERS FROM A SELF-MADE MERCHANT TO HIS SON. Illustrated. *Twenty-second Edition. Cr. 8vo. 3s. 6d.*
OLD GORGON GRAHAM. Illustrated. *Second Edition. Cr. 8vo. 6s.*

'Loyal Serviteur.' THE STORY OF BAYARD. Adapted by AMY G. ANDREWES. Illustrated. *Cr. 8vo. 2s. 6d.*

Lucas (E. V.). THE LIFE OF CHARLES LAMB. Illustrated. *Fifth Edition. Demy 8vo. 7s. 6d. net.*
A WANDERER IN HOLLAND. Illustrated. *Thirteenth Edition. Cr. 8vo. 6s.*
Also Fcap. 8vo. 5s.
A WANDERER IN LONDON. Illustrated. *Twelfth Edition. Cr. 8vo. 6s.*
Also Fcap. 8vo. 5s.
A WANDERER IN PARIS. Illustrated. *Ninth Edition. Cr. 8vo. 6s.*
Also Seventh Edition. Fcap. 8vo. 5s.
THE OPEN ROAD: A Little Book for Wayfarers. *Eighteenth Edition. Fcap. 8vo. 5s.; India Paper, 7s. 6d.*
THE FRIENDLY TOWN: a Little Book for the Urbane. *Sixth Edition. Fcap. 8vo. 5s.; India Paper, 7s. 6d.*
FIRESIDE AND SUNSHINE. *Sixth Edition. Fcap. 8vo. 5s.*
CHARACTER AND COMEDY. *Sixth Edition. Fcap. 8vo. 5s.*
THE GENTLEST ART. A Choice of Letters by Entertaining Hands. *Seventh Edition. Fcap 8vo. 5s.*
THE SECOND POST. *Third Edition. Fcap. 8vo. 5s.*
A SWAN AND HER FRIENDS. Illustrated. *Demy 8vo. 12s. 6d. net.*
HER INFINITE VARIETY: A FEMININE PORTRAIT GALLERY. *Sixth Edition. Fcap. 8vo. 5s.*

GOOD COMPANY: A RALLY OF MEN. *Second Edition. Fcap. 8vo. 5s.*
ONE DAY AND ANOTHER. *Fifth Edition. Fcap. 8vo. 5s.*
OLD LAMPS FOR NEW. *Fourth Edition. Fcap. 8vo. 5s.*
LISTENER'S LURE: AN OBLIQUE NARRATION. *Ninth Edition. Fcap. 8vo. 5s.*
OVER BEMERTON'S: AN EASY-GOING CHRONICLE. *Ninth Edition. Fcap. 8vo. 5s.*
MR. INGLESIDE. *Ninth Edition. Fcap. 8vo. 5s.*
See also Lamb (Charles).

*Lydekker (R. and Others).** REPTILES, AMPHIBIA, AND FISHES. Illustrated. *Demy 8vo. 10s. 6d. net.*

Lydekker (R.). THE OX. Illustrated. *Cr. 8vo. 6s.*

Macaulay (Lord). CRITICAL AND HISTORICAL ESSAYS. Edited by F. C. MONTAGUE. *Three Volumes. Cr. 8vo. 18s.*

McCabe (Joseph). THE DECAY OF THE CHURCH OF ROME. *Third Edition. Demy 8vo. 7s. 6d. net.*
THE EMPRESSES OF ROME. Illustrated. *Demy 8vo. 12s. 6d. net.*

MacCarthy (Desmond) and Russell (Agatha). LADY JOHN RUSSELL: A MEMOIR. Illustrated. *Fourth Edition. Demy 8vo. 10s. 6d. net.*

McCullagh (Francis). THE FALL OF ABD-UL-HAMID. Illustrated. *Demy 8vo. 10s. 6d. net.*

*MacDonagh (Michael).** THE SPEAKER OF THE HOUSE. *Demy 8vo. 10s. 6d. net.*

McDougall (William). AN INTRODUCTION TO SOCIAL PSYCHOLOGY. *Fourth Edition. Cr. 8vo. 5s. net.*
BODY AND MIND: A HISTORY AND A DEFENCE OF ANIMISM. *Demy 8vo. 10s. 6d. net.*

* Mdlle. Mori' (Author of). ST. CATHERINE OF SIENA AND HER TIMES. Illustrated. *Second Edition. Demy 8vo. 7s. 6d. net.*

Maeterlinck (Maurice). THE BLUE BIRD: A FAIRY PLAY IN SIX ACTS. Translated by ALEXANDER TEIXEIRA DE MATTOS. *Twentieth Edition. Fcap. 8vo. Deckle Edges. 3s. 6d. net. Also Twenty-seventh Edition. Fcap. 8vo. Cloth, 1s. net.*
THE BLUE BIRD: A FAIRY PLAY IN SIX ACTS. Translated by ALEXANDER TEIXEIRA DE MATTOS. Illustrated. *Twenty-fifth Edition. Cr. 4to. 21s. net.*
MARY MAGDALENE: A PLAY IN THREE ACTS. Translated by ALEXANDER TEIXEIRA DE MATTOS. *Third Edition. Fcap. 8vo. Deckle Edges. 3s. 6d. net.*

Mahaffy (J. P.). A HISTORY OF EGYPT UNDER THE PTOLEMAIC DYNASTY. Illustrated. *Cr. 8vo. 6s.*

Maitland (F. W.). ROMAN CANON LAW IN THE CHURCH OF ENGLAND. *Royal 8vo. 7s. 6d.*

Marett (R. R.). THE THRESHOLD OF RELIGION. *Cr. 8vo. 3s. 6d. net.*

Marriott (Charles). A SPANISH HOLIDAY. Illustrated. *Demy 8vo. 7s. 6d. net.* THE ROMANCE OF THE RHINE. Illustrated. *Demy 8vo. 10s. 6d. net.*

Marriott (J. A. R.). THE LIFE AND TIMES OF LUCIUS CARY, VISCOUNT FALKLAND. Illustrated. *Second Edition. Demy 8vo. 7s. 6d. net.*

Masefield (John). SEA LIFE IN NELSON'S TIME. Illustrated. *Cr. 8vo. 3s. 6d. net.* A SAILOR'S GARLAND. Selected and Edited. *Second Edition. Cr. 8vo. 3s. 6d. net.*

Masterman (C. F. G.). TENNYSON AS A RELIGIOUS TEACHER. *Second Edition. Cr. 8vo. 6s.* THE CONDITION OF ENGLAND. *Fourth Edition. Cr. 8vo. 6s.*

Medley (D. J.). ORIGINAL ILLUSTRATIONS OF ENGLISH CONSTITUTIONAL HISTORY. *Cr. 8vo. 7s. 6d. net.*

Meldrum (D. S.). HOME LIFE IN HOLLAND. Illustrated. *Second Edition. Demy 8vo. 10s. 6d. net.*

Methuen (A. M. S.). ENGLAND'S RUIN: DISCUSSED IN FOURTEEN LETTERS TO A PROTECTIONIST. *Ninth Edition. Cr. 8vo. 3d. net.*

Meynell (Everard). COROT AND HIS FRIENDS. Illustrated. *Demy 8vo. 10s. 6d. net.*

Miles (Eustace). LIFE AFTER LIFE: OR, THE THEORY OF REINCARNATION. *Cr. 8vo. 2s. 6d. net.* THE POWER OF CONCENTRATION: How to Acquire it. *Third Edition. Cr. 8vo. 3s. 6d. net.*

Millais (J. G.). THE LIFE AND LETTERS OF SIR JOHN EVERETT MILLAIS. Illustrated. *New Edition. Demy 8vo. 7s. 6d. net.*

Milne (J. G.). A HISTORY OF EGYPT UNDER ROMAN RULE. Illustrated. *Cr. 8vo. 6s.*

Moffat (Mary M.). QUEEN LOUISA OF PRUSSIA. Illustrated. *Fourth Edition. Cr. 8vo. 6s.* MARIA THERESA. Illustrated. *10s. 6d. net.*

Money (L. G. Chiozza). RICHES AND POVERTY, 1910. *Tenth and Revised Edition. Demy 8vo. 5s. net.* MONEY'S FISCAL DICTIONARY, 1910. *Second Edition. Demy 8vo. 5s. net.*

Montague (C. E.). DRAMATIC VALUES. *Second Edition. Fcap. 8vo. 5s.*

Moorhouse (E. Hallam). NELSON'S LADY HAMILTON. Illustrated. *Third Edition. Demy 8vo. 7s. 6d. net.*

Morgan (J. H.), THE HOUSE OF LORDS AND THE CONSTITUTION. With an Introduction by the LORD CHANCELLOR. *Cr. 8vo. 1s. net.*

Nevill (Lady Dorothy). UNDER FIVE REIGNS. Edited by her son. Illustrated. *Fifth Edition. Demy 8vo. 15s. net.*

Norway (A. H.). NAPLES. PAST AND PRESENT. Illustrated. *Fourth Edition. Cr. 8vo. 6s.*

Oman (C. W. C.), A HISTORY OF THE ART OF WAR IN THE MIDDLE AGES. Illustrated. *Demy 8vo. 10s. 6d. net.* ENGLAND BEFORE THE NORMAN CONQUEST. With Maps. *Second Edition. Demy 8vo. 10s. 6d. net.*

Oxford (M. N.), A HANDBOOK OF NURSING. *Fifth Edition. Cr. 8vo. 3s. 6d.*

Pakes (W. C. C.). THE SCIENCE OF HYGIENE. Illustrated. *Second and Cheaper Edition. Cr. 8vo. 5s. net.*

Parker (Eric). THE BOOK OF THE ZOO; By DAY AND NIGHT. Illustrated. *Second Edition. Cr. 8vo. 6s.*

Pears (Sir Edwin). TURKEY AND ITS PEOPLE. *Second Edition. Demy 8vo. 12s. 6d. net.*

Petrie (W. M. Flinders). A HISTORY OF EGYPT. Illustrated. *In Six Volumes. Cr. 8vo. 6s. each.*
VOL. I. FROM THE 1ST TO THE XVITH DYNASTY. *Seventh Edition.*
VOL. II. THE XVIITH AND XVIIITH DYNASTIES. *Fourth Edition.*
VOL. III. XIXTH TO XXXTH DYNASTIES.
VOL. IV. EGYPT UNDER THE PTOLEMAIC DYNASTY. J. P. MAHAFFY.
VOL. V. EGYPT UNDER ROMAN RULE. J. G. MILNE.
VOL. VI. EGYPT IN THE MIDDLE AGES. STANLEY LANE-POOLE.
RELIGION AND CONSCIENCE IN ANCIENT EGYPT. Illustrated. *Cr. 8vo. 2s. 6d.*
SYRIA AND EGYPT, FROM THE TELL EL AMARNA LETTERS. *Cr. 8vo. 2s. 6d.*

EGYPTIAN TALES. Translated from the Papyri. First Series, ivth to xiith Dynasty. Illustrated. *Second Edition. Cr. 8vo. 3s. 6d.*

EGYPTIAN TALES. Translated from the Papyri. Second Series, xviiith to xixth Dynasty. Illustrated. *Cr. 8vo. 3s. 6d.*

EGYPTIAN DECORATIVE ART. Illustrated. *Cr. 8vo. 3s. 6d.*

Phelps (Ruth S.). SKIES ITALIAN: A LITTLE BREVIARY FOR TRAVELLERS IN ITALY. *Fcap. 8vo. 5s. net.*

Podmore (Frank). MODERN SPIRITUALISM. *Two Volumes. Demy 8vo. 21s. net.*

MESMERISM AND CHRISTIAN SCIENCE: A Short History of Mental Healing. *Second Edition. Demy 8vo. 10s. 6d. net.*

Pollard (Alfred W.). SHAKESPEARE FOLIOS AND QUARTOS. A Study in the Bibliography of Shakespeare's Plays, 1594-1685. Illustrated. *Folio. 21s. net.*

*Porter (G. R.) THE PROGRESS OF THE NATION. A New Edition. Edited by F. W. HIRST. *Demy 8vo. 21s. net.*

Powell (Arthur E.). FOOD AND HEALTH. *Cr. 8vo. 3s. 6d. net.*

Power (J. O'Connor). THE MAKING OF AN ORATOR. *Cr. 8vo. 6s.*

*Price (Eleanor C.). CARDINAL DE RICHELIEU. Illustrated. *Second Edition. Demy 8vo. 10s. 6d. net.*

Price (L. L.). A SHORT HISTORY OF POLITICAL ECONOMY IN ENGLAND FROM ADAM SMITH TO ARNOLD TOYNBEE. *Seventh Edition. Cr. 8vo. 2s. 6d.*

Pycraft (W. P.). A HISTORY OF BIRDS. Illustrated. *Demy 8vo. 10s. 6d. net.*

*Rappoport (Angelo S.). HOME LIFE IN RUSSIA. Illustrated. *Demy 8vo. 10s. 6d. net.*

Rawlings (Gertrude B.). COINS AND HOW TO KNOW THEM. Illustrated. *Third Edition. Cr. 8vo. 6s.*

Read (C. Stanford), FADS AND FEEDING. *Cr. 8vo. 2s. 6d. net.*

Regan (C. Tate). THE FRESHWATER FISHES OF THE BRITISH ISLES. Illustrated. *Cr. 8vo. 6s.*

Reid (Archdall), THE LAWS OF HEREDITY. *Second Edition. Demy 8vo. 21s. net.*

Robertson (C. Grant). SELECT STATUTES, CASES, AND DOCUMENTS, 1660-1894. *Demy 8vo. 10s. 6d. net.*

ENGLAND UNDER THE HANOVERIANS. Illustrated. *Second Edition. Demy 8vo. 10s. 6d. net.*

Roe (Fred). OLD OAK FURNITURE. Illustrated. *Second Edition. Demy 8vo. 10s. 6d. net.*

Royde-Smith (N. G.). THE PILLOW BOOK: A GARNER OF MANY MOODS. Collected. *Second Edition. Cr. 8vo. 4s. 6d. net.*

POETS OF OUR DAY. Selected, with an Introduction. *Fcap. 8vo. 5s.*

Russell (W. Clark). THE LIFE OF ADMIRAL LORD COLLINGWOOD. Illustrated. *Fourth Edition. Cr. 8vo. 6s.*

*Ryan (P. F. W.). STUART LIFE AND MANNERS: A Social History. Illustrated. *Demy 8vo. 10s. 6d. net.*

St. Francis of Assisi. THE LITTLE FLOWERS OF THE GLORIOUS MESSER, AND OF HIS FRIARS. Done into English, with Notes by WILLIAM HEYWOOD. Illustrated. *Demy 8vo. 5s. net.*

'Saki' (H. H. Munro). REGINALD. *Third Edition. Fcap. 8vo. 2s. 6d. net.*

REGINALD IN RUSSIA. *Fcap. 8vo. 2s. 6d. net.*

Sandeman (G. A. C.). METTERNICH. Illustrated. *Demy 8vo. 10s. 6d. net.*

Selous (Edmund). TOMMY SMITH'S ANIMALS. Illustrated. *Eleventh Edition. Fcap. 8vo. 2s. 6d.*

TOMMY SMITH'S OTHER ANIMALS. Illustrated. *Fifth Edition. Fcap. 8vo. 2s. 6d.*

JACK'S INSECTS. Illustrated. *Cr. 8vo. 6s.*

Shakespeare (William).
THE FOUR FOLIOS, 1623; 1632; 1664; 1685. Each £4 4s. net, or a complete set, £12 12s. net.

THE POEMS OF WILLIAM SHAKESPEARE. With an Introduction and Notes by GEORGE WYNDHAM. *Demy 8vo. Buckram. 10s. 6d.*

Sharp (A.). VICTORIAN POETS. *Cr. 8vo. 2s. 6d.*

Sidgwick (Mrs. Alfred). HOME LIFE IN GERMANY. Illustrated. *Second Edition. Demy 8vo. 10s. 6d. net.*

Sladen (Douglas). SICILY: The New Winter Resort. Illustrated. *Second Edition. Cr. 8vo. 5s. net.*

Smith (Adam). THE WEALTH OF NATIONS. Edited by EDWIN CANNAN. *Two Volumes. Demy 8vo. 21s. net.*

*Smith (G. Herbert). GEMS AND PRECIOUS STONES. Illustrated. *Cr. 8vo. 6s.*

Snell (F. J.). A BOOK OF EXMOOR. Illustrated. *Cr. 8vo. 6s.*

'Stancliffe.' GOLF DO'S AND DONT'S. *Fourth Edition. Fcap. 8vo. 1s. net.*

Stevenson (R. L.). THE LETTERS OF ROBERT LOUIS STEVENSON. Edited by Sir SIDNEY COLVIN. *A New and Enlarged Edition in 4 volumes. Third Edition. Fcap. 8vo. Leather, each 5s. net.*
VAILIMA LETTERS. With an Etched Portrait by WILLIAM STRANG. *Ninth Edition. Cr. 8vo. Buckram. 6s.*
THE LIFE OF R. L. STEVENSON. *See* BALFOUR (G.).

Stevenson (M. I.). FROM SARANAC TO THE MARQUESAS AND BEYOND. Being Letters written by Mrs. M. I. STEVENSON during 1887-88. *Cr. 8vo. 6s. net.*
LETTERS FROM SAMOA, 1891-95. Edited and arranged by M. C. BALFOUR. Illustrated. *Second Edition. Cr. 8vo. 6s. net.*

Storr (Vernon F.). DEVELOPMENT AND DIVINE PURPOSE. *Cr. 8vo. 5s. net.*

Streatfeild (R. A.). MODERN MUSIC AND MUSICIANS. Illustrated. *Second Edition. Demy 8vo. 7s. 6d. net.*

Swanton (E. W.). FUNGI AND HOW TO KNOW THEM. Illustrated. *Cr. 8vo. 6s. net.*

Sykes (Ella C.). PERSIA AND ITS PEOPLE. Illustrated. *Demy 8vo. 10s. 6d. net.*

Symes (J. E.). THE FRENCH REVOLUTION. *Second Edition. Cr. 8vo. 2s. 6d.*

Tabor (Margaret E.). THE SAINTS IN ART. Illustrated. *Fcap. 8vo. 3s. 6d. net.*

Taylor (A. E.). THE ELEMENTS OF METAPHYSICS. *Second Edition. Demy 8vo. 10s. 6d. net.*

Thibaudeau (A. C.). BONAPARTE AND THE CONSULATE. Translated and Edited by G. K. FORTESCUE. Illustrated. *Demy 8vo. 10s. 6d. net.*

Thomas (Edward). MAURICE MAETERLINCK. Illustrated. *Second Edition. Cr. 8vo. 5s. net.*

Thompson (Francis). SELECTED POEMS OF FRANCIS THOMPSON. With a Biographical Note by WILFRID MEYNELL. With a Portrait in Photogravure. *Seventh Edition. Fcap. 8vo. 5s. net.*

Tileston (Mary W.). DAILY STRENGTH FOR DAILY NEEDS. *Eighteenth Edition. Medium 16mo. 2s. 6d. net. Lambskin 3s. 6d. net.* Also an edition in superior binding, 6s.
THE STRONGHOLD OF HOPE. *Medium 16mo. 2s. 6d. net.*

Toynbee (Paget). DANTE ALIGHIERI; HIS LIFE AND WORKS. With 16 Illustrations. *Fourth and Enlarged Edition. Cr. 8vo. 5s. net.*

Trench (Herbert.) DEIRDRE WEDDED, AND OTHER POEMS. *Second and Revised Edition. Large Post 8vo. 6s.*
NEW POEMS. *Second Edition. Large Post 8vo. 6s.*
APOLLO AND THE SEAMAN. *Large Post 8vo. Paper, 1s. 6d. net; cloth, 2s. 6d. net.*

Trevelyan (G. M.). ENGLAND UNDER THE STUARTS. With Maps and Plans. *Fifth Edition. Demy 8vo. 10s. 6d. net.*

Triggs (Inigo H.). TOWN PLANNING: PAST, PRESENT, AND POSSIBLE. Illustrated. *Second Edition. Wide Royal 8vo. 15s. net.*

Underhill (Evelyn). MYSTICISM. A Study in the Nature and Development of Man's Spiritual Consciousness. *Third Edition. Demy 8vo. 15s. net.*

Vaughan (Herbert M.). THE NAPLES RIVIERA. Illustrated. *Second Edition. Cr. 8vo. 6s.*
FLORENCE AND HER TREASURES. Illustrated. *Fcap. 8vo. 5s. net.*

Vernon (Hon. W. Warren). READINGS ON THE INFERNO OF DANTE. With an Introduction by the REV. DR. MOORE. *Two Volumes. Second Edition. Cr. 8vo. 15s. net.*
READINGS ON THE PURGATORIO OF DANTE. With an Introduction by the late DEAN CHURCH. *Two Volumes. Third Edition. Cr. 8vo. 15s. net.*
READINGS ON THE PARADISO OF DANTE. With an Introduction by the BISHOP OF RIPON. *Two Volumes. Second Edition. Cr. 8vo. 15s. net.*

Waddell (Col. L. A.). LHASA AND ITS MYSTERIES. With a Record of the Expedition of 1903-1904. Illustrated. *Third and Cheaper Edition. Medium 8vo. 7s. 6d. net.*

Wagner (Richard). RICHARD WAGNER'S MUSIC DRAMAS: Interpretations, embodying Wagner's own explanations. By ALICE LEIGHTON CLEATHER and BASIL CRUMP. *Fcap. 8vo. 2s. 6d. each.*
THE RING OF THE NIBELUNG. *Fifth Edition.*
TRISTAN AND ISOLDE.

Waterhouse (Elizabeth). WITH THE SIMPLE-HEARTED: Little Homilies to Women in Country Places. *Third Edition. Small Pott 8vo. 2s. net.*
THE HOUSE BY THE CHERRY TREE. A Second Series of Little Homilies to Women in Country Places. *Small Pott 8vo. 2s. net.*
COMPANIONS OF THE WAY. Being Selections for Morning and Evening Reading. Chosen and arranged by ELIZABETH WATERHOUSE. *Large Cr. 8vo. 5s. net.*
THOUGHTS OF A TERTIARY. *Small Pott 8vo. 1s. net.*

Waters (W. G.). ITALIAN SCULPTORS AND SMITHS. Illustrated. *Cr. 8vo.* 7*s.* 6*d. net.*

*Watt (Francis).** EDINBURGH AND THE LOTHIANS. Illustrated. *Second Edition. Cr. 8vo.* 7*s.* 6*d. net.*

Weigall (Arthur E. P.). A GUIDE TO THE ANTIQUITIES OF UPPER EGYPT: From Abydos to the Sudan Frontier. Illustrated. *Cr. 8vo.* 7*s.* 6*d. net.*

Welch (Catharine). THE LITTLE DAUPHIN. Illustrated. *Cr. 8vo.* 6*s.*

Wells (J.). OXFORD AND OXFORD LIFE. *Third Edition. Cr. 8vo.* 3*s.* 6*d.*
A SHORT HISTORY OF ROME. *Eleventh Edition.* With 3 Maps. *Cr. 8vo.* 3*s.* 6*d.*

Westell (W. Percival). THE YOUNG NATURALIST. Illustrated. *Cr. 8vo.* 6*s.*
THE YOUNG ORNITHOLOGIST. Illustrated. *Cr. 8vo.* 5*s.*

Westell (W. Percival)-and Cooper (C. S.). THE YOUNG BOTANIST. Illustrated. *Cr. 8vo.* 3*s.* 6*d. net.*

White (George F.). A CENTURY OF SPAIN AND PORTUGAL, 1788-1898. *Demy 8vo.* 12*s.* 6*d. net.*

Wilde (Oscar). DE PROFUNDIS. *Twelfth Edition. Cr. 8vo.* 5*s. net.*
THE WORKS OF OSCAR WILDE. *In Twelve Volumes. Fcap. 8vo.* 5*s. net each volume.*
I. LORD ARTHUR SAVILE'S CRIME AND THE PORTRAIT OF MR. W. H. II. THE DUCHESS OF PADUA. III. POEMS. IV. LADY WINDERMERE'S FAN. V. A WOMAN OF NO IMPORTANCE. VI. AN IDEAL HUSBAND. VII. THE IMPORTANCE OF BEING EARNEST. VIII. A HOUSE OF POMEGRANATES. IX. INTENTIONS. X. DE PROFUNDIS AND PRISON LETTERS. XI. ESSAYS. XII. SALOMÉ, A FLORENTINE TRAGEDY, and LA SAINTE COURTISANE.

Williams (H. Noel). THE WOMEN BONAPARTES. The Mother and three Sisters of Napoleon. Illustrated. *In Two Volumes. Demy 8vo.* 24*s. net.*

A ROSE OF SAVOY: MARIE ADÉLAÏDE OF SAVOY, DUCHESSE DE BOURGOGNE, MOTHER OF LOUIS XV. Illustrated. *Second Edition. Demy 8vo.* 15*s. net.*

THE FASCINATING DUC DE RICHELIEU: LOUIS FRANÇOIS ARMAND DU PLESSIS (1696-1788). Illustrated. *Demy 8vo.* 15*s. net.*

A PRINCESS OF ADVENTURE: MARIE CAROLINE, DUCHESSE DE BERRY (1798-1870). Illustrated. *Demy 8vo.* 15*s. net.*

Wood (Sir Evelyn). FROM MIDSHIPMAN TO FIELD-MARSHAL. Illustrated. *Fifth and Cheaper Edition. Demy 8vo.* 7*s.* 6*d. net.*

THE REVOLT IN HINDUSTAN. 1857-59. Illustrated. *Second Edition. Cr. 8vo.* 6*s.*

Wood (W. Birkbeck), and Edmonds (Lieut.-Col. J. E.). A HISTORY OF THE CIVIL WAR IN THE UNITED STATES (1861-5). With an Introduction by H. SPENSER WILKINSON. With 24 Maps and Plans. *Third Edition. Demy 8vo.* 12*s.* 6*d. net.*

Wordsworth (W.). THE POEMS. With an Introduction and Notes by NOWELL C. SMITH. *In Three Volumes. Demy 8vo.* 15*s. net.*

Wyllie (M. A.). NORWAY AND ITS FJORDS. Illustrated. *Second Edition. Cr. 8vo.* 6*s.*

Yeats (W. B.). A BOOK OF IRISH VERSE. *Third Edition. Cr. 8vo.* 3*s.* 6*d.*

PART II.—A SELECTION OF SERIES.

Ancient Cities.

General Editor, B. C. A. WINDLE.

Cr. 8vo. 4*s.* 6*d. net each volume.*

With Illustrations by E. H. NEW, and other Artists.

BRISTOL. Alfred Harvey.
CANTERBURY. J. C. Cox.
CHESTER. B. C. A. Windle.
DUBLIN. S. A. O. Fitzpatrick.

EDINBURGH. M. G. Williamson.
LINCOLN. E. Mansel Sympson.
SHREWSBURY. T. Auden.
WELLS and GLASTONBURY. T. S. Holmes.

The Antiquary's Books.

General Editor, J. CHARLES COX.

Demy 8vo. 7s. 6d. net each volume.

With Numerous Illustrations.

ARCHÆOLOGY AND FALSE ANTIQUITIES. R. Munro.

BELLS OF ENGLAND, THE. Canon J. J. Raven. *Second Edition.*

BRASSES OF ENGLAND, THE. Herbert W. Macklin. *Second Edition.*

CELTIC ART IN PAGAN AND CHRISTIAN TIMES. J. Romilly Allen. *Second Edition.*

CASTLES AND WALLED TOWNS OF ENGLAND. A. Harvey.

DOMESDAY INQUEST, THE. Adolphus Ballard.

ENGLISH CHURCH FURNITURE. J. C. Cox and A. Harvey. *Second Edition.*

ENGLISH COSTUME. From Prehistoric Times to the End of the Eighteenth Century. George Clinch.

ENGLISH MONASTIC LIFE. The Right Rev. Abbot Gasquet. *Fourth Edition.*

ENGLISH SEALS. J. Harvey Bloom.

FOLK-LORE AS AN HISTORICAL SCIENCE. Sir G. L. Gomme.

GILDS AND COMPANIES OF LONDON, THE. George Unwin.

MANOR AND MANORIAL RECORDS, THE. Nathaniel J. Hone.

MEDIÆVAL HOSPITALS OF ENGLAND, THE. Rotha Mary Clay.

OLD ENGLISH INSTRUMENTS OF MUSIC. F. W. Galpin. *Second Edition.*

OLD ENGLISH LIBRARIES. James Hutt.

OLD SERVICE BOOKS OF THE ENGLISH CHURCH. Christopher Wordsworth, and Henry Littlehales. *Second Edition.*

PARISH LIFE IN MEDIÆVAL ENGLAND. The Right Rev. Abbot Gasquet. *Third Edition.*

PARISH REGISTERS OF ENGLAND, THE. J. C. Cox.

REMAINS OF THE PREHISTORIC AGE IN ENGLAND. B. C. A. Windle. *Second Edition.*

ROMAN ERA IN BRITAIN, THE. J. Ward.

ROMAN-BRITISH BUILDINGS AND EARTH-WORKS. J. Ward.

ROYAL FORESTS OF ENGLAND, THE. J. C. Cox.

SHRINES OF BRITISH SAINTS. J. C. Wall.

The Arden Shakespeare.

Demy 8vo. 2s. 6d. net each volume.

An edition of Shakespeare in single Plays; each edited with a full Introduction, Textual Notes, and a Commentary at the foot of the page.

ALL'S WELL THAT ENDS WELL.
ANTONY AND CLEOPATRA.
CYMBELINE.
COMEDY OF ERRORS, THE.
HAMLET. *Third Edition.*
JULIUS CAESAR.
KING HENRY IV. PT. I.
KING HENRY V.
KING HENRY VI. PT. I.
KING HENRY VI. PT. II.
KING HENRY VI. PT. III.
KING LEAR.
KING RICHARD III.
LIFE AND DEATH OF KING JOHN, THE.
LOVE'S LABOUR'S LOST.
MACBETH.

MEASURE FOR MEASURE.
MERCHANT OF VENICE, THE.
MERRY WIVES OF WINDSOR, THE.
MIDSUMMER NIGHT'S DREAM, A.
OTHELLO.
PERICLES.
ROMEO AND JULIET.
TAMING OF THE SHREW, THE.
TEMPEST, THE.
TIMON OF ATHENS.
TITUS ANDRONICUS.
TROILUS AND CRESSIDA.
TWO GENTLEMEN OF VERONA, THE.
TWELFTH NIGHT.
VENUS AND ADONIS.

Classics of Art.

Edited by Dr. J. H. W. LAING.

With numerous Illustrations. Wide Royal 8vo.

THE ART OF THE GREEKS. H. B. Walters. 12s. 6d. net.

THE ART OF THE ROMANS. H. B. Walters. 15s. net.

CHARDIN. H. E. A. Furst. 12s. 6d. net.

DONATELLO. Maud Cruttwell. 15s. net.

FLORENTINE SCULPTORS OF THE RENAISSANCE. Wilhelm Bode. Translated by Jessie Haynes. 12s. 6d. net.

GEORGE ROMNEY. Arthur B. Chamberlain. 12s. 6d. net.

GHIRLANDAIO. Gerald S. Davies. *Second Edition.* 10s. 6d.

MICHELANGELO. Gerald S. Davies. 12s. 6d. net.

RUBENS. Edward Dillon. 25s. net.

RAPHAEL. A. P. Oppé. 12s. 6d. net.

REMBRANDT'S ETCHINGS. A. M. Hind.

TITIAN. Charles Ricketts. 12s. 6d. net.

TINTORETTO. Evelyn March Phillipps. 15s. net.

TURNER'S SKETCHES AND DRAWINGS. A. J. FINBERG. 12s. 6d. net. *Second Edition.*

VELAZQUEZ. A. de Beruete. 10s. 6d. net.

The Complete Series.

Fully Illustrated. Demy 8vo.

THE COMPLETE BILLIARD PLAYER. Charles Roberts. 10s. 6d. net.

THE COMPLETE COOK. Lilian Whitling. 7s. 6d. net.

THE COMPLETE CRICKETER. Albert E. Knight. 7s. 6d. net. *Second Edition.*

THE COMPLETE FOXHUNTER. Charles Richardson. 12s. 6d. net. *Second Edition.*

THE COMPLETE GOLFER. Harry Vardon. 10s. 6d. net. *Twelfth Edition.*

THE COMPLETE HOCKEY-PLAYER. Eustace E. White. 5s. net. *Second Edition.*

THE COMPLETE LAWN TENNIS PLAYER. A. Wallis Myers. 10s. 6d. net. *Third Edition, Revised.*

THE COMPLETE MOTORIST. Filson Young. 12s. 6d. net. *New Edition (Seventh).*

THE COMPLETE MOUNTAINEER. G. D. Abraham. 15s. net. *Second Edition.*

THE COMPLETE OARSMAN. R. C. Lehmann. 10s. 6d. net.

THE COMPLETE PHOTOGRAPHER. R. Child Bayley. 10s. 6d. net. *Fourth Edition.*

THE COMPLETE RUGBY FOOTBALLER, ON THE NEW ZEALAND SYSTEM. D. Gallaher and W. J. Stead. 10s. 6d. net. *Second Edition.*

THE COMPLETE SHOT. G. T. Teasdale Buckell. 12s. 6d. net. *Third Edition.*

The Connoisseur's Library.

With numerous Illustrations. Wide Royal 8vo. 25s. net each volume.

ENGLISH FURNITURE. F. S. Robinson.

ENGLISH COLOURED BOOKS. Martin Hardie.

ETCHINGS. Sir F. Wedmore.

EUROPEAN ENAMELS. Henry H. Cunynghame.

GLASS. Edward Dillon.

GOLDSMITHS' AND SILVERSMITHS' WORK. Nelson Dawson. *Second Edition.*

ILLUMINATED MANUSCRIPTS. J. A. Herbert. *Second Edition.*

IVORIES. Alfred Maskell.

JEWELLERY. H. Clifford Smith. *Second Edition.*

MEZZOTINTS. Cyril Davenport.

MINIATURES. Dudley Heath.

PORCELAIN. Edward Dillon.

SEALS. Walter de Gray Birch.

WOOD SCULPTURE. Alfred Maskell. *Second Edition.*

Handbooks of English Church History.

Edited by J. H. BURN. *Crown 8vo.* 2s. 6d. *net each volume.*

THE FOUNDATIONS OF THE ENGLISH CHURCH. J. H. Maude.

THE SAXON CHURCH AND THE NORMAN CONQUEST. C. T. Cruttwell.

THE MEDIÆVAL CHURCH AND THE PAPACY. A. C. Jennings.

THE REFORMATION PERIOD. Henry Gee.

THE STRUGGLE WITH PURITANISM. Bruce Blaxland.

THE CHURCH OF ENGLAND IN THE EIGHTEENTH CENTURY. Alfred Plummer.

Handbooks of Theology.

THE DOCTRINE OF THE INCARNATION. R. L. Ottley. *Fifth Edition, Revised. Demy 8vo.* 12s. 6d.

A HISTORY OF EARLY CHRISTIAN DOCTRINE. J. F. Bethune-Baker. *Demy 8vo.* 10s. 6d.

AN INTRODUCTION TO THE HISTORY OF RELIGION. F. B. Jevons. *Fifth Edition. Demy 8vo.* 10s. 6d.

AN INTRODUCTION TO THE HISTORY OF THE CREEDS. A. E. Burn. *Demy 8vo.* 10s. 6d.

THE PHILOSOPHY OF RELIGION IN ENGLAND AND AMERICA. Alfred Caldecott. *Demy 8vo.* 10s. 6d.

THE XXXIX. ARTICLES OF THE CHURCH OF ENGLAND. Edited by E. C. S. Gibson, *Seventh Edition. Demy 8vo.* 12s. 6d.

The Illustrated Pocket Library of Plain and Coloured Books.

Fcap. 8vo. 3s. 6d. *net each volume.*

WITH COLOURED ILLUSTRATIONS.

OLD COLOURED BOOKS. George Paston. 2s. net.

THE LIFE AND DEATH OF JOHN MYTTON, ESQ. Nimrod. *Fifth Edition.*

THE LIFE OF A SPORTSMAN. Nimrod.

HANDLEY CROSS. R. S. Surtees. *Fourth Edition.*

MR. SPONGE'S SPORTING TOUR. R. S. Surtees. *Second Edition.*

JORROCKS'S JAUNTS AND JOLLITIES. R. S. Surtees. *Third Edition.*

ASK MAMMA. R. S. Surtees.

THE ANALYSIS OF THE HUNTING FIELD. R. S. Surtees.

THE TOUR OF DR. SYNTAX IN SEARCH OF THE PICTURESQUE. William Combe.

THE TOUR OF DR. SYNTAX IN SEARCH OF CONSOLATION. William Combe.

THE THIRD TOUR OF DR. SYNTAX IN SEARCH OF A WIFE. William Combe.

THE HISTORY OF JOHNNY QUAE GENUS. the Author of 'The Three Tours.'

THE ENGLISH DANCE OF DEATH, from the Designs of T. Rowlandson, with Metrical Illustrations by the Author of 'Doctor Syntax.' *Two Volumes.*

THE DANCE OF LIFE: A Poem. The Author of 'Dr. Syntax.'

LIFE IN LONDON. Pierce Egan.

REAL LIFE IN LONDON. An Amateur (Pierce Egan). *Two Volumes.*

THE LIFE OF AN ACTOR. Pierce Egan.

THE VICAR OF WAKEFIELD. Oliver Goldsmith.

THE MILITARY ADVENTURES OF JOHNNY NEWCOMBE. An Officer.

THE NATIONAL SPORTS OF GREAT BRITAIN. With Descriptions and 50 Coloured Plates by Henry Alken.

THE ADVENTURES OF A POST CAPTAIN. A Naval Officer.

GAMONIA. Lawrence Rawstorne.

AN ACADEMY FOR GROWN HORSEMEN. Geoffrey Gambado.

REAL LIFE IN IRELAND. A Real Paddy.

THE ADVENTURES OF JOHNNY NEWCOMBE IN THE NAVY. Alfred Burton.

THE OLD ENGLISH SQUIRE. John Careless.

THE ENGLISH SPY. Bernard Blackmantle. *Two Volumes.* 7s. net.

WITH PLAIN ILLUSTRATIONS.

THE GRAVE: A Poem. Robert Blair.

ILLUSTRATIONS OF THE BOOK OF JOB. Invented and engraved by William Blake.

WINDSOR CASTLE. W. Harrison Ainsworth.

THE TOWER OF LONDON. W. Harrison Ainsworth.

FRANK FAIRLEGH. F. E. Smedley.

HANDY ANDY. Samuel Lover.

THE COMPLEAT ANGLER. Izaak Walton and Charles Cotton.

THE PICKWICK PAPERS. Charles Dickens.

Leaders of Religion.

Edited by H. C. BEECHING. *With Portraits.*

Crown 8vo. 2s. net each volume.

CARDINAL NEWMAN. R. H. Hutton.

JOHN WESLEY. J. H. Overton.

BISHOP WILBERFORCE. G. W. Daniell.

CARDINAL MANNING. A. W. Hutton.

CHARLES SIMEON. H. C. G. Moule.

JOHN KNOX. F. MacCunn. *Second Edition.*

JOHN HOWE. R. F. Horton.

THOMAS KEN. F. A. Clarke.

GEORGE FOX, THE QUAKER. T. Hodgkin. *Third Edition.*

JOHN KEBLE. Walter Lock.

THOMAS CHALMERS. Mrs. Oliphant. *Second Edition.*

LANCELOT ANDREWES. R. L. Ottley. *Second Edition.*

AUGUSTINE OF CANTERBURY. E. L. Cutts.

WILLIAM LAUD. W. H. Hutton. *Third Ed.*

JOHN DONNE. Augustus Jessop.

THOMAS CRANMER. A. J. Mason.

BISHOP LATIMER. R. M. Carlyle and A. J. Carlyle.

BISHOP BUTLER. W. A. Spooner.

The Library of Devotion.

With Introductions and (where necessary) Notes.

Small Pott 8vo, cloth, 2s. ; leather, 2s. 6d. net each volume.

THE CONFESSIONS OF ST. AUGUSTINE. *Seventh Edition.*

THE IMITATION OF CHRIST. *Sixth Edition.*

THE CHRISTIAN YEAR. *Fifth Edition.*

LYRA INNOCENTIUM. *Second Edition.*

THE TEMPLE. *Second Edition.*

A BOOK OF DEVOTIONS. *Second Edition.*

A SERIOUS CALL TO A DEVOUT AND HOLY LIFE. *Fourth Edition.*

A GUIDE TO ETERNITY.

THE INNER WAY. *Second Edition.*

ON THE LOVE OF GOD.

THE PSALMS OF DAVID.

LYRA APOSTOLICA.

THE SONG OF SONGS.

THE THOUGHTS OF PASCAL. *Second Edition.*

A MANUAL OF CONSOLATION FROM THE SAINTS AND FATHERS.

DEVOTIONS FROM THE APOCRYPHA.

THE SPIRITUAL COMBAT.

THE DEVOTIONS OF ST. ANSELM.

BISHOP WILSON'S SACRA PRIVATA.

GRACE ABOUNDING TO THE CHIEF OF SINNERS.

LYRA SACRA : A Book of Sacred Verse. *Second Edition.*

A DAY BOOK FROM THE SAINTS AND FATHERS.

A LITTLE BOOK OF HEAVENLY WISDOM. A Selection from the English Mystics.

LIGHT, LIFE, and LOVE. A Selection from the German Mystics.

AN INTRODUCTION TO THE DEVOUT LIFE.

THE LITTLE FLOWERS OF THE GLORIOUS MESSER ST. FRANCIS AND OF HIS FRIARS.

DEATH AND IMMORTALITY.

THE SPIRITUAL GUIDE. *Second Edition.*

DEVOTIONS FOR EVERY DAY IN THE WEEK AND THE GREAT FESTIVALS.

PRECES PRIVATÆ.

HORÆ MYSTICÆ : A Day Book from the Writings of Mystics of Many Nations.

Little Books on Art.

With many Illustrations. Demy 16mo. 2s. 6d. net each volume.

Each volume consists of about 200 pages, and contains from 30 to 40 Illustrations, including a Frontispiece in Photogravure.

ALBRECHT DÜRER. J. Allen.
ARTS OF JAPAN, THE. E. Dillon. *Third Edition.*
BOOKPLATES. E. Almack.
BOTTICELLI. Mary L. Bonnor.
BURNE-JONES. F. de Lisle.
CHRISTIAN SYMBOLISM. Mrs. H. Jenner.
CHRIST IN ART. Mrs. H. Jenner.
CLAUDE. E. Dillon.
CONSTABLE. H. W. Tompkins. *Second Edition.*
COROT. A. Pollard and E. Birnstingl.
ENAMELS. Mrs. N. Dawson. *Second Edition.*
FREDERIC LEIGHTON. A. Corkran.
GEORGE ROMNEY. G. Paston.
GREEK ART. H. B. Walters. *Fourth Edition.*
GREUZE AND BOUCHER. E. F. Pollard.

HOLBEIN. Mrs. G. Fortescue.
ILLUMINATED MANUSCRIPTS. J. W. Bradley.
JEWELLERY. C. Davenport.
JOHN HOPPNER. H. P. K. Skipton.
SIR JOSHUA REYNOLDS. J. Sime. *Second Edition.*
MILLET. N. Peacock.
MINIATURES. C. Davenport.
OUR LADY IN ART. Mrs. H. Jenner.
RAPHAEL. A. R. Dryhurst.
REMBRANDT. Mrs. E. A. Sharp.
TURNER. F. Tyrrell-Gill.
VANDYCK. M. G. Smallwood.
VELASQUEZ. W. Wilberforce and A. R. Gilbert.
WATTS. R. E. D. Sketchley.

The Little Galleries.

Demy 16mo. 2s. 6d. net each volume.

Each volume contains 20 plates in Photogravure, together with a short outline of the life and work of the master to whom the book is devoted.

A LITTLE GALLERY OF REYNOLDS.
A LITTLE GALLERY OF ROMNEY.
A LITTLE GALLERY OF HOPPNER.

A LITTLE GALLERY OF MILLAIS.
A LITTLE GALLERY OF ENGLISH POETS.

The Little Guides.

With many Illustrations by E. H. NEW and other artists, and from photographs.

Small Pott 8vo, cloth, 2s. 6d. net; leather, 3s. 6d. net, each volume.

The main features of these Guides are (1) a handy and charming form ; (2) illustrations from photographs and by well-known artists ; (3) good plans and maps ; (4) an adequate but compact presentation of everything that is interesting in the natural features, history, archaeology, and architecture of the town or district treated.

CAMBRIDGE AND ITS COLLEGES. A. H. Thompson. *Third Edition, Revised.*
CHANNEL ISLANDS, THE. E. E. Bicknell.
ENGLISH LAKES, THE. F. G. Brabant.
ISLE OF WIGHT, THE. G. Clinch.
MALVERN COUNTRY, THE. B. C. A. Windle.
NORTH WALES. A. T. Story.
OXFORD AND ITS COLLEGES. J. Wells. *Ninth Edition.*

SHAKESPEARE'S COUNTRY. B. C. A. Windle. *Fourth Edition.*
ST. PAUL'S CATHEDRAL. G. Clinch.
WESTMINSTER ABBEY. G. E. Troutbeck. *Second Edition.*

BERKSHIRE. F. G. Brabant.
BUCKINGHAMSHIRE. E. S. Roscoe.
CHESHIRE. W. M. Gallichan.

THE LITTLE GUIDES—*continued.*

CORNWALL. A. L. Salmon.
DERBYSHIRE. J. C. Cox.
DEVON. S. Baring-Gould. *Second Edition.*
DORSET. F. R. Heath. *Second Edition.*
ESSEX. J. C. Cox.
HAMPSHIRE. J. C. Cox.
HERTFORDSHIRE. H. W. Tompkins.
KENT. G. Clinch.
KERRY. C. P. Crane.
MIDDLESEX. J. B. Firth.
MONMOUTHSHIRE. G. W. Wade and J. H. Wade.
NORFOLK. W. A. Dutt. *Second Edition, Revised.*
NORTHAMPTONSHIRE. W. Dry. *Second Ed.*
NORTHUMBERLAND. J. E. Morris.
NOTTINGHAMSHIRE. L. Guilford.
OXFORDSHIRE. F. G. Brabant.

SOMERSET. G. W. and J. H. Wade.
STAFFORDSHIRE. C. E. Masefield.
SUFFOLK. W. A. Dutt.
SURREY. J. C. Cox.
SUSSEX. F. G. Brabant. *Third Edition.*
WILTSHIRE. F. R. Heath.
YORKSHIRE, THE EAST RIDING. J. E. Morris.
YORKSHIRE, THE NORTH RIDING. J. E. Morris.
YORKSHIRE, THE WEST RIDING. J. E. Morris. *Cloth, 3s. 6d. net; leather, 4s. 6d. net.*

BRITTANY. S. Baring-Gould.
NORMANDY. C. Scudamore.
ROME. C. G. Ellaby.
SICILY. F. H. Jackson.

The Little Library.

With Introductions, Notes, and Photogravure Frontispieces.

Small Pott 8vo.   Each Volume, cloth, 1s. 6d. net.

Anon. A LITTLE BOOK OF ENGLISH LYRICS. *Second Edition.*

Austen (Jane). PRIDE AND PREJUDICE. *Two Volumes.*
NORTHANGER ABBEY.

Bacon (Francis). THE ESSAYS OF LORD BACON.

Barham (R. H.). THE INGOLDSBY LEGENDS. *Two Volumes.*

Barnet (Annie). A LITTLE BOOK OF ENGLISH PROSE.

Beckford (William). THE HISTORY OF THE CALIPH VATHEK.

Blake (William). SELECTIONS FROM THE WORKS OF WILLIAM BLAKE.

Borrow (George). LAVENGRO. *Two Volumes.*
THE ROMANY RYE.

Browning (Robert). SELECTIONS FROM THE EARLY POEMS OF ROBERT BROWNING.

Canning (George). SELECTIONS FROM THE ANTI-JACOBIN: with GEORGE CANNING's additional Poems.

Cowley (Abraham). THE ESSAYS OF ABRAHAM COWLEY.

Crabbe (George). SELECTIONS FROM THE POEMS OF GEORGE CRABBE.

Craik (Mrs.). JOHN HALIFAX, GENTLEMAN. *Two Volumes.*

Crashaw (Richard). THE ENGLISH POEMS OF RICHARD CRASHAW.

Dante Alighieri. THE INFERNO OF DANTE. Translated by H. F. CARY.
THE PURGATORIO OF DANTE. Translated by H. F. CARY.
THE PARADISO OF DANTE. Translated by H. F. CARY.

Darley (George). SELECTIONS FROM THE POEMS OF GEORGE DARLEY.

Deane (A. C.). A LITTLE BOOK OF LIGHT VERSE.

Dickens (Charles). CHRISTMAS BOOKS. *Two Volumes.*

Ferrier (Susan). MARRIAGE. *Two Volumes.*
THE INHERITANCE. *Two Volumes.*

Gaskell (Mrs.). CRANFORD. *Second Ed.*

Hawthorne (Nathaniel). THE SCARLET LETTER.

Henderson (T. F.). A LITTLE BOOK OF SCOTTISH VERSE.

Keats (John). POEMS.

Kinglake (A. W.). EOTHEN. *Second Edition.*

THE LITTLE LIBRARY—*continued.*

Lamb (Charles). ELIA, AND THE LAST ESSAYS OF ELIA.

Locker (F.). LONDON LYRICS.

Longfellow (H. W.). SELECTIONS FROM THE POEMS OF H. W. LONGFELLOW.

Marvell (Andrew). THE POEMS OF ANDREW MARVELL.

Milton (John). THE MINOR POEMS OF JOHN MILTON.

Moir (D. M.). MANSIE WAUCH.

Nichols (J. B. B.). A LITTLE BOOK OF ENGLISH SONNETS.

Rochefoucauld (La). THE MAXIMS OF LA ROCHEFOUCAULD.

Smith (Horace and James). REJECTED ADDRESSES.

Sterne (Laurence). A SENTIMENTAL JOURNEY.

Tennyson (Alfred, Lord). THE EARLY POEMS OF ALFRED, LORD TENNYSON.
IN MEMORIAM.
THE PRINCESS.
MAUD.

Thackeray (W. M.). VANITY FAIR. *Three Volumes.*
PENDENNIS. *Three Volumes.*
ESMOND.
CHRISTMAS BOOKS.

Vaughan (Henry). THE POEMS OF HENRY VAUGHAN.

Walton (Izaak). THE COMPLEAT ANGLER.

Waterhouse (Elizabeth). A LITTLE BOOK OF LIFE AND DEATH. *Thirteenth Edition.*

Wordsworth (W.). SELECTIONS FROM THE POEMS OF WILLIAM WORDSWORTH.

Wordsworth (W.) and Coleridge (S. T.). LYRICAL BALLADS. *Second Edition.*

The Little Quarto Shakespeare.

Edited by W. J. CRAIG. With Introductions and Notes.

Pott 16mo. In 40 Volumes. Leather, price 1s. net each volume.
Mahogany Revolving Book Case. 10s. net.

Miniature Library.

EUPHRANOR : A Dialogue on Youth. Edward FitzGerald. *Demy 32mo. Leather, 2s. net.*

THE LIFE OF EDWARD, LORD HERBERT OF CHERBURY. Written by himself. *Demy 32mo. Leather, 2s. net.*

POLONIUS : or Wise Saws and Modern Instances. Edward FitzGerald. *Demy 32mo. Leather, 2s. net.*

THE RUBÁIYÁT OF OMAR KHAYYÁM. Edward FitzGerald. *Fourth Edition. Leather, 1s. net.*

The New Library of Medicine.

Edited by C. W. SALEEBY. *Demy 8vo.*

CARE OF THE BODY, THE. F. Cavanagh. *Second Edition. 7s. 6d. net.*

CHILDREN OF THE NATION, THE. The Right Hon. Sir John Gorst. *Second Edition. 7s. 6d. net.*

CONTROL OF A SCOURGE, THE : or, How Cancer is Curable. Chas. P. Childe. *7s. 6d. net.*

DISEASES OF OCCUPATION. Sir Thomas Oliver. *10s. 6d. net. Second Edition.*

DRINK PROBLEM, THE, in its Medico-Sociological Aspects. Edited by T. N. Kelynack. *7s. 6d. net.*

DRUGS AND THE DRUG HABIT. H. Sainsbury.

FUNCTIONAL NERVE DISEASES. A. T. Schofield. *7s. 6d. net.*

HYGIENE OF MIND, THE. T. S. Clouston. *Fifth Edition. 7s. 6d. net.*

INFANT MORTALITY. Sir George Newman. *7s. 6d. net.*

PREVENTION OF TUBERCULOSIS (CONSUMPTION), THE. Arthur Newsholme. *10s. 6d. net. Second Edition.*

AIR AND HEALTH. Ronald C. Macfie. *7s. 6d. net. Second Edition.*

The New Library of Music.

Edited by ERNEST NEWMAN. *Illustrated. Demy 8vo. 7s. 6d. net.*

BRAHMS. J. A. Fuller-Maitland. *Second Edition.*
GIROLAMO SAVONAROLA. E. L. S. Horsburgh.

HANDEL. R. A. Streatfeild. *Second Edition*
HUGO WOLF. Ernest Newman.

Oxford Biographies.

Illustrated. Fcap. 8vo. Each volume, cloth, 2s. 6d. net; leather, 3s. 6d. net.

DANTE ALIGHIERI. Paget Toynbee. *Third Edition.*
GIROLAMO SAVONAROLA. E. L. S. Horsburgh. *Fourth Edition.*
JOHN HOWARD. E. C. S. Gibson.
ALFRED TENNYSON. A. C. Benson. *Second Edition.*
SIR WALTER RALEIGH. I. A. Taylor.
ERASMUS. E. F. H. Capey.

THE YOUNG PRETENDER. C. S. Terry.
ROBERT BURNS. T. F. Henderson.
CHATHAM. A. S. M'Dowall.
FRANCIS OF ASSISI. Anna M. Stoddart.
CANNING. W. Alison Phillips.
BEACONSFIELD. Walter Sichel.
JOHANN WOLFGANG GOETHE. H. G. Atkins.
FRANÇOIS FÉNELON. Viscount St. Cyres.

Romantic History.

Edited by MARTIN HUME. *Illustrated. Demy 8vo.*

A series of attractive volumes in which the periods and personalities selected are such as afford romantic human interest, in addition to their historical importance.

THE FIRST GOVERNESS OF THE NETHERLANDS, MARGARET OF AUSTRIA. Eleanor E. Tremayne. 10s. 6d. net.
TWO ENGLISH QUEENS AND PHILIP. Martin

Hume. 15s. net.
THE NINE DAYS' QUEEN. Richard Davey. With a Preface by Martin Hume. *Second Edition.* 10s. 6d. net.

The States of Italy.

Edited by E. ARMSTRONG and R. LANGTON DOUGLAS.

Illustrated. Demy 8vo.

A HISTORY OF MILAN UNDER THE SFORZA. Cecilia M. Ady. 10s. 6d. net.
A HISTORY OF PERUGIA. W. Heywood. 12s. 6d. net.

A HISTORY OF VERONA. A. M. Allen. 12s. 6d. net.

The Westminster Commentaries.

General Editor, WALTER LOCK.

THE ACTS OF THE APOSTLES. Edited by R. D. Rackham. *Demy 8vo. Fifth Edition.* 10s. 6d.

THE FIRST EPISTLE OF PAUL THE APOSTLE TO THE CORINTHIANS. Edited by H. L. Goudge. *Third Edition. Demy 8vo.* 6s.

THE BOOK OF EXODUS. Edited by A. H. M'Neile. With a Map and 3 Plans. *Demy 8vo.* 10s. 6d.

THE BOOK OF EZEKIEL. Edited by H. A. Redpath. *Demy 8vo.* 10s. 6d.

THE BOOK OF GENESIS. Edited with Introduction and Notes by S. R. Driver. *Eighth Edition. Demy 8vo.* 10s. 6d.

THE BOOK OF THE PROPHET ISAIAH. Edited by G. W. Wade. *Demy 8vo.* 10s. 6d.

ADDITIONS AND CORRECTIONS IN THE SEVENTH EDITION OF THE BOOK OF GENESIS. S. R. Driver. *Demy 8vo.* 1s.

THE BOOK OF JOB. Edited by E. C. S. Gibson. *Second Edition. Demy 8vo.* 6s.

THE EPISTLE OF ST. JAMES. Edited with Introduction and Notes by R. J. Knowling. *Second Edition. Demy 8vo.* 6s.

Methuen's Shilling Library.

Fcap. 8vo.

DE PROFUNDIS. Oscar Wilde.

THE LORE OF THE HONEY-BEE. Tickner Edwardes.

LETTERS FROM A SELF-MADE MERCHANT TO HIS SON. George Horace Lorimer.

SELECTED POEMS. Oscar Wilde.

THE LIFE OF ROBERT LOUIS STEVENSON. Graham Balfour.

THE LIFE OF JOHN RUSKIN. W. G. Collingwood.

THE CONDITION OF ENGLAND. G. F. G. Masterman.

PART III.—A SELECTION OF WORKS OF FICTION

Albanesi (E. Maria). SUSANNAH AND ONE OTHER. *Fourth Edition. Cr. 8vo.* 6s.
LOVE AND LOUISA. *Second Edition. Cr. 8vo.* 6s.
THE BROWN EYES OF MARY. *Third Edition. Cr. 8vo.* 6s.
I KNOW A MAIDEN. *Third Edition. Cr. 8vo.* 6s.
THE INVINCIBLE AMELIA; OR, THE POLITE ADVENTURESS. *Third Edition. Cr. 8vo.* 3s. 6d.
THE GLAD HEART. *Fifth Edition. Cr. 8vo.* 6s.

Bagot (Richard). A ROMAN MYSTERY. *Third Edition. Cr. 8vo.* 6s.
THE PASSPORT. *Fourth Edition. Cr. 8vo.* 6s.
ANTHONY CUTHBERT. *Fourth Edition. Cr. 8vo.* 6s.
LOVE'S PROXY. *Cr. 8vo.* 6s.
DONNA DIANA. *Second Edition. Cr. 8vo.* 6s.
CASTING OF NETS. *Twelfth Edition. Cr. 8vo.* 6s.
THE HOUSE OF SERRAVALLE. *Third Edition. Cr. 8vo.* 6s.

Bailey (H. C.). STORM AND TREASURE. *Third Edition. Cr. 8vo.* 6s.
THE LONELY QUEEN. *Third Edition. Cr. 8vo.* 6s.

Baring-Gould (S.). IN THE ROAR OF THE SEA. *Eighth Edition. Cr. 8vo.* 6s.
MARGERY OF QUETHER. *Second Edition. Cr. 8vo.* 6s.
THE QUEEN OF LOVE. *Fifth Edition. Cr. 8vo.* 6s.
JACQUETTA. *Third Edition. Cr. 8vo.* 6s.
KITTY ALONE. *Fifth Edition. Cr. 8vo.* 6s.
NOÉMI. Illustrated. *Fourth Edition. Cr. 8vo.* 6s.
THE BROOM-SQUIRE. Illustrated. *Fifth Edition. Cr. 8vo.* 6s.
DARTMOOR IDYLLS. *Cr. 8vo.* 6s.
GUAVAS THE TINNER. Illustrated. *Second Edition. Cr. 8vo.* 6s.
BLADYS OF THE STEWPONEY. Illustrated. *Second Edition. Cr. 8vo.* 6s.
PABO THE PRIEST. *Cr. 8vo.* 6s.
WINEFRED. Illustrated. *Second Edition. Cr. 8vo.* 6s.
ROYAL GEORGIE. Illustrated. *Cr. 8vo.* 6s.

CHRIS OF ALL SORTS. *Cr. 8vo.* 6s.
IN DEWISLAND. *Second Edition. Cr. 8vo.* 6s.
THE FROBISHERS. *Cr. 8vo.* 6s.
MRS. CURGENVEN OF CURGENVEN. *Fifth Edition. Cr. 8vo.* 6s.

Barr (Robert). IN THE MIDST OF ALARMS. *Third Edition. Cr. 8vo.* 6s.
THE COUNTESS TEKLA. *Fifth Edition. Cr. 8vo.* 6s.
THE MUTABLE MANY. *Third Edition. Cr. 8vo.* 6s.

Begbie (Harold). THE CURIOUS AND DIVERTING ADVENTURES OF SIR JOHN SPARROW, BART. ; OR, THE PROGRESS OF AN OPEN MIND. *Second Edition. Cr. 8vo.* 6s.

Belloc (H.). EMMANUEL BURDEN, MERCHANT. Illustrated. *Second Edition. Cr. 8vo.* 6s.
A CHANGE IN THE CABINET. *Third Edition. Cr. 8vo.* 6s.

Bennett (Arnold). CLAYHANGER. *Tenth Edition. Cr. 8vo.* 6s.
THE CARD. *Sixth Edition. Cr. 8vo.* 6s.
HILDA LESSWAYS. *Seventh Edition. Cr. 8vo.* 6s.

Benson (E. F.). DODO: A DETAIL OF THE DAY. *Sixteenth Edition. Cr. 8vo.* 6s.

Birmingham (George A.). SPANISH GOLD. *Sixth Edition. Cr. 8vo.* 6s.
THE SEARCH PARTY. *Fifth Edition. Cr. 8vo.* 6s.
LALAGE'S LOVERS. *Third Edition. Cr. 8vo.* 6s.
*THE ADVENTURES OF DR. WHITTY. *Cr. 8vo.* 6s.

Bowen (Marjorie). I WILL MAINTAIN. *Seventh Edition. Cr. 8vo.* 6s.
DEFENDER OF THE FAITH. *Fourth Edition. Cr. 8vo.* 6s.

Castle (Agnes and Egerton). FLOWER O' THE ORANGE, and Other Tales. *Third Edition. Cr. 8vo.* 6s.

Clifford (Mrs. W. K.). THE GETTING WELL OF DOROTHY. Illustrated. *Second Edition. Cr. 8vo.* 3s. 6d.

Conrad (Joseph). THE SECRET AGENT: A Simple Tale. *Fourth Ed. Cr. 8vo.* 6s.
A SET OF SIX. *Fourth Edition. Cr. 8vo.* 6s.
UNDER WESTERN EYES. *Second Ed. Cr. 8vo.* 6s.

Corelli (Marie). A ROMANCE OF TWO WORLDS. *Thirty-first Ed. Cr. 8vo.* 6s.
VENDETTA. *Twenty-ninth Edition. Cr. 8vo.* 6s.
THELMA : A NORWEGIAN PRINCESS. *Forty-second Edition. Cr. 8vo.* 6s.
ARDATH : THE STORY OF A DEAD SELF. *Twentieth Edition. Cr. 8vo.* 6s.

THE SOUL OF LILITH. *Seventeenth Edition. Cr. 8vo.* 6s.
WORMWOOD : A DRAMA OF PARIS. *Eighteenth Edition. Cr. 8vo.* 6s.
BARABBAS: A DREAM OF THE WORLD'S TRAGEDY. *Forty-fifth Edition. Cr. 8vo.* 6s.
THE SORROWS OF SATAN. *Fifty-seventh Edition. Cr. 8vo.* 6s.
THE MASTER CHRISTIAN. *Thirteenth Edition. 179th Thousand. Cr. 8vo.* 6s.
TEMPORAL POWER : A STUDY IN SUPREMACY. *Second Edition. 150th Thousand. Cr. 8vo.* 6s.
GOD'S GOOD MAN : A SIMPLE LOVE STORY. *Fifteenth Edition. 154th Thousand. Cr. 8vo.* 6s.
HOLY ORDERS: THE TRAGEDY OF A QUIET LIFE. *Second Edition. 120th Thousand. Crown 8vo.* 6s.
THE MIGHTY ATOM. *Twenty-ninth Edition. Cr. 8vo.* 6s.
BOY: a Sketch. *Twelfth Edition. Cr. 8vo.* 6s.
CAMEOS. *Fourteenth Edition. Cr. 8vo.* 6s.
THE LIFE EVERLASTING. *Fifth Ed. Cr. 8vo.* 6s.

Crockett (S. R.). LOCHINVAR. Illustrated. *Third Edition. Cr. 8vo.* 6s.
THE STANDARD BEARER. *Second Edition. Cr. 8vo.* 6s.

Croker (B. M.). THE OLD CANTONMENT. *Second Edition. Cr. 8vo.* 6s.
JOHANNA. *Second Edition. Cr. 8vo.* 6s.
THE HAPPY VALLEY. *Fourth Edition. Cr. 8vo.* 6s.
A NINE DAYS' WONDER. *Fourth Edition. Cr. 8vo.* 6s.
PEGGY OF THE BARTONS. *Seventh Edition. Cr. 8vo.* 6s.
ANGEL. *Fifth Edition. Cr. 8vo.* 6s.
KATHERINE THE ARROGANT. *Sixth Edition. Cr. 8vo.* 6s.
BABES IN THE WOOD. *Fourth Edition. Cr. 8vo.* 6s.

Doyle (A. Conan). ROUND THE RED LAMP. *Twelfth Edition. Cr. 8vo.* 6s.

Duncan (Sara Jeannette) (Mrs. Everard Cotes). A VOYAGE OF CONSOLATION. Illustrated. *Third Edition. Cr. 8vo.* 6s.
COUSIN CINDERELLA. *Second Edition. Cr. 8vo.* 6s.
THE BURNT OFFERING. *Second Edition. Cr. 8vo.* 6s.

Fenn (G. Manville). SYD BELTON : THE BOY WHO WOULD NOT GO TO SEA. Illustrated. *Second Ed. Cr. 8vo.* 3s. 6d.

Findlater (J. H.). THE GREEN GRAVES OF BALGOWRIE. *Fifth Edition. Cr. 8vo.* 6s.
THE LADDER TO THE STARS. *Second Edition. Cr. 8vo.* 6s.

FICTION

Findlater (Mary). A NARROW WAY. *Third Edition. Cr. 8vo. 6s.*
OVER THE HILLS. *Second Edition. Cr. 8vo. 6s.*
THE ROSE OF JOY. *Third Edition. Cr. 8vo. 6s.*
A BLIND BIRD'S NEST. Illustrated. *Second Edition. Cr. 8vo. 6s.*

Fry (B. and C. B.). A MOTHER'S SON. *Fifth Edition. Cr. 8vo. 6s.*

Gibbon (Perceval). MARGARET HARDING. *Third Edition. Cr. 8vo. 6s.*

Gissing (George). THE CROWN OF LIFE. *Cr. 8vo. 6s.*

Harraden (Beatrice). IN VARYING MOODS. *Fourteenth Edition. Cr. 8vo. 6s.*
HILDA STRAFFORD and THE REMITTANCE MAN. *Twelfth Ed. Cr. 8vo. 6s.*
INTERPLAY. *Fifth Edition. Cr. 8vo. 6s.*

Hichens (Robert). THE PROPHET OF BERKELEY SQUARE. *Second Edition. Cr. 8vo. 6s.*
TONGUES OF CONSCIENCE. *Third Edition. Cr. 8vo. 6s.*
FELIX. *Eighth and Cheaper Edition. Cr. 8vo. 2s. net.*
THE WOMAN WITH THE FAN. *Eighth Edition. Cr. 8vo. 6s.*
DYEWAYS. *Cr. 8vo. 6s.*
THE GARDEN OF ALLAH. *Twenty-first Edition. Cr. 8vo. 6s.*
THE BLACK SPANIEL. *Cr. 8vo. 6s.*
THE CALL OF THE BLOOD. *Seventh Edition. Cr. 8vo. 6s.*
BARBARY SHEEP. *Second Edition. Cr. 8vo. 6s.*
THE DWELLER ON THE THRESHOLD. *Cr. 8vo. 6s.*

Hope (Anthony). THE GOD IN THE CAR. *Eleventh Edition. Cr. 8vo. 6s.*
A CHANGE OF AIR. *Sixth Edition. Cr. 8vo. 6s.*
A MAN OF MARK. *Seventh Ed. Cr. 8vo. 6s.*
THE CHRONICLES OF COUNT ANTONIO. *Sixth Edition. Cr. 8vo. 6s.*
PHROSO. Illustrated. *Eighth Edition. Cr. 8vo. 6s.*
SIMON DALE. Illustrated. *Eighth Edition. Cr. 8vo. 6s.*
THE KING'S MIRROR. *Fifth Edition. Cr. 8vo. 6s.*
QUISANTE. *Fourth Edition. Cr. 8vo. 6s.*
THE DOLLY DIALOGUES. *Cr. 8vo. 6s.*
A SERVANT OF THE PUBLIC. Illustrated. *Fourth Edition. Cr. 8vo. 6s.*
TALES OF TWO PEOPLE. *Third Edition. Cr. 8vo. 6s.*
THE GREAT MISS DRIVER. *Fourth Edition. Cr. 8vo. 6s.*
MRS. MAXON PROTESTS. *Third Edition. Cr. 8vo. 6s.*

Hutten (Baroness von). THE HALO. *Fifth Edition. Cr. 8vo. 6s.*

Hyne (C. J. Cutcliffe). MR. HORROCKS, PURSER. *Fifth Edition. Cr. 8vo. 6s.*

'Inner Shrine' (Author of the). THE WILD OLIVE. *Third Edition. Cr. 8vo. 6s.*

Jacobs (W. W.). MANY CARGOES. *Thirty-second Edition. Cr. 8vo. 3s. 6d.*
SEA URCHINS. *Sixteenth Edition. Cr. 8vo. 3s. 6d.*
A MASTER OF CRAFT. Illustrated. *Ninth Edition. Cr. 8vo. 3s. 6d.*
LIGHT FREIGHTS. Illustrated. *Eighth Edition. Cr. 8vo. 3s. 6d.*
THE SKIPPER'S WOOING. *Eleventh Edition. Cr. 8vo. 3s. 6d.*
AT SUNWICH PORT. Illustrated. *Tenth Edition. Cr. 8vo. 3s. 6d.*
DIALSTONE LANE. Illustrated. *Eighth Edition. Cr. 8vo. 3s. 6d.*
ODD CRAFT. Illustrated. *Fourth Edition. Cr. 8vo. 3s. 6d.*
THE LADY OF THE BARGE. Illustrated. *Ninth Edition. Cr. 8vo. 3s. 6d.*
SALTHAVEN. Illustrated. *Third Edition. Cr. 8vo. 3s. 6d.*
SAILORS' KNOTS. Illustrated. *Fifth Edition. Cr. 8vo. 3s. 6d.*
SHORT CRUISES. *Third Edition. Cr. 8vo. 3s. 6d.*

James (Henry). THE GOLDEN BOWL. *Third Edition. Cr. 8vo. 6s.*
THE FINER GRAIN. *Third Edition. Cr. 8vo. 6s.*

Le Queux (William). THE HUNCHBACK OF WESTMINSTER. *Third Edition. Cr. 8vo. 6s.*
THE CLOSED BOOK. *Third Edition. Cr. 8vo. 6s.*
THE VALLEY OF THE SHADOW. Illustrated. *Third Edition. Cr. 8vo. 6s.*
BEHIND THE THRONE. *Third Edition. Cr. 8vo. 6s.*

London (Jack). WHITE FANG. *Eighth Edition. Cr. 8vo. 6s.*

Lucas (E. V.). LISTENER'S LURE : AN OBLIQUE NARRATION. *Eighth Edition. Fcap. 8vo. 5s.*
OVER BEMERTON'S : AN EASY-GOING CHRONICLE. *Ninth Edition. Fcap 8vo. 5s.*
MR. INGLESIDE. *Eighth Edition. Cr. 8vo. 6s.*

Lyall (Edna). DERRICK VAUGHAN, NOVELIST. *44th Thousand. Cr. 8vo. 3s. 6d.*

Macnaughtan (S.). THE FORTUNE OF CHRISTINA M'NAB. *Fifth Edition. Cr. 8vo. 6s.*
PETER AND JANE. *Fourth Edition. Cr. 8vo. 6s.*

Malet (Lucas). COLONEL ENDERBY'S WIFE. *Fifth Edition. Cr. 8vo.* 6s.
A COUNSEL OF PERFECTION. *Second Edition. Cr. 8vo.* 6s.
THE WAGES OF SIN. *Sixteenth Edition. Cr. 8vo.* 6s.
THE CARISSIMA. *Fifth Ed. Cr. 8vo.* 6s.
THE GATELESS BARRIER. *Fifth Edition. Cr. 8vo.* 6s.
THE HISTORY OF SIR RICHARD CALMADY. *Ninth Edition. Cr. 8vo.* 2s. net.

Mann (Mrs. M. E.). THE PARISH NURSE. *Fourth Edition. Cr. 8vo.* 6s.
A SHEAF OF CORN. *Second Edition. Cr. 8vo.* 6s.
THE HEART-SMITER. *Second Edition. Cr. 8vo.* 6s.
AVENGING CHILDREN. *Second Edition. Cr. 8vo.* 6s.
ASTRAY IN ARCADY. *Second Edition. Cr. 8vo.* 6s.
THERE WAS A WIDOW. *Second Edition. Cr. 8vo.* 6s.

Marsh (Richard). THE COWARD BE-HIND THE CURTAIN. *Cr. 8vo.* 6s.
THE SURPRISING HUSBAND. *Second Edition. Cr. 8vo.* 6s.
LIVE MEN'S SHOES. *Second Edition. Cr. 8vo.* 6s.

Marshall (Archibald). MANY JUNES. *Second Edition. Cr. 8vo.* 6s.
THE SQUIRE'S DAUGHTER. *Third Edition. Cr. 8vo.* 6s.
THE ELDEST SON. *Third Edition. Cr. 8vo.* 6s.

Mason (A. E. W.). CLEMENTINA. Illustrated. *Seventh Edition. Cr. 8vo.* 2s. net.

Maxwell (W. B.). VIVIEN. *Tenth Edition. Cr. 8vo.* 6s.
THE RAGGED MESSENGER. *Third Edition. Cr. 8vo.* 6s.
FABULOUS FANCIES. *Cr. 8vo.* 6s.
THE GUARDED FLAME. *Seventh Edition. Cr. 8vo.* 6s.
ODD LENGTHS. *Second Ed. Cr. 8vo.* 6s.
HILL RISE. *Fourth Edition. Cr. 8vo.* 6s.
THE COUNTESS OF MAYBURY: BE-TWEEN YOU AND I. *Fourth Edition. Cr. 8vo.* 6s.
THE REST CURE. *Fourth Edition. Cr. 8vo.* 6s.

Meade (L. T.). DRIFT. *Second Edition. Cr. 8vo.* 6s.
RESURGAM. *Second Edition. Cr. 8vo.* 6s.
VICTORY. *Cr. 8vo.* 6s.
A GIRL OF THE PEOPLE. Illustrated. *Fourth Edition. Cr. 8vo.* 3s. 6d.
HEPSY GIPSY. Illustrated. *Cr. 8vo.* 2s. 6d.
THE HONOURABLE MISS: A STORY OF AN OLD-FASHIONED TOWN. Illustrated. *Second Edition. Cr. 8vo.* 3s. 6d.

Mitford (Bertram). THE SIGN OF THE SPIDER. Illustrated. *Seventh Edition. Cr. 8vo.* 3s. 6d.

Molesworth (Mrs.). THE RED GRANGE. Illustrated. *Second Edition. Cr. 8vo.* 3s. 6d.

Montague (C. E.). A HIND LET LOOSE. *Third Edition. Cr. 8vo.* 6s.

Morrison (Arthur). TALES OF MEAN STREETS. *Seventh Edition. Cr. 8vo.* 6s.
A CHILD OF THE JAGO. *Sixth Edition. Cr. 8vo.* 6s.
THE HOLE IN THE WALL. *Fourth Edition. Cr. 8vo.* 6s.
DIVERS VANITIES. *Cr. 8vo.* 6s.

Nesbit (E.), (Mrs. H. Bland). THE RED HOUSE. Illustrated. *Fifth Edition. Cr. 8vo.* 6s.
DORMANT. *Second Edition. Cr. 8vo.* 6s.

Ollivant (Alfred). OWD BOB, THE GREY DOG OF KENMUIR. With a Frontispiece. *Eleventh Ed. Cr. 8vo.* 6s.
THE TAMING OF JOHN BLUNT. *Second Edition. Cr. 8vo.* 6s.

Onions (Oliver). GOOD BOY SELDOM: A ROMANCE OF ADVERTISEMENT. *Second Edition. Cr. 8vo.* 6s.

Oppenheim (E. Phillips). MASTER OF MEN. *Fifth Edition. Cr. 8vo.* 6s.
THE MISSING DELORA. Illustrated. *Fourth Edition. Cr. 8vo.* 6s.

Orczy (Baroness). FIRE IN STUBBLE. *Third Edition. Cr. 8vo.* 6s.

Oxenham (John). A WEAVER OF WEBS. Illustrated. *Fifth Ed. Cr. 8vo.* 6s.
THE GATE OF THE DESERT. *Eighth Edition. Cr. 8vo.* 2s. net.
PROFIT AND LOSS. *Fourth Edition. Cr. 8vo.* 6s.
THE LONG ROAD. *Fourth Edition. Cr. 8vo.* 6s.
THE SONG OF HYACINTH, AND OTHER STORIES. *Second Edition. Cr. 8vo.* 6s.
MY LADY OF SHADOWS. *Fourth Edition. Cr. 8vo.* 6s.
LAURISTONS. *Fourth Edition. Cr. 8vo.* 6s.
THE COIL OF CARNE. *Sixth Edition. Cr. 8vo.* 6s.

Pain (Barry). THE EXILES OF FALOO. *Second Edition. Crown 8vo.* 6s.

Parker (Gilbert). PIERRE AND HIS PEOPLE. *Seventh Edition. Cr. 8vo.* 6s.
MRS. FALCHION. *Fifth Edition. Cr. 8vo.* 6s.
THE TRANSLATION OF A SAVAGE. *Fourth Edition. Cr. 8vo.* 6s.
THE TRAIL OF THE SWORD. Illustrated. *Tenth Edition. Cr. 8vo.* 6s.

WHEN VALMOND CAME TO PONTIAC: The Story of a Lost Napoleon. *Seventh Edition. Cr. 8vo. 6s.*
AN ADVENTURER OF THE NORTH. The Last Adventures of 'Pretty Pierre.' *Fifth Edition. Cr. 8vo. 6s.*
THE SEATS OF THE MIGHTY. Illustrated. *Seventeenth Edition. Cr. 8vo. 6s.*
THE BATTLE OF THE STRONG: a Romance of Two Kingdoms. Illustrated. *Seventh Edition. Cr. 8vo. 6s.*
THE POMP OF THE LAVILETTES. *Third Edition. Cr. 8vo. 3s. 6d.*
NORTHERN LIGHTS. *Fourth Edition. Cr. 8vo. 6s.*

Pasture (Mrs. Henry de la). THE TYRANT. *Fourth Edition. Cr. 8vo. 6s.*

Pemberton (Max). THE FOOTSTEPS OF A THRONE. Illustrated. *Fourth Edition. Cr. 8vo. 6s.*
I CROWN THEE KING. Illustrated. *Cr. 8vo. 6s.*
LOVE THE HARVESTER: A STORY OF THE SHIRES. Illustrated. *Third Edition. Cr. 8vo. 3s. 6d.*
THE MYSTERY OF THE GREEN HEART. *Third Edition. Cr. 8vo. 6s.*

Perrin (Alice). THE CHARM. *Fifth Edition. Cr. 8vo. 6s.*

Phillpotts (Eden). LYING PROPHETS. *Third Edition. Cr. 8vo. 6s.*
CHILDREN OF THE MIST. *Sixth Edition. Cr. 8vo. 6s.*
THE HUMAN BOY. With a Frontispiece. *Seventh Edition. Cr. 8vo. 6s.*
SONS OF THE MORNING. *Second Edition. Cr. 8vo. 6s.*
THE RIVER. *Fourth Edition. Cr. 8vo. 6s.*
THE AMERICAN PRISONER. *Fourth Edition. Cr. 8vo. 6s.*
THE SECRET WOMAN. *Fourth Edition. Cr. 8vo. 6s.*
KNOCK AT A VENTURE. *Third Edition. Cr. 8vo. 6s.*
THE PORTREEVE. *Fourth Edition. Cr. 8vo. 6s.*
THE POACHER'S WIFE. *Second Edition. Cr. 8vo. 6s.*
THE STRIKING HOURS. *Second Edition. Cr. 8vo. 6s.*
DEMETER'S DAUGHTER. *Third Edition. Cr. 8vo. 6s.*

Pickthall (Marmaduke). SAÏD THE FISHERMAN. *Eighth Edition. Cr. 8vo. 6s.*

'Q' (A. T. Quiller Couch). THE WHITE WOLF. *Second Edition. Cr. 8vo. 6s.*
THE MAYOR OF TROY. *Fourth Edition. Cr. 8vo. 6s.*

MERRY-GARDEN AND OTHER STORIES. *Cr. 8vo. 6s*
MAJOR VIGOUREUX. *Third Edition. Cr. 8vo. 6s.*

Ridge (W. Pett). ERB. *Second Edition. Cr. 8vo. 6s.*
A SON OF THE STATE. *Third Edition. Cr. 8vo. 3s. 6d.*
A BREAKER OF LAWS. *Cr. 8vo. 3s. 6d.*
MRS. GALER'S BUSINESS. Illustrated. *Second Edition. Cr. 8vo. 6s.*
THE WICKHAMSES. *Fourth Edition. Cr. 8vo. 6s.*
NAME OF GARLAND. *Third Edition. Cr. 8vo. 6s.*
SPLENDID BROTHER. *Fourth Edition. Cr. 8vo. 6s.*
NINE TO SIX-THIRTY. *Third Edition. Cr. 8vo. 6s.*
THANKS TO SANDERSON. *Second Edition. Cr. 8vo. 6s.*

Robins (Elizabeth). THE CONVERT. *Third Edition. Cr. 8vo. 6s.*

Russell (W. Clark). MY DANISH SWEETHEART. Illustrated. *Fifth Edition. Cr. 8vo. 6s.*
HIS ISLAND PRINCESS. Illustrated. *Second Edition. Cr. 8vo. 6s.*
ABANDONED. *Second Edition. Cr. 8vo. 6s.*
MASTER ROCKAFELLAR'S VOYAGE. Illustrated. *Fourth Edition. Cr. 8vo. 3s. 6d.*

Sidgwick (Mrs. Alfred). THE KINSMAN. Illustrated. *Third Edition. Cr. 8vo. 6s.*
THE SEVERINS. *Sixth Edition. Cr. 8vo. 6s.*
THE LANTERN-BEARERS. *Third Ed. Cr. 8vo. 6s.*
ANTHEA'S GUEST. *Fifth Edition. Cr. 8vo. 6s.*

Somerville (E. Œ.) and Ross (Martin). DAN RUSSEL THE FOX. Illustrated. *Fourth Edition. Cr. 8vo. 6s.*

Thurston (E. Temple). MIRAGE. *Fourth Edition. Cr. 8vo. 6s.*

Watson (H. B. Marriott). TWISTED EGLANTINE. Illustrated. *Third Edition. Cr. 8vo. 6s.*
THE HIGH TOBY. *Third Edition. Cr. 8vo. 6s.*
THE PRIVATEERS. Illustrated. *Second Edition. Cr. 8vo. 6s.*
ALISE OF ASTRA. *Third Edition. Cr. 8vo. 6s.*

Webling (Peggy). THE STORY OF VIRGINIA PERFECT. *Third Edition. Cr. 8vo. 6s.*
THE SPIRIT OF MIRTH. *Fifth Edition. Cr. 8vo. 6s.*

Weyman (Stanley). UNDER THE RED ROBE. Illustrated. *Twenty-third Edition.* *Cr. 8vo.* 6s.

Whitby (Beatrice). ROSAMUND. *Second Edition.* *Cr. 8vo.* 6s.

Williamson (C. N. and A. M.). THE LIGHTNING CONDUCTOR: The Strange Adventures of a Motor Car. Illustrated. *Seventeenth Edition.* *Cr. 8vo.* 6s. Also *Cr. 8vo.* 1s. net.
THE PRINCESS PASSES : A Romance of a Motor. Illustrated. *Ninth Edition.* *Cr. 8vo.* 6s.
MY FRIEND THE CHAUFFEUR. Illustrated. *Twelfth Edition.* *Cr. 8vo.* 2s. net.
LADY BETTY ACROSS THE WATER. *Eleventh Edition.* *Cr. 8vo.* 6s.

THE CAR OF DESTINY AND ITS ERRAND IN SPAIN. Illustrated. *Fifth Edition.* *Cr. 8vo.* 6s.
THE BOTOR CHAPERON. Illustrated. *Sixth Edition.* *Cr. 8vo.* 6s.
SCARLET RUNNER. Illustrated. *Third Edition.* *Cr. 8vo.* 6s.
SET IN SILVER. Illustrated. *Fourth Edition.* *Cr. 8vo.* 6s.
LORD LOVELAND DISCOVERS AMERICA. *Second Edition.* *Cr. 8vo.* 6s.
THE GOLDEN SILENCE. *Sixth Edition.* *Cr. 8vo.* 6s.
THE GUESTS OF HERCULES. *Cr. 8vo.* 6s.

Wyllarde (Dolf). THE PATHWAY OF THE PIONEER (Nous Autres). *Sixth Edition.* *Cr. 8vo.* 6s.
THE UNOFFICIAL HONEYMOON. *Sixth Edition.* *Cr. 8vo.* 6s.

Methuen's Two-Shilling Novels.

Cr. 8vo.   2s. net.

THE GATE OF THE DESERT. John Oxenham.
THE SEVERINS. Mrs. Alfred Sidgwick.
CLEMENTINA. A. E. W. Mason.

THE PRINCESS VIRGINIA. C. N. and A. M. Williamson.
COLONEL ENDERBY'S WIFE. Lucas Malet.

Books for Boys and Girls.

Illustrated.   Crown 8vo.   3s. 6d.

CROSS AND DAGGER. The Crusade of the Children, 1212. W. Scott Durrant.

THE GETTING WELL OF DOROTHY. Mrs. W. K. Clifford.

ONLY A GUARD-ROOM DOG. Edith E. Cuthell.

MASTER ROCKAFELLAR'S VOYAGE. W. Clark Russell.

SYD BELTON: The Boy who would not go to Sea. G. Manville Fenn.

THE RED GRANGE. Mrs. Molesworth.
A GIRL OF THE PEOPLE. L. T. Meade.
HEPSY GIPSY. L. T. Meade. 2s. 6d.
THE HONOURABLE MISS. L. T. Meade.
THERE WAS ONCE A PRINCE. Mrs. M. E. Mann.

Methuen's Shilling Novels.

JANE. Marie Corelli.
UNDER THE RED ROBE. Stanley J. Weyman.
LADY BETTY ACROSS THE WATER. C. N. & A. M. Williamson.

MIRAGE. E. Temple Thurston.
VIRGINIA PERFECT. Peggy Webling.
SPANISH GOLD. G. A. Birmingham.
BARBARY SHEEP. Robert Hichens.

The Novels of Alexandre Dumas.

Medium 8vo. Price 6d. Double Volumes, 1s.

Actá.
The Adventures of Captain Pamphile.
Amaury.
The Bird of Fate.
The Black Tulip.
The Castle of Eppstein.
Catherine Blum.
Cécile.
The Châtelet.
The Chevalier D'Harmental. (Double volume.)
Chicot the Jester.
Chicot Redivivus.
The Comte de Montgommery.
Conscience.
The Convict's Son.
The Corsican Brothers; and Otho the Archer.
Crop-Eared Jacquot.
Dom Gorenflot.
The Duc d'Anjou.
The Fatal Combat.
The Fencing Master.
Fernande.
Gabriel Lambert.
Georges.
The Great Massacre.
Henri de Navarre.
Hélène de Chaverny.
The Horoscope.

Leone-Leona.
Louise de la Vallière. (Double volume.)
The Man in the Iron Mask. (Double volume.)
Maître Adam.
The Mouth of Hell.
Nanon. (Double volume.)
Olympia.
Pauline; Pascal Bruno; and Bontekoe.
Père la Ruine.
The Porte Saint-Antoine.
The Prince of Thieves.
The Reminiscences of Antony.
St. Quentin.
Robin Hood.
Samuel Gelb.
The Snowball and the Sultanetta.
Sylvandire.
The Taking of Calais.
Tales of the Supernatural.
Tales of Strange Adventure.
Tales of Terror.
The Three Musketeers. (Double volume.)
Tourney of the Rue St. Antoine.
The Tragedy of Nantes.
Twenty Years After. (Double volume.)
The Wild-Duck Shooter.
The Wolf-Leader.

Methuen's Sixpenny Books.

Medium 8vo.

Albanesi (E. Maria). LOVE AND LOUISA.
I KNOW A MAIDEN.
THE BLUNDER OF AN INNOCENT.
PETER A PARASITE.

Anstey (F.). A BAYARD OF BENGAL.

Austen (J.). PRIDE AND PREJUDICE.

Bagot (Richard). A ROMAN MYSTERY.
CASTING OF NETS.
DONNA DIANA.

Balfour (Andrew). BY STROKE OF SWORD.

Baring-Gould (S.). FURZE BLOOM.
CHEAP JACK ZITA.
KITTY ALONE.
URITH.
THE BROOM SQUIRE.
IN THE ROAR OF THE SEA.
NOÉMI.
A BOOK OF FAIRY TALES. Illustrated.
LITTLE TU'PENNY.
WINEFRED.
THE FROBISHERS.
THE QUEEN OF LOVE.
ARMINELL.
BLADYS OF THE STEWPONEY.
CHRIS OF ALL SORTS.

Barr (Robert). JENNIE BAXTER.
IN THE MIDST OF ALARMS.
THE COUNTESS TEKLA.
THE MUTABLE MANY.

Benson (E. F.). DODO.
THE VINTAGE.

Brontë (Charlotte). SHIRLEY.

Brownell (C. L.). THE HEART OF
JAPAN.

Burton (J. Bloundelle). ACROSS THE
SALT SEAS.

Caffyn (Mrs.). ANNE MAULEVERER.

Capes (Bernard). THE LAKE OF
WINE.
THE GREAT SKENE MYSTERY.

Clifford (Mrs. W. K.). A FLASH OF
SUMMER.
MRS. KEITH'S CRIME.

Corbett (Julian). A BUSINESS IN
GREAT WATERS.

Croker (Mrs. B. M.). ANGEL.
A STATE SECRET.
PEGGY OF THE BARTONS.
JOHANNA.

Dante (Alighieri). THE DIVINE
COMEDY (Cary).

Doyle (A. Conan). ROUND THE RED
LAMP.

Duncan (Sara Jeannette). THOSE
DELIGHTFUL AMERICANS.

Eliot (George). THE MILL ON THE
FLOSS.

Findlater (Jane H.). THE GREEN
GRAVES OF BALGOWRIE.

Gallon (Tom). RICKERBY'S FOLLY.

Gaskell (Mrs.). CRANFORD.
MARY BARTON.
NORTH AND SOUTH.

Gerard (Dorothea). HOLY MATRI-
MONY.
THE CONQUEST OF LONDON.
MADE OF MONEY.

Gissing (G.). THE TOWN TRAVELLER.
THE CROWN OF LIFE.

Glanville (Ernest). THE INCA'S
TREASURE.
THE KLOOF BRIDE.

Gleig (Charles). BUNTER'S CRUISE.

Grimm (The Brothers). GRIMM'S
FAIRY TALES.

Hope (Anthony). A MAN OF MARK.
A CHANGE OF AIR.
THE CHRONICLES OF COUNT
ANTONIO.
PHROSO.
THE DOLLY DIALOGUES.

Hornung (E. W.). DEAD MEN TELL
NO TALES.

Hyne (C. J. C.). PRINCE RUPERT THE
BUCCANEER.

Ingraham (J. H.). THE THRONE OF
DAVID.

Le Queux (W.). THE HUNCHBACK
OF WESTMINSTER.
THE CROOKED WAY.
*THE VALLEY OF THE SHADOW.

Levett-Yeats (S. K.). THE TRAITOR'S
WAY.
ORRAIN.

Linton (E. Lynn). THE TRUE HIS-
TORY OF JOSHUA DAVIDSON.

Lyall (Edna). DERRICK VAUGHAN.

Malet (Lucas). THE CARISSIMA.
A COUNSEL OF PERFECTION.

Mann (Mrs. M. E.). MRS. PETER
HOWARD.
A LOST ESTATE.
THE CEDAR STAR.
ONE ANOTHER'S BURDENS.
THE PATTEN EXPERIMENT.
A WINTER'S TALE.

Marchmont (A. W.). MISER HOAD-
LEY'S SECRET.
A MOMENT'S ERROR.

Marryat (Captain). PETER SIMPLE.
JACOB FAITHFUL.

March (Richard). A METAMORPHOSIS
THE TWICKENHAM PEERAGE.
THE GODDESS.
THE JOSS.

Mason (A. E. W.). CLEMENTINA.

Mathers (Helen). HONEY.
GRIFF OF GRIFFITHSCOURT.
SAM'S SWEETHEART.
THE FERRYMAN.

Meade (Mrs. L. T.). DRIFT.

Miller (Esther). LIVING LIES.

Mitford (Bertram). THE SIGN OF THE
SPIDER.

Montresor (F. F.). THE ALIEN.

Morrison (Arthur). THE HOLE IN
THE WALL.

Nesbit (E.). THE RED HOUSE.

Norris (W. E.). HIS GRACE.
GILES INGILBY.
THE CREDIT OF THE COUNTY.
LORD LEONARD THE LUCKLESS.
MATTHEW AUSTEN.
CLARISSA FURIOSA.

Oliphant (Mrs.). THE LADY'S WALK.
SIR ROBERT'S FORTUNE.
THE PRODIGALS.
THE TWO MARYS.

Oppenheim (E. P.). MASTER OF MEN.

Parker (Gilbert). THE POMP OF THE
LAVILETTES.
WHEN VALMOND CAME TO PONTIAC.
THE TRAIL OF THE SWORD.

Pemberton (Max). THE FOOTSTEPS
OF A THRONE.
I CROWN THEE KING.

Phillpotts (Eden). THE HUMAN BOY.
CHILDREN OF THE MIST.
THE POACHER'S WIFE.
THE RIVER.

'Q.' (A. T. Quiller Couch). THE
WHITE WOLF.

Ridge (W. Pett). A SON OF THE STATE.
LOST PROPERTY.
GEORGE and THE GENERAL.
A BREAKER OF LAWS.
ERB.

Russell (W. Clark). ABANDONED.
A MARRIAGE AT SEA.
MY DANISH SWEETHEART.
HIS ISLAND PRINCESS.

Sergeant (Adeline). THE MASTER OF
BEECHWOOD.
BALBARA'S MONEY.
THE YELLOW DIAMOND.
THE LOVE THAT OVERCAME.

Sidgwick (Mrs. Alfred). THE KINS-
MAN.

Surtees (R. S.). HANDLEY CROSS.
MR. SPONGE'S SPORTING TOUR.
ASK MAMMA.

Walford (Mrs. L. B.). MR. SMITH.
COUSINS.
THE BABY'S GRANDMOTHER.
TROUBLESOME DAUGHTERS.

Wallace (General Lew). BEN-HUR.
THE FAIR GOD.

Watson (H. B. Marriott). THE ADVEN-
TURERS.
CAPTAIN FORTUNE.

Weekes (A. B.). PRISONERS OF WAR.

Wells (H. G.). THE SEA LADY.

Whitby (Beatrice). THE RESULT OF
AN ACCIDENT.

White (Percy). A PASSIONATE PIL-
GRIM.

Williamson (Mrs. C. N.). PAPA.

Books for Travellers.

Crown 8vo. 6s. each.

Each volume contains a number of Illustrations in Colour.

A WANDERER IN PARIS. E. V. Lucas.

A WANDERER IN HOLLAND. E. V. Lucas.

A WANDERER IN LONDON. E. V. Lucas.

THE NORFOLK BROADS. W. A. Dutt.

THE NEW FOREST. Horace G. Hutchinson.

NAPLES. Arthur H. Norway.

THE CITIES OF UMBRIA. Edward Hutton.

THE CITIES OF SPAIN. Edward Hutton.

FLORENCE AND THE CITIES OF NORTHERN TUSCANY, WITH GENOA. Edward Hutton.

ROME. Edward Hutton.

VENICE AND VENETIA. Edward Hutton.

THE BRETONS AT HOME. F. M. Gostling.

THE LAND OF PARDONS (Brittany). Anatole Le Braz.

A BOOK OF THE RHINE. S. Baring-Gould.

THE NAPLES RIVIERA. H. M. Vaughan.

DAYS IN CORNWALL. C. Lewis Hind.

THROUGH EAST ANGLIA IN A MOTOR CAR. J. E. Vincent.

THE SKIRTS OF THE GREAT CITY. Mrs. A. G. Bell.

ROUND ABOUT WILTSHIRE. A. G. Bradley.

SCOTLAND OF TO-DAY. T. F. Henderson and Francis Watt.

NORWAY AND ITS FJORDS. M. A. Wyllie.

Some Books on Art.

ART AND LIFE. T. Sturge Moore. Illustrated. *Cr. 8vo. 5s. net.*

AIMS AND IDEALS IN ART. George Clausen. Illustrated. *Second Edition. Large Post 8vo. 5s. net.*

SIX LECTURES ON PAINTING. George Clausen. Illustrated. *Third Edition. Large Post 8vo. 3s. 6d. net.*

FRANCESCO GUARDI, 1712-1793. G. A. Simonson. Illustrated. *Imperial 4to. £2 2s. net.*

ILLUSTRATIONS OF THE BOOK OF JOB. William Blake. *Quarto. £1 1s. net.*

JOHN LUCAS, PORTRAIT PAINTER, 1828-1874. Arthur Lucas. Illustrated. *Imperial 4to. £3 3s. net.*

ONE HUNDRED MASTERPIECES OF PAINTING. With an Introduction by R. C. Witt. Illustrated. *Second Edition. Demy 8vo. 10s. 6d. net.*

ONE HUNDRED MASTERPIECES OF SCULPTURE. With an Introduction by G. F. Hill. Illustrated. *Demy 8vo. 10s. 6d. net.*

A ROMNEY FOLIO. With an Essay by A. B. Chamberlain. *Imperial Folio. £15 15s. net.*

THE SAINTS IN ART. Margaret E. Tabor. Illustrated. *Fcap. 8vo. 3s. 6d. net.*

SCHOOLS OF PAINTING. Mary Innes. Illustrated. *Cr. 8vo. 5s. net.*

THE POST IMPRESSIONISTS. C. Lewis Hind. Illustrated. *Royal 8vo. 7s. 6d. net.*

CELTIC ART IN PAGAN AND CHRISTIAN TIMES. J. R. Allen. Illustrated. *Second Edition. Demy 8vo. 7s. 6d. net.*

"CLASSICS OF ART." See page 14.

"THE CONNOISSEUR'S LIBRARY." See page 14.

"LITTLE BOOKS ON ART." See page 17.

"THE LITTLE GALLERIES." See page 17.

Some Books on Italy.

A HISTORY OF MILAN UNDER THE SFORZA. Cecilia M. Ady. Illustrated. *Demy 8vo.* 10s. 6d. net.

A HISTORY OF VERONA. A. M. Allen. Illustrated. *Demy 8vo.* 12s. 6d. net.

A HISTORY OF PERUGIA. William Heywood. Illustrated. *Demy 8vo.* 12s. 6d. net.

THE LAKES OF NORTHERN ITALY. Richard Bagot. Illustrated. *Fcap. 8vo.* 5s. net.

WOMAN IN ITALY. W. Boulting. Illustrated. *Demy 8vo.* 10s. 6d. net.

OLD ETRURIA AND MODERN TUSCANY. Mary L. Cameron. Illustrated. *Second Edition. Cr. 8vo.* 6s. net.

FLORENCE AND THE CITIES OF NORTHERN TUSCANY, WITH GENOA. Edward Hutton. Illustrated. *Second Edition. Cr. 8vo.* 6s.

SIENA AND SOUTHERN TUSCANY. Edward Hutton. Illustrated. *Second Edition. Cr. 8vo.* 6s.

IN UNKNOWN TUSCANY. Edward Hutton. Illustrated. *Second Edition. Demy 8vo.* 7s. 6d. net.

VENICE AND VENETIA. Edward Hutton. Illustrated. *Cr. 8vo.* 6s.

VENICE ON FOOT. H. A. Douglas. Illustrated. *Fcap. 8vo.* 5s. net.

VENICE AND HER TREASURES. H. A. Douglas. Illustrated. *Fcap. 8vo.* 5s. net.

FLORENCE: Her History and Art to the Fall of the Republic. F. A. Hyett. *Demy 8vo.* 7s. 6d. net.

FLORENCE AND HER TREASURES. H. M. Vaughan. Illustrated. *Fcap. 8vo.* 5s. net.

COUNTRY WALKS ABOUT FLORENCE. Edward Hutton. Illustrated. *Fcap. 8vo.* 5s. net.

NAPLES : Past and Present. A. H. Norway. Illustrated. *Third Edition. Cr. 8vo.* 6s.

THE NAPLES RIVIERA. H. M. Vaughan. Illustrated. *Second Edition. Cr. 8vo.* 6s.

SICILY: The New Winter Resort. Douglas Sladen. Illustrated. *Second Edition. Cr. 8vo.* 5s. net.

SICILY. F. H. Jackson. Illustrated. *Small Pott 8vo. Cloth,* 2s. 6d. net; *leather,* 3s. 6d. net.

ROME. Edward Hutton. Illustrated. *Second Edition. Cr. 8vo.* 6s.

A ROMAN PILGRIMAGE. R. E. Roberts. Illustrated. *Demy 8vo.* 10s. 6d. net.

ROME. C. G. Ellaby. Illustrated. *Small Pott 8vo. Cloth,* 2s. 6d. net; *leather,* 3s. 6d. net.

THE CITIES OF UMBRIA. Edward Hutton. Illustrated. *Fourth Edition. Cr. 8vo.* 6s.

THE LIVES OF S. FRANCIS OF ASSISI. Brother Thomas of Celano. *Cr. 8vo.* 5s. net.

LORENZO THE MAGNIFICENT. E. L. S. Horsburgh. Illustrated. *Second Edition. Demy 8vo.* 15s. net.

GIROLAMO SAVONAROLA. E. L. S. Horsburgh. Illustrated. *Cr. 8vo.* 5s. net.

ST. CATHERINE OF SIENA AND HER TIMES. By the Author of " Mdlle Mori." Illustrated. *Second Edition. Demy 8vo.* 7s. 6d. net.

DANTE AND HIS ITALY. Lonsdale Ragg. Illustrated. *Demy 8vo.* 12s. 6d. net.

DANTE ALIGHIERI: His Life and Works. Paget Toynbee. Illustrated. *Cr. 8vo.* 5s. net.

THE MEDICI POPES. H. M. Vaughan. Illustrated. *Demy 8vo.* 15s. net.

SHELLEY AND HIS FRIENDS IN ITALY. Helen R. Angeli. Illustrated. *Demy 8vo.* 10s. 6d. net.

HOME LIFE IN ITALY. Lina Duff Gordon. Illustrated. *Second Edition. Demy 8vo.* 10s. 6d. net.

SKIES ITALIAN : A Little Breviary for Travellers in Italy. Ruth S. Phelps. *Fcap. 8vo.* 5s. net.

www.ingramcontent.com/pod-product-compliance
Lightning Source LLC
Chambersburg PA
CBHW030312270326
41926CB00010B/1336